GNOCCHI

(NYOH-KKEE)

GNOCCHI SOLO GNOCCHI

A Comprehensive Tribute To Italy's Other Favorite First Course

CHRISTINE Y. HICKMAN

Belle Cose &
Buon Appetito!

Christine "Marcella"

To my dear friend Anna Maria Rodriquez D'Amato, my "gnocchi mother," with whom I made my first gnocchi over 25 years ago.

And to Italy, my second home, and the Italians with whom I share *l'amore e la passione per la buona cucina* — the love and the passion for good food.

CONTENTS

FOREWORD

/ David Tanis

If you have ever attempted to make gnocchi at home without a seasoned, wise and loving nonna at your elbow, you probably have encountered problems.

Most cooks' first gnocchi attempts are fraught and clumsy, with unsatisfying results; even if you manage to make a dough and form it into little shapes, the resulting gnocchi are usually less than ethereal. And a sad, heavy dumpling that lands with a thud is not at all what you want.

Enter Christine Hickman, the least nonna-like teacher imaginable (physique-wise, at least), who has spent half a lifetime diligently pursuing and studying the ins and outs of gnocchi-making. She will lead you to gnocchi perfection.

Christine wisely notes that gnocchi made with potato — the kind most non-Italians think of when they hear the word — are the most difficult type to make.

Instead she counsels us to begin with the kinds of gnocchi that are more likely to succeed on the first go, made with fresh ricotta, eggs and a little flour. The recipe for Basic Ricotta Gnocchi, page 90, is easy to master, and is an excellent place to start. The oftener you make them, the better they will be, as you become familiar with the simple dough's personality. Or try the spinach and ricotta malfatti, page 106, for gnocchi you can form with a spoon.

With Christine's help, commit to the potato gnocchi. Even if the first try fails, persevere. There are clear explanations of the methods and techniques and all sorts of encouraging guidance. Accept that gnocchi expertise can only be truly learned from hands-on trial and error — practice, practice. Success is well within reach. And you'll find plenty of variations beyond plain potato, and inspired vegetable gnocchi, from parsnip to pumpkin.

Then there are canederli, the savory gnocchi made from breadcrumbs; baked polenta or semolina gnocchi smothered in cheese; and even a few sweet dessert gnocchi recipes.

A little melted butter is often the best and easiest sauce for gnocchi, but Christine provides a wonderfully varied assortment of tasty sauces — tomato-y, lemon-y, pesto-y, wild mushroom-y, Umbrian herb-y and otherwise — to catapult your gnocchi to greater heights.

Sometimes single-subject cookbooks are disappointing. Not this one. Christine's personal and well-researched gnocchi collection is deliciously fascinating.

Brava!

INTRODUCTION

It's early summer in Perugia, and the jasmine outside the kitchen window is perfuming my small house in *centro*. Its delicate scent is just one reminder of why I look forward to my return to Italy every year, a journey I've been fortunate to make for over 30 years. I return to teach, to cook with the abundance of quality ingredients that exist here, and to reconnect with a country I've grown to love.

My first trip to Italy set a pattern of learning the language during the winter and returning to Italy every summer for two to four weeks, choosing a new "central spot" each time and traveling out from there to learn more about this beautiful country's food and culture.

On one of those very early trips, I ate my first gnocchi at a small restaurant in San Gimignano that made its own from scratch. Why I chose gnocchi over pasta as a first course at that moment, I'm not sure — but my first bite was heavenly. There were more than 20 gnocchi on my plate, and every one was perfect, neither mushy nor gummy. After that, I searched for gnocchi on every restaurant menu before I agreed to dine there. My husband Mark began to question my sanity, but I was in gnocchi heaven.

At about the same time, as I was toying with the idea of making food a serious career, I decided I needed some restaurant experience. With the help of a friend, I arranged a two-week job at a French restaurant in San Francisco to get a taste of what happens behind the scenes, which was far different than I had imagined. A restaurant kitchen is more stressful and difficult than I had fantasized — and no one cleans up after you!

Nonetheless, I was still intrigued. I worked for various caterers in Santa Fe, New Mexico, mostly as an onsite finish chef, and eventually landed a job at Café Escalera, an upscale Mediterranean restaurant where I baked the daily bread and breakfast items and helped in the dessert department. At Escalera, I worked with David Tanis, my most influential mentor, and Deborah Madison, who were the restaurant's executive and pastry chefs. I learned more from just being in the kitchen, observing and working with these knowledgeable chefs and other talented people, than from any previous experience.

Most importantly, I was able to solidify a personal philosophy of cooking and eating that I had been forming over the years. It was the perfect springboard for my next step: creating my own small catering company. Marcella — a name I chose while beginning my Italian studies — became my business name: Sono Marcella.

During our 1993 trip to Italy, Mark suggested I find a summer job as an apprentice in an Italian restaurant. I asked about the opportunity in every restaurant we dined in where the food was of a quality and variety that interested me, and the following summer I worked for three to four months in La Fontana in Castiglione del Lago, a hotel restaurant near Perugia. As a prep chef at La Fontana, I learned firsthand about Italian basics and cooking styles and further refined my skills.

Although gnocchi was not on the menu at La Fontana, one evening we had a special request for potato gnocchi from an important client. My co-worker (and now dear friend) Anna Maria Rodriguez D'Amato volunteered to make them, and I was thrilled to help. The opportunity to learn about gnocchi from an experienced cook was a gift I hadn't expected. Anna Maria's skillful hands were amazing to watch form the dough, and when I tried myself and was clumsy, I asked her for her secret. She replied: *"Ascolta. Marcellina, tu devi praticare. Fai, fai e fai ancora di più."* ("Listen. Little Marcella, you need to practice. You make and make and make even more.")

I began to search out recipes and to make my own potato gnocchi, using all the tips I had learned from Anna Maria, and practicing — making more and more and more. It was gnocchi heaven all over again.

That summer of hands-on cooking also strengthened my resolve to continue returning to Italy, to continue learning the language, and to focus on the "Italian kitchen" as my catering and teaching specialty.

Mark and I continued traveling to other areas of Italy where I learned more about regional specialties, and more about gnocchi as well. The innumerable varieties of this humble dish opened a whole new world for me and planted a seed — a book in the future? I searched various libraries and bookstores in Italy and was able to find only one book in Italian dedicated to gnocchi. So, for the time being, I kept the seed dormant.

I used what I'd learned from my Italian experience when catering in Santa Fe, and I sometimes felt frustrated at not being able to find the same quality ingredients to recreate a dish. I quickly learned just how much raw ingredients differ depending on the soil, the air, the water, the altitude. I realized that some American ingredients would never match those I use in Italy, nor can they be shipped or brought back in my luggage. So I've learned to enjoy all I can while I'm there — and to remind myself and my students of that fact with the following quotation (source unknown):

> *To take a local dish and put it in a faraway place and pretend it's the same, it doesn't make sense. Food is more than the fuel we put in our bodies. It's the spiritual connection that nourishes you and keeps you alive.*

In May 1999, we arrived in Perugia and looked at a house with two small terraces, a view of Assisi, and light that entered from three directions. Even though it needed some work, I was smitten and began a nine-month reconstruction project.

Once the house was ready, it seemed a natural progression to begin teaching while I was spending summers in Italy. Having small dinner parties catered is not part of the Italian culture. So the first class I taught was in Italian — American desserts to Italian participants — and it worked. I then decided to focus on teaching "La Cucina Italiana" to tourists who want to spend a day in the kitchen while visiting this amazing country. I began teaching in Santa Fe as well, the first subject being gnocchi — although the seed of the gnocchi book continued to lie dormant.

A few years ago I felt inspired to begin research for my gnocchi book in earnest and spent many hours collecting information and ideas, adding to what I already knew. I'd taught numerous classes on gnocchi and had focused on the subject for a very long time, but was distracted by other life priorities and put the work aside — again.

During that pause, Mark and I began a yearly, sometimes semiannual, trek to the Dolomites in northern Italy, where various kinds of gnocchi share a prominent place on menus, next to the pasta. Some of the best gnocchi I've ever eaten have been on those trips and in unusual places — like a restaurant hidden along a hiking path. At each place, I asked chefs for gnocchi tips. Some would talk openly; others didn't care to share their secrets.

Italy is a small but highly diverse country, and I've been fortunate to travel from the northern high mountain areas of the Alps to the stunningly beautiful, warm sandy beaches of Sardinia and Sicily. While ingredients (and recipes) vary greatly from one region to another, local pride in history, customs, and traditional foods that have survived centuries remains strong in every corner of the country.

In the past, recipes were passed down from mother to daughter. Today, however, Italians' interest in and use of cookbooks is growing and regional foods are being reinterpreted, reflecting a more rapid exchange of information and a wider, faster transportation of food-stuffs. Still, *Io mangio solo Italiano* (I only eat Italian) is something I hear frequently — which, loosely translated, means eating only the regional food with which one is familiar. I find a certain romance in that.

The focus of my business has changed over the years; I now cater less and teach more. I've enjoyed passing on all I've learned from the Italians about their culture and cuisine; hopefully, I can pass some of the passion for food that I share with them to my students as well. It's this shared passion for good food that has brought me back to Italy over and over and over again, and inspired me to write this book.

That seed from long ago? It has finally blossomed into *Gnocchi — Solo Gnocchi*.

This book is an in-depth exploration of gnocchi — and only gnocchi.

More than a collection of recipes — although there are more than 160 recipes for gnocchi, sauces and a few basics such as broth included here — it's also a distillation of my years of research into the history of gnocchi, and my decades of experience hunting gnocchi in all the regions of Italy where they are made.

Many Americans know only the gummy, sticky, potato gnocchi that have given this quintessential Italian comfort food a bad name. I was lucky. My first mouthful of gnocchi — on November 2, 1988, at La Mangiatoia in San Gimignano — was so *squisito*, sublime, that I noted it in my diary. And it ignited a passion for gnocchi that continues to this day.

The irony is that Italians generally don't use cookbooks. And the cookbooks that do exist tend to be short on detailed instruction. The authors assume you already know how to execute the basic techniques. Even Anna Maria Rodriquez D'Amato, my gnocchi mentor, can't conceive of a book dedicated to gnocchi. You learn these things from your mother, she says: Why would anyone want a book on the subject?

But I want Americans to know how Italians make gnocchi — and to help Americans duplicate the wide varieties of Italian gnocchi using the best equivalent ingredients found in the United States. My intention is to bring my love of gnocchi — as defined by the Italians — and my 30 years of intense study and teaching of the subject together, and to share that knowledge with Americans who are interested in the subject — historically, traditionally, and contemporarily.

This book comes from my heart as much as from my mind and hands; it's born of my desire to pay tribute to my many years living in Italy, and to the Italians who have taught and befriended me in the best way I know how: at the stove.

A BRIEF HISTORY OF GNOCCHI

Gnocchi (nyoh-kkee) refers to small Italian dumplings. It is one of the most mispronounced Italian food words and should not be confused with two similar terms:

Gnocco (nyoh-kko) a knucklehead, idiot, lump — or a single dumpling
Gnocca (nyoh-kkah) a "hot babe," a compliment that describes a beautiful woman

One of the oldest preparations in the history of food, gnocchi have been documented as far back as Roman times: Gnocchi alla Romana, made from cooked semolina flour and milk, spread evenly on a surface, cut and baked with a layer of cheese, is *un piatto povero* — a simple dish made with inexpensive, widely available ingredients. The earliest written recipes for gnocchi appear in the 14th century.

Gnocchi made with potato, known and loved worldwide, date back to the 17th century — well after Spanish explorers introduced potatoes from South America to Italian kitchens. Two hundred years later, Pellegrino Artusi, the "grandfather" of Italian cuisine, published the first recipe for the potato gnocchi we know today.

In my experience, American chefs' (and home cooks') search for gnocchi of ethereal lightness has led them to lose sight of what gnocchi were — and are: small soft dumplings, tender, yet sturdy enough to hold their own when combined with sauce, the quintessential Italian comfort food.

In Italy, gnocchi are made from various nut- and grain-based flours, potatoes — with or without egg — vegetables, cheese, or breadcrumbs. They can be savory or sweet; boiled, baked, fried, or stuffed; and sauced in a wide variety of ways. There are as many gnocchi variations as there are pastas. But gnocchi are NOT pasta, not just flour and water — at least they haven't been for a long time.

Historically, gnocchi are closely linked to pasta, and sometimes the difference between the two can be confusing, particularly to non-Italians. Both are served as a first course, as are risotto, soups, and polenta. But regardless of that link, by today's accepted Italian definition, "all gnocchi 'shapes' made of flour and water are considered 'pasta' while all dumplings made of different ingredients are called gnocchi." Probably the most confusing example is gnocchetti Sardi, a small pasta shape that looks like gnocchi (thus the name "little gnocchi") but is made with semolina flour and water and is a specialty of the island of Sardinia.

Gnocchi are more common in northern Italy, a natural result of living where the mountains and longer winters make one yearn for comforting food. Gnocchi based on bread or buckwheat and nut flours all originated in the border regions of the north, although many variations are also found in other areas. In some parts of Italy, the gnocchi are given other names — canederli, malfatti, gnudi, and strangolapreti, for example — and may include local vegetables, ricotta, and different flours.

Particularly in Rome, gnocchi are a Thursday specialty in many a trattoria or osteria (less formal Italian restaurants). The custom has unknown origins, but it follows the Roman proverb of "Giovedì gnocchi, venerdì pesce, Sabato trippa" — Gnocchi on Thursday, fish on Friday, tripe on Saturday, as well as the Roman Catholic tradition of fasting on Friday. However it began, the tradition lives on.

Perhaps the oldest gnocchi tradition is celebrated in Verona during carnival season, as it has been every year since 1531. During a terrible famine, a local doctor, Tomasso da Vaco, is credited with quelling a citizens' uprising by paying for and distributing food to the townspeople, and ordering that the tradition be continued every year thereafter. Called the *Bacanal del Gnocco*, it's celebrated annually on the last Friday of carnival with huge cauldrons of gnocchi and sauce served to those who attend. Each year an old man with a white beard sticks a golden fork in an enormous gnocco and rides through town on a mule, tossing candies to the spectators.

Those who have visited Italy may be aware of the annual *sagre*, or fairs, that honor the earth's bounties. Usually held in small towns, these events celebrating prized regional produce and traditional dishes offer visitors an excellent opportunity to learn about Italian fare and customs while locals gather at community tables, enjoy the food and chance to visit with others, and dance into the late evening. Gnocchi is often the focus of these fairs, with female volunteers providing their expertise and energy to make thousands of servings for people attending the *sagra* over a period of days.

In spite of their humble beginnings, gnocchi can be found today on the menus of some of the most elite Italian restaurants in Europe, the U.S., and around the world, the gnocchi taking their rightful place next to pasta as a first course. Creative chefs are inventing new sauces as well, increasing gnocchi's popularity and piquing the interest of home cooks.

ABOUT THESE RECIPES

Some of the recipes in these pages are traditional; some are collected from restaurant chefs and Italian friends; others are my own creations. All recipes include headnotes, suggestions for saucing, and background information specific to the dish. All the recipes have been tested and retested by students in my classes, by home cooks, and by professional chefs.

Read the full recipe and assemble the ingredients before you start to work so you can be sure you have all the components and tools needed, and are familiar with specific details of the process.

I've not noted a "total time" for preparing a recipe because not all cooks work at the same pace. The information can be misleading — not to mention frustrating — when it takes you a half hour to prep a recipe that claims it can be done in 15 minutes. If you're working on a tight schedule, do what you can ahead of time — for example, many sauces can be made ahead and held or reheated before serving; vegetables that will be worked into the dough can be cooked hours or days ahead and refrigerated until needed.

Always start with the least amount of flour specified in a recipe, then test the dough for the proper consistency. You can always add more flour; you can't remove it if the dough is too dry or stiff.

Salt should be used with personal discretion and always adjusted before serving. Recipes that include a salty ingredient (capers, olives, salted meats, etc.) may not require any additional salt. As with flour, salt can be added but not removed from a dish. Salt also brings out the natural sweetness in vegetables such as tomatoes and should be used instead of sugar to enhance the flavor.

Follow the Italian rule: When sautéing garlic or onions, always place them in a cold pan and cook them slowly until they begin to sizzle and release a mild aroma. Putting garlic and/or onions into hot oil shocks their delicate flavor and puts them in danger of burning.

*Eggs are large unless otherwise noted.

*Olive oil is always extra-virgin.

*Butter is always unsalted.

*Salt is kosher salt unless otherwise specified.

*Peperoncini are tiny red-hot Italian chili peppers usually used dried, and not to be confused with peperoni or bell peppers. You will find them bottled with other dried spices. Use sparingly; they are very potent.

*Always buy whole chunks of genuine Parmigiano-Reggiano and grate it just before using. Once grated, the cheese begins to dry out.

*Fennel can be substituted for celery in any of the recipes. The flavor and texture are similar.

*Use only fresh herbs. The difference in flavor is remarkable. If absolutely necessary, dried herbs can be substituted to taste. Dried herbs vary in their potency, so no equivalent substitutions for the fresh herbs are suggested.

Restaurants in Italy often use a trick when preparing gnocchi a few hours in advance for service later in the day. Instead of freezing the gnocchi, they cook them immediately, drain them when done, coat them evenly and liberally with olive oil, place them on a tray and refrigerate them. When they need to retrieve a portion, they reheat the correct number in boiling water for a minute or two, toss it with sauce, and serve it immediately.

In an excllent guide to fearless deep-frying, the website Food 52 notes that if you insert a wooden skewer into the oil, the oil will bubble around the stick when the temperature is hot enough for frying. (Alternatively, you can use a popcorn kernel to test for readiness; it will pop somewhere between 325 and 350 degrees Fahrenheit.)

Practice, practice, practice!

Don't expect success the first time you make gnocchi and don't expect the gnocchi to be the same every time you make them. There are too many variables — the age and dryness of the flour, moisture in the potatoes, or the humidity in the room, for example — but the more you make gnocchi, the better you'll be at knowing when the dough feels right and when it needs some tweaking.

Traditional boiled potato gnocchi are the most difficult to master, a fact that has given gnocchi, in general, a bad rap over the years. To gain confidence and experience, I suggest starting with any of the ricotta, canederli (bread), or alla Romana recipes before taking on the potato-based variety.

Most importantly, *all gnocchi experts test the dough* before shaping the whole batch of gnocchi. I don't know a single experienced gnocchi-maker who skips this step, and they all have a story about a time when they didn't test and the batch failed.

Finally, embrace any imperfections and rejoice in the fact that your gnocchi are handmade.

*** *Read the Gnocchi Tips before you start, and refer to the step by step images (pages 18), or my YouTube video (https://www.youtube.com/watch?v=iz1K5HFLzKA). You will find a wealth of information there that can help..*

POTATO GNOCCHI

The plain texture and mild flavor of a simple potato-based gnocchi can be a particularly good foil for a large variety of sauces. When various meats, cheeses, or vegetables are added to the dough, the gnocchi can take on an entirely different dimension, especially when served with a buttery sauce that accents the additions.

Let's be clear: The basic recipe for potato gnocchi is very simple — but these are the most difficult gnocchi to prepare. Even today, after years of gnocchi-making, my potato gnocchi aren't always perfect — so don't get discouraged if yours aren't either. Gnocchi are handmade and should be appreciated as such. Not all the gnocchi have to look the same.

You need to practice, practice, practice to learn the "feel" of the dough that will make the best gnocchi, as well as test a few gnocchi before shaping and cooking a full batch. Much like making bread, mastering the technique can be deeply satisfying — and your family and friends will be happy to reap the benefits of your work.

Read the Gnocchi Tips that follow before you start, and refer to my YouTube video for help. (https://www.youtube.com/watch?v=iz1K5HFLzKA) You will find a wealth of information there that can help prevent failures.

Perhaps the most important gnocchi tip I ever received was from Anna Maria Rodriquez-D'Amato, the Italian friend who inspired me to make my own gnocchi: "Practice, practice, and practice some more," she said. And I can't repeat it often enough.

Don't expect your potato gnocchi to be perfect the first time, or even every time thereafter. Changes in ingredients and even the weather will affect the outcome. It takes experience to know and remember what good gnocchi dough feels like, and to trust yourself to reproduce it. And don't plan on making gnocchi for a dinner party unless you've made it before. That said, don't feel intimidated or discouraged if, after a couple of tries, you're not satisfied with your results. Watch the YouTube video again and practice. You'll eventually get there!

POTATO GNOCCHI TIPS

/ CHOOSING AND COOKING THE POTATO

I recommend that American cooks use Yukon Golds for potato gnocchi as they have more of the nutty flavor of the yellow-fleshed boiling potatoes preferred by the Italian and Provençal cooks who have mastered gnocchi. Italians traditionally boil the potatoes for gnocchi; however, I've found that baking or microwaving works better with the yellow-gold variety found in the U.S. — and that it produces what I consider a more authentic result. Russets are not grown in Italy and are not recommended as they make a grainier-textured gnocchi.

/ RICING THE POTATO

Use a ricer or food mill to process the cooked potatoes. Never mash or blend them in a food processor; this compresses the potatoes and will make the gnocchi dense. Always rice the potatoes while they're warm; this releases moisture and keeps the gnocchi light. Cool to room temperature before adding remaining ingredients.

/ THE FLOUR

The basic recipes for potato gnocchi suggest using a combination of cake and all-purpose flours, but you can use only all-purpose flour for any and all of the recipes in this book if you prefer. Read the flour section in The Full Pantry chapter for more detailed information.

The amount of flour you will need to add to the potato is determined by the amount of moisture in the ingredients — something that can change every time you make the recipe. It's better to let the ingredients and your experience dictate how much flour to add. Start with the minimum amount suggested in the recipe, shape a few gnocchi, and cook them. If they are mushy or fall apart, you can add more flour and test again. Work as quickly as possible so the flour doesn't absorb extra moisture and become sticky. If you keep unshaped dough at room temperature for more than 30 minutes, it will sweat and become too wet to use successfully.

/ OTHER ADDITIONS

If you are adding vegetables — such as squash purée or finely chopped spinach — to the basic dough, drain them well before you mix them in, or dry them out by heating and stirring over medium heat until all the excess liquid has evaporated. Cool the mixture before adding it to the dough. You can complete this step while the potatoes are cooking.

For potato or ricotta gnocchi, you may choose to mix one to two tablespoons of finely chopped herbs, such as sage or rosemary, into the dough along with the flour. Herbed gnocchi are simply buttered and served alongside meat stews or roasts such as beef, pork, or the traditional rabbit.

/ MIXING THE GNOCCHI

Use a light hand when mixing in the remaining ingredients and forming the gnocchi. Do not overwork or overmix the dough, as this will toughen the gnocchi. A rubber spatula or flexible curved plastic bowl scraper works well for this process.

/ SHAPING THE GNOCCHI

Gnocchi that are formed into ropes and then cut do not need to be shaped further with a fork or gnocchi paddle.

If you want to take the extra step to create the more traditional shape — one that forms a small pocket and ridges that help the sauce cling to the gnocchi — you will need to use a wooden gnocchi paddle, the back of a fork, or a box grater. My personal preference is a paddle because the tooth of the wood makes forming much easier. Or, if you want a pocket without the ridges, you can flip the gnocchi using the tip of your middle finger on a clean work surface. Anna Maria, my gnocchi mentor, always shapes gnocchi this way — and very rapidly I might add — rather than using a tool for ridges. (See page 246 for more information on gnocchi-shaping tools, and refer to the YouTube link, https://www.youtube.com/watch?v=iz1K5HFLzKA, for visual guidance and instructions.) Toss the gnocchi lightly with flour after shaping. You can store uncooked gnocchi on a floured tray in the refrigerator for up to an hour, then remove and finish cooking them when you're ready to serve.

/ FREEZING GNOCCHI

You can also freeze uncooked gnocchi in a single layer on a baking sheet lined with parchment or waxed paper until they are firm. Put the frozen gnocchi in plastic bags and store them in the freezer for up to two weeks. Never thaw frozen gnocchi before cooking them. Frozen gnocchi will require only a few more minutes cooking time. Read the Freezing Notes on page 250 for more information.

/ COOKING THE GNOCCHI

You can cook all the gnocchi as you form them, toss them immediately with a generous amount of olive oil to coat, and refrigerate them up to two days, reheating for just a minute or two in simmering water before serving.

Use ABUNDANT simmering water! Gnocchi need room to swim — but vigorously boiling water can cause them to break apart. If you don't have a large stockpot, it's best to cook fewer at a time in a smaller pot and serve each batch as soon as it is done. You could also use two or three pots simultaneously. With few exceptions, gnocchi cook in only two to four minutes. If you overload the pot, they will form a compact mass at the bottom and be inedible.

Add salt to the pot AFTER the water comes to a simmer to prevent salt corrosion on the bottom of the pot. The cooking water should taste like the sea.

If you want to sauté your gnocchi to add another dimension to a dish, first cook the gnocchi just until they float. Do not overcook; they should remain firm. Use a slotted spoon to transfer them to a bowl of ice water for just a minute or two, drain well, and place them on an oiled baking sheet.

To sauté, heat one tablespoon each unsalted butter and olive oil in a large skillet or sauté pan over medium-high heat, and toss the gnocchi quickly until browned and crisp. This procedure works best with the ricotta or potato gnocchi, and compliments sauces that are more delicate. Robust tomato and ragù sauces overwhelm the tender fried crust.

You can add your sauce directly to the sauté pan to heat it with the sautéed gnocchi or you can toss the gnocchi and hot sauce together in a separate bowl.

/ SERVING THE GNOCCHI

Toss cooked gnocchi gently with the warm sauce. Treat the gnocchi tenderly, or they may break apart. For garnishes, use fresh herb sprigs such as rosemary, sage, thyme, basil, or mint, choosing the one that best complements the sauce. Hard grating cheeses, such as an aged pecorino or Asiago, can be substituted for the Parmigiano-Reggiano served as a garnish or at the table.

BASIC POTATO GNOCCHI WITH EGG

/ serves 6

2 pounds Yukon Gold potatoes, skin pricked 5 to 6 times with a fork
1 cup unbleached all-purpose flour + ½ cup cake flour
OR 1½ cups unbleached all-purpose flour
1 large egg
1 teaspoon kosher salt

Bake the potatoes at 400°F, or microwave them on high, until tender when deeply pierced with a small knife. Allow to cool just enough to handle them comfortably. Peel while still warm and pass them through the fine disk of a food mill or potato ricer into a large bowl or onto a clean counter. Cool to room temperature.

Whisk the two flours together in a small bowl. In another bowl, whisk the egg and salt together until just combined. With a rubber spatula or a flexible curved plastic bowl scraper, fold the egg mixture lightly into the potatoes with a cutting/folding motion similar to what you would use when mixing a cake. Sprinkle the dough with all but ¼ cup of the flour and cut it lightly into the potatoes. Do not overmix or gnocchi will be tough.

Gather the dough into a smooth ball and place it on a lightly floured board. Take a walnut-sized portion of dough, roll it into a 2-inch log, and cut the log into thirds. Test cook the three gnocchi in a small deep saucepan of simmering water until they rise to the surface. Check the texture and add more flour to the dough if necessary — 1/8 cup at a time — until the additional tests indicate you've reached the desired consistency. The gnocchi should hold together when cooked without being gummy.

Divide the remaining dough into four to six pieces and roll each piece into a finger-thick rope on a lightly floured board. Cut each rope into ¾-inch pieces. You can press each piece over a wooden gnocchi or butter paddle or the reversed tines of a fork to create the small pockets and ridges that help the sauce cling to the gnocchi — or

simply cut the ropes and leave the gnocchi unshaped. Place the finished gnocchi close together, but not touching, on a lightly floured tray. Set aside or refrigerate up to an hour while making the sauce.

Bring a very large, deep pot of water — no less than 1 gallon — to a simmer. Add 1 to 2 tablespoons salt and drop in the gnocchi, cooking no more than half the batch at a time. Stir a couple of times with a wooden spoon so the gnocchi move gently. The water should remain at a simmer rather than a rolling boil.

Have ready warmed serving bowls and a large mixing bowl with half your chosen sauce portioned into it. As the gnocchi rise to the surface, remove them with a slotted spoon, toss with the sauce, garnish as desired, and serve immediately. Repeat with the remaining gnocchi and sauce.

Alternatively, you can cook all the gnocchi at the same time in two separate pots and toss them all together in a large serving bowl with the appropriate amount of sauce.

These gnocchi can be frozen after forming for up to two weeks. See Freezer Notes, page 250.

To egg or not to egg?

Opposite is a basic potato gnocchi recipe without egg, and I encourage you to try this before deciding which version — with or without egg — is your favorite. Many an Italian purist will argue that the addition of egg masks the potato flavor, while others suggest it contributes to the workability and texture of the dough.

I've found truth in both arguments; however, my personal choice is to add a beaten egg or egg yolk. The addition of egg helps bring the dough together much more quickly without the need to overwork it — a very important factor in producing tender gnocchi. The proportion of flour to potato will change with either approach, so it's important to follow the recipes as written.

BASIC POTATO GNOCCHI WITHOUT EGG

/ serves 6

2 pounds Yukon Gold potatoes, skin pricked 5 to 6 times with a fork
2/3 cup unbleached all-purpose flour + 1/3 cup cake flour
OR 1 cup unbleached all-purpose flour
1 teaspoon kosher salt
Additional flour for shaping the gnocchi

Bake the potatoes at 400°F, or microwave them on high, until tender when deeply pierced with a small knife. Allow to cool just enough to handle them comfortably. Peel while still warm and pass them through the fine disk of a food mill or potato ricer into a large bowl or onto a clean counter. Cool to room temperature.

Whisk the two flours and the salt together in a small bowl. Sprinkle the potatoes with all but ¼ cup of the flour mixture. With a rubber spatula or a flexible curved plastic bowl scraper, mix the flours lightly into the potatoes with a cutting/folding motion similar to what you would use when mixing a cake. Do not overmix or gnocchi will be tough.

Gather the dough into a smooth ball and place it on a lightly floured board. Take a walnut-sized portion of dough, roll it into a 2-inch log, and cut the log into thirds. Test cook the three gnocchi in a small deep saucepan of simmering water until they rise to the surface. Check the texture and add more flour to the dough if necessary — 1/8 cup at a time — until the additional tests indicate you've reached the desired consistency. The gnocchi should hold together when cooked without being gummy.

Divide the remaining dough into four to six pieces and roll each piece into a finger-thick rope on a lightly floured board. Cut each rope into ¾-inch pieces. You can press each piece over a wooden gnocchi or butter paddle or the reversed tines of a fork to create the small pockets and ridges that help the sauce cling to the gnocchi — or simply cut the ropes and leave the gnocchi unshaped. Place the finished gnocchi close together, but not touching, on a lightly floured tray. Set aside or refrigerate up to an hour while making the sauce.

Bring a very large, deep pot of water — no less than 1 gallon — to a simmer. Add 1 to 2 tablespoons salt and drop in the gnocchi, cooking no more than half the batch at a time. Stir a couple of times with a wooden spoon so the gnocchi move gently. The water should remain at a simmer rather than a rolling boil.

Have ready warmed serving bowls and a large mixing bowl with half your chosen sauce portioned into it. As the gnocchi rise to the surface, remove them with a slotted spoon, toss with the sauce, garnish as desired, and serve immediately. Repeat with the remaining gnocchi and sauce.

Alternatively, you can cook all the gnocchi at the same time in two separate pots and toss them all together in a large serving bowl with the appropriate amount of sauce.

These gnocchi can be frozen after forming for up to two weeks. See Freezer Notes, page 250.

POTATO GNOCCHI

/ Step-By-Step

1 Potato ricer, bowl, and Yukon Gold potatoes

2 Peel the potatoes while warm

3 Begin ricing the potatoes

4 Finish ricing the potatoes

5 Fold in the beaten egg/salt mixture

6 Sprinkle with flour

7 Fold in the flour

8 Bring the dough together

9 Form a smooth ball

10 Divide the dough into thirds

11 Begin forming a rope

12 Form a long rope about ½-inch diameter

13   Cut into ¾-inch lengths

14   Shape with a gnocchi paddle

15   Make ridges in the gnocchi

16   Finished gnocchi ready to cook

Claudio Brugalossi is the chef/owner of La Taverna, one of the top-rated restaurants in Italy. He came from a restaurant family and began working at the age of 17 as a dishwasher in Rome at Le Sans Souci, Italy's only Michelin-starred restaurant at the time. His career expanded from there; he became a chef and, for three years, was chef-owner of Claudio's, a restaurant in Midland, Texas. Then he moved to Tampa, Florida, and worked as chef de cuisine at Armani's Restaurant at Hyatt Regency Westshore before returning to Italy, settling in Perugia, and opening La Taverna in 1988.

I met Claudio through his American wife Sherry, with whom I have shared a friendship of nearly 20 years after meeting her by chance in the local alimentari (grocery store). I was impressed with Claudio, his restaurant, his staff, and, more than anything, his dedication to cooking and serving the highest quality Italian cuisine possible. He's been an ongoing and important source of inspiration for me ever since, and a valuable source of information regarding gnocchi.

A CHEF'S-EYE VIEW OF GNOCCHI

Dimmi Claudio, per favore, cosa pensi di un libro dedicato solo al soggetto di gnocchi, tutti i tipi possibile? Il titolo del libro e Gnocchi Solo Gnocchi. *Sarebbe utile?*

Si si … non credo che ci sia già in America.

Io, ho schelto questo soggetto perché sono appassionata di gnocchi e non trovo un libro scritto in profondità sul soggetto.

Ma, fai bene.

Quando sono in America e di pomeriggio non lavoro, vado a Barnes & Noble e mi leggo qualche libro di cucina ed io non l'ho mai visto sinceramente.

E qui in Italia? Dimmi più di dove e come i gnocchi sono mangiati.

I gnocchi sono molto popolare. E un piatto di famiglia..di casa, più che ristorante. I ristoranti che servono gnocchi sono trattorie che hanno la cucina molto tradizionale, molto povera.

Alora, negli Stati Uniti vengono più populare a causa della popolarità della cucina italiana, e sono serviti in ristoranti mentre in Italia tradizionalmente solo trattorie e non ristoranti?

Normalmente, sì. Io, però a La Taverna, li faccio ogni tanto nel inverno con ragù Umbro, o Gorgonzola. Io mi piaciono molto, ma e daverro un piatto pesante, per l'inverno. Mi piace anche canederli tradizionale fate con formaggio e o speck dentro, come fanno in Alto Adige; saltati al burro e poi Parmiggiano, e gratinato. Tanto burro — tanto burro.

E per quanto riguardo le patate, le migliori per fare gnocchi di patate?

Le migliori patate sono quelle gialle, senza dubbio. E ti vengono meglio al forno. Me, forati perché tutta l'acqua va via, e hai bosogno di mettere meno farina. Poi si sbuccia caldo.

Grazie, Claudio, per tutto nel corso degli anni.

Please tell me, Claudio, what do you think of a book dedicated only to the subject of gnocchi, all the kinds possible? The title of the book is Gnocchi Solo Gnocchi. *Would it be useful?*

Yes, yes. I don't believe there is already one in America.

I chose this subject because I'm passionate about gnocchi and I don't find an in-depth book on the subject.

It's a great idea. When I'm in America, and in the afternoon when I don't work, I go to Barnes & Noble and I read cookbooks, and I have never seen one, sincerely.

And here in Italy? Tell me more of where and how gnocchi are eaten.

Gnocchi are very popular. It's a family dish, eaten at home more than in restaurants. The restaurants that serve gnocchi are trattorias that have very traditional cuisine, very peasant-style.

So, in the United States they are becoming more popular due to the interest in Italian cuisine and are served in restaurants, while in Italy, they are traditionally served only in trattorias and not restaurants?

Normally, yes. But at La Taverna, I make them once in a while in the winter, with Umbrian ragù or with Gorgonzola. I like them a lot, but it's really a heavy dish, for the winter. I also like traditional canederli with or without speck inside, like they're made in Alto Adige — sautéed in butter, then some Parmigiano, and gratinéed. Lots of butter — lots of butter.

And regarding the potato, the best for making potato gnocchi?

The best potatoes are the yellow ones, without a doubt. And they work better for you in the oven, pierced so all the water goes away and you need to use less flour. Then you peel while warm.

Thanks, Claudio, for everything over the years.

AFFOGATI (MEAT & POTATO GNOCCHI)

/ serves 4-6

Typical gnocchi from Friulia-Venezia Giulia, Italia's most northeastern region, this variation is sometimes called gnocchi affogati, or drowned gnocchi, because they're served in a rich broth. Although liver is traditional, other ground meat, such as pork or veal, can be substituted for the liver with equally good results. If you wish to make an even more substantial dish, try one of the Additional Sauce Suggestions listed below.

1½ pounds Yukon Gold potatoes, skin pricked 5-6
    times with a fork

½ cup finely grated fresh Parmigiano-Reggiano
    + more for serving

½-¾ cups unbleached all-purpose flour

¼ pound lean ground beef

¼ pound veal liver, very finely chopped

1 tablespoon marjoram leaves, chopped

2 tablespoons parsley, finely chopped

2 teaspoons kosher salt

Freshly ground black pepper to taste

A few gratings of nutmeg

2 large eggs, beaten

1 small onion, finely chopped

¼ cup unsalted butter

6 cups rich chicken or beef broth,
    preferably homemade

Bake the potatoes at 400°F, or microwave them on high, until tender when deeply pierced with a small knife. Allow to cool just enough to handle them comfortably. Peel while still warm and pass them through the fine disk of a food mill or potato ricer into a large bowl or onto a clean counter. Cool to room temperature.

In a bowl, thoroughly mix the meats with the grated Parmigiano-Reggiano, flour, chopped herbs, salt, pepper, and freshly grated nutmeg. Mix in the beaten eggs. Add to the riced potatoes and lightly mix to form a uniform dough. Sprinkle with ½ cup flour and mix together using a folding motion until the flour is evenly incorporated.

With a tablespoon or 1-inch scoop, form small balls of dough and place close together, but not touching, on a parchment-lined tray. If the dough doesn't hold its shape, add more flour, 2 tablespoons at a time, to stiffen the dough. Sprinkle lightly with flour and set aside or refrigerate up to an hour while making the sauce.

In a sauté pan, cook the butter and chopped onion until softened, being careful not to brown either. Add the gnocchi and cook over medium heat, turning constantly, to evenly brown the exterior of the gnocchi, about 10 minutes. Be careful not to burn the onions.

Meanwhile, bring the broth to a simmer in a soup pot.

As the gnocchi finish browning, transfer them to the simmering broth and cook an additional 15 minutes. When ready to serve, divide the cooked gnocchi between warmed serving bowls and top with the broth. Shower with freshly grated Parmigiano-Reggiano.

Alternatively, you can omit the browning step and add the gnocchi directly to the simmering broth. Cook 15 to 20 minutes and serve as directed above.

Do not freeze.

Additional Sauce Suggestions: Parmigiano-Reggiano Cream, Creamy Leek Sauce, Basic Tomato Sauce, Roasted Red Pepper Purée

POTATO-BUCKWHEAT GNOCCHI

/ serves 6 to 8 generously

Buckwheat, or grano saraceno, *which is actually a fruit seed, has a very long history in the cuisine of northern Italy, particularly in the regions of Lombardia and Piemonte. It adds an earthy flavor to Lombardy's* pizzoccheri — *a pasta similar to fettuccine made with two-thirds buckwheat flour and one-third wheat flour — traditionally served with cabbage, potatoes, sage, and an Alpine cheese such as Gruyère, fontina, or Taleggio. While gnocchi made with buckwheat flour alone tend to be too heavy for most gnocchi aficionados, mixing the flour with potato makes them lighter in texture. The dough is also easier to work with as the lack of gluten means the finished gnocchi actually benefit from extra kneading rather than risk the dough becoming tough from overworking it. These gnocchi have a nutty flavor that I particularly enjoy with Creamy Leek or Cabbage & Cheese Sauce, or just a few shavings of aged Gruyère cheese.*

2 pounds Yukon Gold potatoes, skin pricked 5-6 times with a fork

1 cup buckwheat flour + more for forming

1 large egg

1 teaspoon kosher salt

Bake the potatoes at 400°F, or microwave them on high, until tender when deeply pierced with a small knife. Allow to cool just enough to handle them comfortably. Peel while still warm and pass them through the fine disk of a food mill or potato ricer into a large bowl or onto a clean counter. Cool to room temperature.

Beat the egg and salt until just combined. With a rubber spatula or a flexible curved plastic bowl scraper, fold the egg mixture lightly into the potatoes using a cutting/folding motion similar to mixing a cake. Sprinkle with all but ¼ cup of the flour and cut lightly into the potatoes.

Gather the dough into a smooth ball and place it on a lightly floured board. Take a walnut-sized portion of dough, roll it into a 2-inch log, and cut the log into thirds. Test cook the three gnocchi in a small deep saucepan of simmering water until they rise to the surface. Check the texture and add more flour to the dough if necessary — ⅛ cup at a time — until the additional tests indicate you've reached the desired consistency. The gnocchi should hold together when cooked without being gummy.

Divide the remaining dough into four to six pieces and roll each piece into a finger-thick rope on a lightly floured board. Cut each rope into ¾-inch pieces. You can press each piece over a wooden gnocchi or butter paddle or the reversed tines of a fork to create the small pockets and ridges that help the sauce cling to the gnocchi — or simply cut the ropes and leave the gnocchi unshaped. Place the finished gnocchi close together, but not touching, on a lightly floured tray. Set aside or refrigerate up to an hour while making the sauce.

Bring a very large, deep pot of water to boil — no less than 1 gallon — add 1 to 2 tablespoons of salt, and drop in the gnocchi, cooking no more than half the batch at a time. Stir a couple of times with a wooden spoon so the gnocchi move gently. The water should remain at a simmer rather than a rolling boil.

Have ready warmed serving bowls and a large mixing bowl with half your chosen sauce portioned into it. As the gnocchi rise to the surface, remove them with a slotted spoon, toss with the sauce, garnish as desired, and serve immediately. Repeat with the remaining gnocchi and sauce.

Alternatively, you can cook all the gnocchi at the same time in two separate pots and toss them all together in a large serving bowl with the appropriate amount of sauce.

Do not freeze.

Sauce Suggestions: Shaved Gruyère or Fontina Cheese, Wild Mushroom & Blueberry Sauce, Cabbage & Cheese Sauce, Creamy Lemon, Peas & Prosciutto Sauce, Creamy Leek Sauce, Italian Brodo or other light soups

POTATO-ROASTED PEPPER GNOCCHI

/ serves 6

Tiny pieces of sweet roasted red pepper make a surprising textural and flavorful addition to traditional potato gnocchi. Roast your own peppers — the flavor difference between fresh and canned is remarkable. Instructions for roasting peppers are on page 228.

2 pounds Yukon gold potatoes, skin pierced 5 to 6 times

1 cup unbleached all-purpose flour + more for
  shaping the gnocchi

½ cup cake flour

3 medium red bell peppers, about 1¼ pounds total,
  roasted, cored, seeded, skinned, and very finely diced

1 egg, beaten

1 teaspoon salt

¼ cup finely chopped fresh basil (optional)

Bake the potatoes at 400°F, or microwave them on high, until tender when deeply pierced with a small knife. Allow to cool just enough to handle them comfortably. Peel while still warm and pass them through the fine disk of a food mill or potato ricer into a large bowl or onto a clean counter. Cool to room temperature.

Squeeze any extra moisture from the peppers and pat dry between paper towels.

Whisk the two flours together in a large bowl and set aside. In another bowl, whisk the egg and salt until just combined. Add the finely chopped peppers and basil (if using) to the potatoes and mix lightly using a folding motion similar to mixing a cake. Sprinkle with 1¼ cups of the flour mixture, and mix lightly into the potatoes using the same cutting motion. Do not overmix or gnocchi will be tough.

Gather the dough into a smooth ball and place it on a lightly floured board. Take a walnut-sized portion of dough, roll it into a 2-inch log, and cut the log into thirds. Test cook the three gnocchi in a small deep saucepan of simmering water until they rise to the surface. Check the texture and add more flour to the dough if necessary — ⅛ cup at a time — until the additional tests indicate you've reached the desired consistency. The gnocchi should hold together when cooked without being gummy.

Divide the remaining dough into four to six pieces and roll each piece into a finger-thick rope on a lightly floured board. Cut each rope into ¾-inch pieces. You can press each piece over a wooden gnocchi or butter paddle or the reversed tines of a fork to create the small pockets and ridges that help the sauce cling to the gnocchi — or simply cut the ropes and leave the gnocchi unshaped. Place the finished gnocchi close together, but not touching, on a lightly floured tray. Set aside or refrigerate up to an hour while making the sauce.

Bring a very large, deep pot of water — no less than 1 gallon — to a simmer. Add 1 to 2 tablespoons salt and drop in the gnocchi, cooking no more than half the batch at a time. Stir a couple of times with a wooden spoon so the gnocchi move gently. The water should remain at a simmer rather than a rolling boil.

Have ready warmed serving bowls and a large mixing bowl with half your chosen sauce portioned into it. As the gnocchi rise to the surface, remove them with a slotted spoon, toss with the sauce, garnish as desired, and serve immediately. Repeat with the remaining gnocchi and sauce.

Alternatively, you can cook all the gnocchi at the same time in two separate pots and toss them all together in a large serving bowl with the appropriate amount of sauce. These gnocchi can be frozen for up to two weeks after forming. See Freezer Notes, page 250.

Sauce Suggestions: Tomato & Olive Sauce, Roasted Eggplant Sauce, Fennel Pollen-Cream Sauce, Olive-Mint Pesto, Pine Nut-Butter Sauce

POTATO-CHESTNUT GNOCCHI

/ serves 6 to 8

You might say Italians have a love affair with chestnuts. Ground into flour, they can be the central ingredient for many a dessert or bread; puréed, they are often a substitute for potatoes. When chestnut season arrives in October, roasted chestnut vendors take to the streets to satisfy many a passerby with a tasty snack. Often eaten with tangerines and a sip of amaretto, they make a perfect fall dessert. Here, chestnut flour is blended with potato to make gnocchi that will celebrate the best of the fall season.

2 pounds Yukon Gold potatoes
1⅓ cups chestnut flour
⅔ cup unbleached all-purpose flour

1 large egg
1½ teaspoons kosher salt

Bake the potatoes at 400°F, or microwave them on high, until tender when deeply pierced with a small knife. Allow to cool just enough to handle them comfortably. Peel while still warm and pass them through the fine disk of a food mill or potato ricer into a large bowl or onto a clean counter. Cool to room temperature.

Whisk the two flours together in a small bowl. Beat the egg with the salt until just combined, then mix lightly into the potatoes using a folding motion similar to mixing a cake. Sprinkle with all but ¼ cup of the flour and cut lightly into the potatoes. Do not overmix or gnocchi will be tough.

Gather the dough into a smooth ball and place it on a lightly floured board. Take a walnut-sized portion of dough, roll it into a 2-inch log, and cut the log into thirds. Test cook the three gnocchi in a small deep saucepan of simmering water until they rise to the surface. Check the texture and add more flour to the dough if necessary — ⅛ cup at a time — until the additional tests indicate you've reached the desired consistency. The gnocchi should hold together when cooked without being gummy.

Divide the remaining dough into four to six pieces and roll each piece into a finger-thick rope on a lightly floured board. Cut each rope into ¾-inch pieces. You can press each piece over a wooden gnocchi or butter paddle or the reversed tines of a fork to create the small pockets and ridges that help the sauce cling to the gnocchi, or simply cut the ropes and leave the gnocchi unshaped. Place the finished gnocchi close together, but not touching, on a lightly floured tray. Set aside or refrigerate up to an hour while making the sauce.

Bring a very large, deep pot of water — no less than 1 gallon — to a simmer. Add 1 to 2 tablespoons salt and drop in the gnocchi, cooking no more than half the batch at a time. Stir a couple of times with a wooden spoon so the gnocchi move gently. The water should remain at a simmer rather than a rolling boil.

Have ready warmed serving bowls and a large mixing bowl with half your chosen sauce portioned into it. As the gnocchi rise to the surface, remove them with a slotted spoon, toss with the sauce, garnish as desired, and serve immediately. Repeat with the remaining gnocchi and sauce.

Alternatively, you can cook all the gnocchi at the same time in separate pots and toss them all together in a large serving bowl with the appropriate amount of sauce.

These gnocchi can be frozen for up to two weeks after forming. See Freezer Notes, page 250.

Sauce Suggestions: Pestos, Basic Fontina Sauce, Sage-Butter Sauce, Mushroom Sauce, Creamy Roasted Garlic and Parmigano-Reggiano Sauce, Thyme-Garlic Butter Sauce, Pancetta, Radicchio, Pine Nut & Rosemary Sauce

POTATO-FISH GNOCCHI

/ serves 6

These gnocchi are light, soft, and delicate, and make a great main course with a simple salad. Be sure to use a mildly flavored fish, as suggested, and a simple sauce that will enhance the flavor. They're equally good simply dribbled with unsalted butter. Traditionally, Italians don't serve Parmigiano-Reggiano with any seafood dish. There are a number of theories as to why this is the accepted practice in Italy, such as the religious tradition of meat and dairy consumption being forbidden on Fridays. I tend to agree with the Italians that cheese overwhelms the delicate flavor of the fish, but there's no golden rule.

1 pound Yukon Gold potatoes, skin pricked 5-6 times
1 large egg
¾-1 cup unbleached all-purpose flour
½ pound delicate fish such as lake fish, sole, or
    flounder, coarsely chopped

1 small onion, finely chopped (about ⅔ cup)
1 clove garlic, minced
2 tablespoons extra-virgin olive oil
½ cup dry white wine
Salt and freshly ground pepper to taste

Put the olive oil, garlic, and onions in a medium sauté pan and cook over medium-low heat until the ingredients begin to soften, about 3 minutes. Add the chopped fish and cook another minute or two. Add the wine and continue cooking until all the wine is evaporated and the mixture is very, very dry. Season with salt and pepper and set aside to cool.

Bake the potatoes at 400°F, or microwave them on high, until tender when deeply pierced with a small knife. Allow to cool just enough to handle them comfortably. Peel while still warm and pass them through the fine disk of a food mill or potato ricer into a large bowl or onto a clean counter. Cool to room temperature.

With an eggbeater, whip the fish mixture until smooth and uniform. Add the egg and beat gently to combine.

With a rubber spatula or a flexible curved plastic bowl scraper, mix the fish mixture lightly into the potatoes using a cutting/folding motion similar to mixing a cake. Sprinkle with ¾ cup of the flour and cut lightly into the potatoes. Do not overmix or gnocchi will be tough. Cover with plastic wrap or a bowl and let rest 15 to 30 minutes while preparing the sauce of your choice.

Gather the dough into a smooth ball and place it on a lightly floured board. Take a walnut-sized portion of dough, roll it into a 2-inch log, and cut the log into thirds. Test cook the three gnocchi in a small deep saucepan of simmering water until they rise to the surface. Check the texture and add more flour to the dough if necessary — ⅛ cup at a time — until the additional tests indicate you've

reached the desired consistency. The gnocchi should hold together when cooked without being gummy.

Divide the remaining dough into four to six pieces and roll each piece into a finger-thick rope on a lightly floured board. Cut each rope into ¾-inch pieces. Press each piece over a wooden gnocchi or butter paddle or the reversed tines of a fork to create the small pockets and ridges that help the sauce cling — or simply cut the ropes and leave the gnocchi unshaped. Place the finished gnocchi close together, but not touching, on a lightly floured tray.

Bring a very large, deep pot of water — no less than 1 gallon — to a simmer. Add 1 to 2 tablespoons salt and drop in the gnocchi, cooking no more than half the batch at a time. Stir a couple of times with a wooden spoon so the gnocchi move gently. The water should remain at a simmer rather than a rolling boil.

Have ready warmed serving bowls and a large mixing bowl with half your chosen sauce portioned into it. As the gnocchi rise to the surface, remove them with a slotted spoon, toss with the sauce, garnish as desired, and serve immediately. Repeat with the remaining gnocchi and sauce.

Alternatively, you can cook all the gnocchi at the same time in two separate pots and toss them all together in a large serving bowl with the appropriate amount of sauce.

Do not freeze.

Sauce Suggestions: Lemon & Garlic Sauce, Thyme-Garlic Butter Sauce, Uncooked Fresh Tomato Sauce, Oven-Roasted Cherry Tomatoes

POTATO-ASPARAGUS GNOCCHI WITH SHRIMP & ALMONDS

/ serves 4 generously

Seafood and gnocchi may seem an odd combination, but along the coastal areas of Italy where fresh seafood is prevalent, it is often used in both the sauce and the gnocchi themselves. Sometimes pieces of fish are worked into the dough; at other times seafood is used in the sauce. The following recipe is an example of a popular combination of flavors that use spring asparagus in the gnocchi and shrimp in the light cream sauce.

/ GNOCCHI

¾ pound Yukon Gold potatoes

¾ pound asparagus, trimmed

2 tablespoons extra-virgin olive oil

½ cup finely grated fresh Parmigiano-Reggiano

2 egg yolks

¾ cup unbleached all-purpose flour

¾ cup cake flour

½ teaspoon kosher salt

Pinch freshly grated nutmeg

Freshly ground white pepper to taste

Additional flour for shaping the gnocchi

/ SAUCE

½ pound cleaned small shrimp

2 cloves garlic, minced

2 tablespoons extra-virgin olive oil

Salt to taste

¼ cup heavy cream

⅓ cup slivered almonds, lightly toasted

Fresh basil, thyme, or mint for garnish

Shredded asparagus for garnish

/ MAKE THE GNOCCHI

Preheat oven to 400°F. Line a baking sheet with aluminum foil. Cut the asparagus into 1-inch pieces, coat with olive oil, sprinkle lightly with salt and spread evenly on baking sheet. Roast in oven until soft when pierced with a knife, about 15 minutes. Set aside to cool.

Bake the potatoes at 400°F, or microwave them on high, until tender when deeply pierced with a small knife, and allow to cool just enough to handle. Peel while still warm and pass through the fine disk of a food mill or potato ricer into a large bowl or onto a clean counter. Cool to room temperature.

Beat together the egg yolks, freshly grated Parmigiano-Reggiano, ½ teaspoon salt, white pepper, and nutmeg. Set aside.

In a blender, purée the asparagus until smooth and creamy. Measure ½ cup and set the rest aside for another use.

With a rubber spatula or a flexible curved plastic bowl scraper, blend the riced potatoes, asparagus purée, and egg together with a light cutting/folding motion similar to what you would use when mixing a cake.

Whisk the two flours together in a small bowl. Sprinkle potato mixture with all but ¼ cup of flour and cut/fold the flours lightly into the potato/asparagus until it begins to hold together. Do not overmix or gnocchi will be tough.

Gather the dough into a smooth ball and place it on a lightly floured board. Take a walnut-sized portion of dough, roll it into a 2-inch log, and cut the log into thirds. Test cook the three gnocchi in a small, deep saucepan of simmering water until they rise to the surface. Check the texture and add more flour to the dough if necessary — ⅛ cup at a time — until additional tests indicate you've reached the desired consistency. The gnocchi should hold together when cooked without being gummy.

Divide the remaining dough into four to six pieces and roll each piece into a finger-thick rope on a lightly floured board. Cut each rope into ¾-inch pieces. You can press each piece over a wooden gnocchi or butter paddle or the reversed tines of a fork to create the small pockets and ridges that help the sauce cling to the gnocchi — or simply cut the ropes and leave the gnocchi unshaped.

Place the finished gnocchi close together, but not touching, on a lightly floured tray. Refrigerate while making the sauce.

Bring a very large, deep pot of water — no less than 1 gallon — to a simmer, and add 1 to 2 tablespoons salt.

/ MAKE THE SAUCE

In a sauté pan, heat 2 tablespoons extra-virgin olive oil with the minced garlic over medium-high heat until it begins to sizzle. Add the shrimp and cook until they begin to turn pale, a minute or two. Lower the heat, add the cream, and allow the sauce to thicken slightly while you cook the gnocchi.

Drop gnocchi into the simmering water, cooking not more than half the batch at a time. Stir a couple of times with a wooden spoon so the gnocchi move gently. The water should remain at a simmer rather than a rolling boil.

Have ready four heated serving bowls and a large bowl with half the sauce portioned into it. As the gnocchi rise to the surface, remove with a slotted spoon, toss with the sauce, garnish with herb of choice, asparagus slivers, and toasted almonds. Serve immediately.

Repeat with the remaining gnocchi and sauce.

These gnocchi can be frozen for up to two weeks after forming. See Freezer Notes, page 250.

Inspired by a gnocchi dish served at Battibecco Restaurant in Corciano, Italy

POTATO GNOCCHI WITH ASIAGO CHEESE & BASIL

/ serves 6

The idea for this recipe came from Lisa Lavagetto, a friend who also shared the wonderful Oxtail Ragù recipe on page 198. I adapted it using techniques I learned in Italy and added some chopped basil. These gnocchi are rich in egg and cheese and have a wonderful texture. They are well suited for many sauces, only some of which are listed below.

1½ pounds Yukon Gold potatoes, skin pricked 5-6 times with a fork

1-1½ cups unbleached all-purpose flour + more for shaping

3 large egg yolks

1 teaspoon kosher salt

4 ounces finely grated young Asiago cheese (1½ cups loosely packed)

¼ cup finely chopped fresh basil, optional

Bake the potatoes at 400˚F, or microwave them on high, until tender when deeply pierced with a small knife. Allow to cool just enough to handle them comfortably. Peel while still warm and pass them through the fine disk of a food mill or potato ricer into a large bowl or onto a clean counter. Cool to room temperature.

In another bowl, whisk the egg and salt together until just combined. With a rubber spatula or a flexible curved plastic bowl scraper, fold the egg mixture lightly into the potatoes with a cutting/folding motion similar to what you would use when mixing a cake. Sprinkle with the grated Asiago cheese, the basil, and 1 cup of the flour, and cut lightly into the potatoes. Do not overmix or gnocchi will be tough.

Gather the dough into a smooth ball and place it on a lightly floured board. Take a walnut-sized portion of dough, roll it into a 2-inch log, and cut the log into thirds. Test cook the three gnocchi in a small deep saucepan of simmering water until they rise to the surface. Check the texture and add more flour to the dough if necessary — ⅛ cup at a time — until the additional tests indicate you've reached the desired consistency. The gnocchi should hold together when cooked without being gummy.

Divide the remaining dough into four to six pieces and roll each piece into a finger-thick rope on a lightly floured board. Cut each rope into ¾-inch pieces. You can press each piece over a wooden gnocchi or butter paddle or the reversed tines of a fork to create the small pockets and ridges that help the sauce cling to the gnocchi — or simply cut the ropes and leave the gnocchi unshaped. Place the finished gnocchi close together, but not touching, on a lightly floured tray. Set aside or refrigerate up to an hour while making the sauce.

Bring a very large, deep pot of water to simmer — no less than 1 gallon — add 1 to 2 tablespoons salt and drop in the gnocchi, cooking no more than half the batch at a time. Stir a couple of times with a wooden spoon so the gnocchi move gently. The water should remain at a simmer rather than a rolling boil.

Have ready warmed serving bowls and a large mixing bowl with half your chosen sauce portioned into it. As the gnocchi rise to the surface, remove them with a slotted spoon, toss with the sauce, garnish as desired, and serve immediately. Repeat with the remaining gnocchi and sauce.

Alternatively, you can cook all the gnocchi at the same time in two separate pots and toss them all together in a large serving bowl with the appropriate amount of sauce.

These gnocchi can be frozen for up to two weeks after forming. See Freezer Notes, page 250.

Sauce Suggestions: All Tomato Sauces, Lemon & Garlic Sauce, all Ragùs

POTATO GNOCCHI WITH COCOA, RAISINS & CINNAMON

/ serves 6 to 8

The reaction to this recipe is always the same — one of incredulity. I agree that it seems "out of bounds" to mix or serve chocolate with potato gnocchi, but, in fact, it's a very traditional recipe from the Piemonte region of Italy, where chocolate and hazelnuts reign as a popular combination and where gianduja *(commercially known as Nutella) was born. If you give it a try, you'll find out just how wonderful this recipe can be. It's often served as a first course since the sugar is minimal and the chocolate is unsweetened. But you can also top it with heavy sweetened cream, whipped or not, and enjoy it as dessert.*

1½ pounds Yukon gold potatoes

2 large eggs

1¾ cups unbleached all-purpose flour
 + more for shaping

¾ teaspoon salt

1-2 tablespoons unsweetened
 cocoa for the gnocchi (optional)

2 teaspoons sugar

½ cup golden raisins

3 tablespoons finely diced
 candied citron or lemon peel

½ teaspoon ground cinnamon

2 tablespoons unsweetened cocoa for the topping

¼ pound freshly grated smoked ricotta
 OR equal parts smoked mozzarella and ricotta salata

½ cup toasted, skinned, and coarsely chopped hazelnuts

¼ pound unsalted butter

Make the topping: Soak the raisins in tepid water to cover for 30 minutes. Drain and blot dry. In a bowl, lightly toss the raisins, candied citron or lemon peel, 1 teaspoon sugar, cinnamon, and the remaining cocoa. Set the grated cheese and hazelnuts aside in separate bowls while making the gnocchi.

Bake the potatoes at 400°F, or microwave them on high, until tender when deeply pierced with a small knife. Allow to cool just enough to handle them comfortably. Peel while still warm and pass them through the fine disk of a food mill or potato ricer into a large bowl. Cool to room temperature.

In another bowl, beat the eggs, salt, and 1 teaspoon sugar until combined. Mix lightly into the potatoes using a folding motion similar to mixing a cake. Sprinkle with all but ¼ cup of the flour and the optional cocoa, if using, and cut lightly into the potatoes. Do not overmix or gnocchi will be tough.

Gather the dough into a smooth ball and place it on a lightly floured board. Take a walnut-sized portion of dough, roll it into a 2-inch log, and cut the log into thirds. Test cook the three gnocchi in a small deep saucepan of simmering water until they rise to the surface. Check the texture and add more flour to the dough if necessary — ⅛ cup at a time — until the additional tests indicate you've reached the desired consistency. The gnocchi should hold together when cooked without being gummy.

Divide the remaining dough into four to six pieces and roll each piece into a finger-thick rope on a lightly floured board. Cut each rope into ¾-inch pieces. You can press each piece over a wooden gnocchi or butter paddle or the reversed tines of a fork to create the small pockets and ridges that help the sauce cling to the gnocchi — or simply cut the ropes and leave the gnocchi unshaped. Place the finished gnocchi close together, but not touching, on a lightly floured tray. Set aside or refrigerate up to an hour.

Melt the butter in a large sauté pan and keep warm. Bring a very large, deep pot of water — no less than 1 gallon — to a simmer. Add 1 to 2 tablespoons salt and drop in the gnocchi, cooking no more than half the batch at a time. Stir a couple of times with a wooden spoon so the gnocchi move gently. The water should remain at a simmer rather than a boil.

As the gnocchi rise to the surface, remove with a slotted spoon and toss with melted butter. Divide among warm, shallow serving bowls and sprinkle with reserved topping, grated cheese, and hazelnuts. Serve immediately. Repeat with the remaining gnocchi and topping.

Alternatively, you can cook all the gnocchi at the same time in two separate pots.

These gnocchi can be frozen after forming for up to two weeks. See Freezer Notes, page 250.

POTATO-POLENTA GNOCCHI

/ serves 6 to 8 generously

The addition of polenta to potato gnocchi is common in northern Italian regions where polenta is a staple. These delicately flavored and smoothly textured gnocchi are wonderful without any additions. Be sure to use finely ground polenta or corn flour rather than corn meal or the gnocchi will be gritty. A variety of herbs can be added to taste and the prosciutto can be replaced with other cured sausages such as Coppa, Soppressata, or Culatello. Be sure to grind or very finely chop the sausage or the gnocchi will be difficult to form. I often buy prosciutto ends for this purpose as they're sold at a reduced price.

2 pounds Yukon Gold potatoes
1 cup all-purpose unbleached flour
½ cup finely milled polenta
½ cup finely chopped or ground prosciutto
2 eggs

2 tablespoons finely chopped fresh herbs such as
   rosemary, marjoram, or sage
1 teaspoon kosher salt
Finely grated fresh Parmigiano-Reggiano for serving

Bake the potatoes at 400°F, or microwave them on high, until tender when deeply pierced with a small knife. Allow to cool just enough to handle them comfortably. Peel while still warm and pass them through the fine disk of a food mill or potato ricer into a large bowl or onto a clean counter. Cool to room temperature.

Whisk 1 cup unbleached all-purpose flour and 1 cup polenta meal together in a small bowl. Beat the egg and salt together until just combined. With a rubber spatula or a flexible curved plastic bowl scraper, mix the eggs lightly into the potatoes using a cutting/folding motion similar to mixing a cake. Sprinkle with the flour-hazelnut mixture and cut lightly into the potatoes. Do not overmix or gnocchi will be tough.

Gather the dough into a smooth ball and place it on a lightly floured board. Take a walnut-sized portion of dough, roll it into a 2-inch log, and cut the log into thirds. Test cook the three gnocchi in a small, deep saucepan of simmering water until they rise to the surface. Check the texture and add more flour to the dough if necessary — ⅛ cup at a time — until the additional tests indicate you've reached the desired consistency. The gnocchi should hold together when cooked without being gummy.

Divide the remaining dough into four to six pieces and roll each piece into a finger-thick rope on a lightly floured board. Cut each rope into ¾-inch pieces. You can press each piece over a wooden gnocchi or butter paddle or the reversed tines of a fork to create the small pockets and ridges that help the sauce cling to the gnocchi — or simply cut the ropes and leave the gnocchi unshaped. Place the finished gnocchi close together, but not touching, on a lightly floured tray. Set aside or refrigerate up to an hour while making the sauce.

Bring a very large, deep pot of water — no less than 1 gallon — to a simmer. Add 1 to 2 tablespoons salt and drop in the gnocchi, cooking no more than half the batch at a time. Stir a couple of times with a wooden spoon so the gnocchi move gently. The water should remain at a simmer rather than a rolling boil.

Have ready warmed serving bowls and a large mixing bowl with half your chosen sauce portioned into it. As the gnocchi rise to the surface, remove them with a slotted spoon, toss with the sauce, garnish as desired, and serve immediately. Repeat with the remaining gnocchi and sauce. Pass freshly grated Parmigiano-Reggiano at the table, if desired.

Alternatively, you can cook all the gnocchi at the same time in two separate pots and toss them all together in a large serving bowl with the appropriate amount of sauce.

Note: This is a good gnocchi for garnishing soup: Cook, drain, and cool the gnocchi. Shake them in a bag or toss them in a bowl with coarse cornmeal until they are well coated. Sauté or deep fry in olive oil until crisp and brown.

These gnocchi can be frozen for up to two weeks after forming. See Freezer Notes, page 250.

Sauce Suggestions: Uncooked Fresh Tomato Sauce, all Mushroom Sauces, Oven-Roasted Cherry Tomatoes

POTATO-HAZELNUT GNOCCHI

/ serves 6 to 8

Replacing some of the unbleached wheat flour in the dough with nut flour adds a different flavor and textural dimension to potato gnocchi. This recipe that uses hazelnut flour is particularly tasty. It makes a soft, supple dough that's easy to form, and the cooked gnocchi have an earthy depth of flavor that can stand on its own with just butter and cheese — or you can choose from a variety of other suggested sauces. My favorite is Sage Pesto.

2 pounds Yukon Gold potatoes

1-1½ cups unbleached all-purpose flour

1 cup hazelnut meal, available at most
   natural food stores

1 large egg

1 teaspoon kosher salt

Bake the potatoes at 400°F, or microwave them on high, until tender when deeply pierced with a small knife. Allow to cool just enough to handle them comfortably. Peel while still warm and pass them through the fine disk of a food mill or potato ricer into a large bowl or onto a clean counter. Cool to room temperature.

Whisk 1 cup unbleached all-purpose flour and 1 cup hazelnut meal together in a small bowl. Beat the egg and salt together until just combined. With a rubber spatula or a flexible curved plastic bowl scraper, mix the eggs lightly into the potatoes using a cutting/folding motion similar to mixing a cake. Sprinkle with the flour-hazelnut mixture and cut lightly into the potatoes. Do not overmix or gnocchi will be tough.

Gather the dough into a smooth ball and place it on a lightly floured board. Take a walnut-sized portion of dough, roll it into a 2-inch log, and cut the log into thirds. Test cook the three gnocchi in a small deep saucepan of simmering water until they rise to the surface. Check the texture and add more flour to the dough if necessary — ⅛ cup at a time — until the additional tests indicate you've reached the desired consistency. The gnocchi should hold together when cooked without being gummy.

Divide the remaining dough into four to six pieces and roll each piece into a finger-thick rope on a lightly floured board. Cut each rope into ¾-inch pieces. You can press each piece over a wooden gnocchi or butter paddle or the

reversed tines of a fork to create the small pockets and ridges that help the sauce cling to the gnocchi — or simply cut the ropes and leave the gnocchi unshaped. Place the finished gnocchi close together, but not touching, on a lightly floured tray. Set aside or refrigerate up to an hour while making the sauce.

Bring a very large, deep pot of water — no less than 1 gallon — to a simmer. Add 1 to 2 tablespoons salt and drop in the gnocchi, cooking no more than half the batch at a time. Stir a couple of times with a wooden spoon so the gnocchi move gently. The water should remain at a simmer rather than a rolling boil.

Have ready warmed serving bowls and a large mixing bowl with half your chosen sauce portioned into it. As the gnocchi rise to the surface, remove them with a slotted spoon, toss with the sauce, garnish as desired, and serve immediately. Repeat with the remaining gnocchi and sauce.

Alternatively, you can cook all the gnocchi at the same time in two separate pots and toss them all together in a large serving bowl with the appropriate amount of sauce.

These gnocchi can be frozen for up to two weeks after forming. See Freezer Notes, page 250.

Sauce Suggestions: Sage Pesto, Sage-Butter Sauce, Zucchini Pesto, Avocado-Arugula Sauce, Savory Fig Sauce, all Mushroom Sauces

POTATO GNOCCHI WITH ROLLED OATS & RICOTTA

/ serves 6

You will find oats used in many ways in the Italian cuisine — just not for breakfast. Yet the first thing that came to mind when I tasted these was how wonderful they would be in a pool of warm milk, dribbled with honey, sprinkled with toasted nuts, and topped with some bits of fruit. That's how I enjoy oatmeal, and these gnocchi are a perfect replacement for that breakfast cereal. I can't imagine someone rising early enough to make gnocchi for breakfast, so make a double batch and stash some in the freezer.

If you'd rather eat these gnocchi as a savory dish, see the sauce suggestions below. They're very tender and have the added flavor and texture of oats. Be sure to use quick-cooking oats as they're smaller in size and make the gnocchi easier to shape.

1 pound Yukon Gold potatoes, skin pricked 5-6 times

2 cups rolled oats, preferably quick-cooking

1 tablespoon unsalted butter at room temperature

1 large egg

2 large egg yolks

1 teaspoon kosher salt

¾-1 cup all-purpose flour + more for shaping

2 cups whole milk ricotta (OR a 15-ounce container), placed in a cheesecloth-lined colander set in a bowl and drained at least 30 minutes before using

Bake the potatoes at 400˚F, or microwave them on high, until tender when deeply pierced with a small knife. Allow to cool just enough to handle them comfortably. Peel while still warm and pass them through the fine disk of a food mill or potato ricer into a large bowl or onto a clean counter. Cool to room temperature.

In another bowl, whisk the drained ricotta, egg, and salt together until just combined. With a rubber spatula or a flexible curved plastic bowl scraper, fold the egg mixture lightly into the potatoes using a cutting/folding motion similar to mixing a cake. Sprinkle with ¾ cup of the flour and cut lightly into the potatoes. Do not overmix or gnocchi will be tough.

Gather the dough into a smooth ball and place on a lightly floured board. Cover with a towel or plastic wrap and let rest 30 minutes to 2 hours at room temperature.

Gather the dough into a smooth ball and place it on a lightly floured board. Take a walnut-sized portion of dough, roll it into a 2-inch log, and cut the log into thirds. Test cook the three gnocchi in a small deep saucepan of simmering water until they rise to the surface. Check the texture and add more flour to the dough if necessary — ⅛ cup at a time — until the additional tests indicate you've reached the desired consistency. The gnocchi should hold together when cooked without being gummy.

Divide the remaining dough into four to six pieces and roll each piece into a finger-thick rope on a lightly floured board. Cut each rope into ¾-inch pieces. Because the dough is coarse, I don't recommend shaping these with a gnocchi paddle. Place the finished gnocchi close together, but not touching, on a lightly floured tray. Set aside or refrigerate up to an hour while making the sauce.

Bring a very large, deep pot of water — no less than 1 gallon — to a simmer. Add 1 to 2 tablespoons salt and drop in the gnocchi, cooking no more than half the batch at a time. Stir a couple of times with a wooden spoon so the gnocchi move gently. The water should remain at a simmer rather than a rolling boil.

Have ready warmed serving bowls and a large mixing bowl with half your chosen sauce portioned into it. As the gnocchi rise to the surface, remove them with a slotted spoon, toss with the sauce, garnish as desired, and serve immediately. Repeat with the remaining gnocchi and sauce. Serve immediately.

Alternatively, you can cook all the gnocchi at the same time in two separate pots and toss them all together in a large serving bowl with the appropriate amount of sauce.

These gnocchi can be frozen after forming for up to two weeks. See Freezer Notes, page 250.

Sauce Suggestions: All Ragùs, Tomato, Vegetable, and Cream Sauces

POTATO-PORCINI GNOCCHI

/ serves 6

Porcini mushrooms have a distinct, woodsy aroma and flavor that is highly prized in Italian cuisine. They are readily available in the dry form and add an intriguing element to mushroom sauces. Although relatively expensive, only a small amount is needed to flavor these potato-based gnocchi. When possible, purchase Italian porcini as their flavor is much stronger than the American variety. Look for dried porcini without a lot of dirty bits in the bottom of the package; it will make cleaning them much easier. Served with the Parmigiano-Reggiano Cream Sauce on page 183, this is a rich and satisfying version of potato gnocchi for porcini lovers. They are also good added to a simple soup or broth garnished with Parmigiano-Reggiano shavings.

2 pounds Yukon Gold potatoes, skin pricked 5 to 6 times

1-1½ cups loosely packed dried porcini mushrooms
    (about 1.5 ounces)

¼ cup finely grated fresh Parmigiano-Reggiano

½ cup unbleached all-purpose flour

½ cup cake flour

1 teaspoon kosher salt

¼ teaspoon freshly ground black pepper

2 egg yolks

Place the porcini mushrooms in a bowl with just enough boiling water to cover. Set aside for 10 minutes. Drain the mushrooms by lifting them from the liquid. Strain the remaining liquid through a double layer of cheesecloth and reserve 1 cup for the sauce. Finely chop the porcini and set aside.

Bake the potatoes at 400°F, or microwave them on high, until tender. Allow to cool just enough to handle them. Peel while still warm and pass them through the fine disk of a food mill or potato ricer into a large bowl. Cool to room temperature. Whisk the two flours together in a small bowl. In another bowl, whisk the egg yolks, salt, and pepper together until combined.

With a rubber spatula, mix the eggs and the chopped the porcini lightly into the potatoes using a cutting/folding motion. Sprinkle with the grated cheese and all but ¼ cup of the flour, and cut lightly into the potatoes. Do not overmix or gnocchi will be tough.

Gather the dough into a smooth ball and place it on a lightly floured board. Take a walnut-sized portion of dough, roll it into a 2-inch log, and cut the log into thirds. Test cook the three gnocchi in a small deep saucepan of simmering water until they rise to the surface. Check the texture and add more flour to the dough if necessary — ⅛ cup at a time. The gnocchi should hold together when cooked.

Divide the remaining dough into four to six pieces and roll each piece into a finger-thick rope on a lightly floured board.

Cut each rope into ¾-inch pieces. You can press each piece over a wooden gnocchi or butter paddle or the reversed tines of a fork to create the small pockets and ridges that help the sauce cling to the gnocchi — or simply cut the ropes and leave the gnocchi unshaped. Place the finished gnocchi close together, on a lightly floured tray. Refrigerate no more than 1 hour while finishing the Parmigiano-Reggiano Cream Sauce (page 183).

Bring a large, deep pot of water — no less than 1 gallon — to a simmer. Add 1 to 2 tablespoons salt and drop in the gnocchi, cooking no more than half the batch at a time. Stir a couple of times with a wooden spoon so the gnocchi move gently. The water should remain at a simmer.

Have ready warmed serving bowls and a large mixing bowl with half the sauce portioned into it. As the gnocchi rise to the surface, remove them with a slotted spoon, toss with the sauce, garnish as desired, and serve immediately. Repeat with the remaining gnocchi and sauce.

Alternatively, you can cook all the gnocchi at the same time in two separate pots and toss them all together in a large serving bowl with the appropriate amount of sauce.

These gnocchi can be frozen for up to two weeks after forming. See Freezer Notes, page 250.

Additional Sauce Suggestions: Creamy Leek Sauce, Thyme-Garlic Butter Sauce, Sagrantino Cream Sauce

POTATO-MEYER LEMON & BLACK PEPPER GNOCCHI

/ serves 6

Although regular lemons can be substituted, this is a unique way for Meyer lemon lovers to indulge their passion. Meyer lemons originated in China and are thought to be a cross between a regular lemon and a mandarin orange. They have a slightly sweet, less acidic flavor than other lemon varieties. The black pepper in the recipe is supposed to be a dominant flavor, although you can reduce the amount of pepper used if you prefer. I like to serve these gnocchi with the optional bottagara garnish. A salted, cured fish roe, the bottarga adds a delicate and rich flavor to the dish. The combination of the three ingredients is unusual — and wonderful.

2 pounds Yukon Gold potatoes, skin pricked 5 to 6 times

1 cup unbleached all-purpose flour +
    ½ cup cake flour

OR 1½ cups unbleached all-purpose flour

1 large egg

1 teaspoon kosher salt

Additional flour for shaping the gnocchi

½ cup mascarpone

Finely grated zest of 2 large Meyer lemons

1 tablespoon freshly ground black pepper

Bake the potatoes at 400°F, or microwave them on high, until tender when deeply pierced with a small knife. Allow to cool just enough to handle them comfortably. Peel while still warm and pass them through the fine disk of a food mill or potato ricer into a large bowl or onto a clean counter. Cool to room temperature.

Whisk the two flours, the lemon zest, and the pepper together in a small bowl. In another bowl, whisk the egg and salt together then whisk in the mascarpone until just combined. With a rubber spatula or a flexible curved plastic bowl scraper, fold the egg mixture lightly into the potatoes with a cutting/folding motion similar to what you would use when mixing a cake. Sprinkle the dough with all but ¼ cup of the flour and cut it lightly into the potatoes. Do not overmix or gnocchi will be tough.

Gather the dough into a smooth ball and place it on a lightly floured board. Take a walnut-sized portion of dough, roll it into a 2-inch log, and cut the log into thirds. Test cook the three gnocchi in a small, deep saucepan of simmering water until they rise to the surface. Check the texture and add more flour to the dough if necessary — ⅛ cup at a time — until the additional tests indicate you've reached the desired consistency. The gnocchi should hold together when cooked without being gummy.

Divide the remaining dough into four to six pieces and roll each piece into a finger-thick rope on a lightly floured board. Cut each rope into ¾-inch pieces. You can press each piece over a wooden gnocchi or butter paddle or the reversed tines of a fork to create the small pockets and ridges that help the sauce cling to the gnocchi — or simply cut the ropes and leave the gnocchi unshaped. Place the finished gnocchi close together, but not touching, on a lightly floured tray. Set aside or refrigerate up to an hour while making the sauce.

Bring a very large, deep pot of water — no less than 1 gallon — to a simmer. Add 1 to 2 tablespoons salt and drop in the gnocchi, cooking no more than half the batch at a time. Stir a couple of times with a wooden spoon so the gnocchi move gently. The water should remain at a simmer rather than a rolling boil.

Have ready warmed serving bowls and a large mixing bowl with half your chosen sauce portioned into it. As the gnocchi rise to the surface, remove them with a slotted spoon, toss with the sauce, garnish as desired, and serve immediately. Repeat with the remaining gnocchi and sauce.

Alternatively, you can cook all the gnocchi at the same time in two separate pots and toss them all together in a large serving bowl with the appropriate amount of sauce.

These gnocchi can be frozen for up to two weeks after forming. See Freezer Notes, page 250.

Sauce Suggestions: Meyer Lemon-Butter Sauce, Pine Nut-Butter Sauce, Garlic Scape Pesto, Arugula Pesto

Inspired by a recipe in Food & Wine, *March 2008*

POTATO-WINTER SQUASH GNOCCHI

/ serves 6

Gnocchi di Zucca is one of the best-known traditional gnocchi. Typical of the northern regions of Italy, Friuli-Venezia Giulia, it's sometimes mixed with potato and sometimes made with squash alone. Either way, it's best to prepare the squash by roasting it. Roasting the squash until the pieces are browned adds a depth of flavor to the finished gnocchi. The best substitutes for an Italian winter squash, are the common butternut squash easily found in American supermarkets, or the sweet, low-moisture kabocha.

1½-2 pounds butternut squash

2-3 tablespoons extra-virgin olive oil

1 pound Yukon Gold potatoes, skin pricked 5 to 6 times

1 large egg

1 teaspoon kosher salt

Pinch of cinnamon or freshly ground nutmeg

¼ teaspoon freshly ground white pepper

1-1¼ cups unbleached all-purpose flour

+ more for shaping the gnocchi

Finely grated fresh Parmigiano-Reggiano for the table

Preheat the oven to 400°F. Line a baking sheet with parchment paper. Peel and seed the squash, then cut into 1-inch pieces and toss with the olive oil. Spread squash evenly on the baking sheet and roast in middle of the oven for about 25 minutes, or until squash is tender and lightly browned. Set aside to cool.

Bake the potatoes at 400°F, or microwave them on high, until tender. Allow to cool. Peel while still warm and pass them through the fine disk of a food mill or potato ricer into a large bowl. Cool to room temperature.

Pass the squash through a food mill or ricer into a separate bowl and add 1 cup lightly packed purée to the potatoes. Reserve the remaining squash for another use.

With a rubber spatula, lightly mix the potato and squash together, using a cutting/folding motion until only light streaks remain in the batter.

Beat the egg, salt, and freshly ground pepper together. Cut the egg mixture lightly into the potato-squash until mostly combined. Sprinkle with all but ¼ cup of the flour and fold lightly into the potato. Do not overmix or gnocchi will be tough.

Gather the dough into a smooth ball and place it on a lightly floured board. Take a walnut-sized portion of dough, roll it into a 2-inch log, and cut the log into thirds. Test cook the three gnocchi in a small, deep saucepan of simmering water until they rise to the surface. Check the texture and add more flour to the dough if necessary — ⅛ cup at a time — until the additional tests indicate you've reached the desired consistency.

Divide the remaining dough into four to six pieces and roll each piece into a finger-thick rope on a lightly floured board. Cut each rope into ¾-inch pieces. You can press each piece over a wooden gnocchi or butter paddle or the reversed tines of a fork to create the small pockets and ridges that help the sauce cling to the gnocchi — or simply cut the ropes and leave the gnocchi unshaped. Place the finished gnocchi close together, but not touching on a lightly floured tray. Set aside or refrigerate up to an hour while making the sauce.

Bring a very large, deep pot of water — no less than 1 gallon — to a simmer. Add 1 to 2 tablespoons salt and drop in the gnocchi, cooking no more than half the batch at a time. Stir a couple of times with a wooden spoon so the gnocchi move gently. The water should remain at a simmer.

Have ready warmed serving bowls and a large mixing bowl with half your chosen sauce portioned into it. As the gnocchi rise to the surface, remove them with a slotted spoon, toss with the sauce, garnish as desired, and serve immediately. Repeat with the remaining gnocchi and sauce.

Alternatively, you can cook all the gnocchi at the same time in two separate pots and toss them all together in a large serving bowl.

These gnocchi can be frozen for up to two weeks after forming. See Freezer Notes, page 250.

Sauce Suggestions: Poppy-Seed Mint Butter Sauce, Browned Butter & Sage with Smoked Ricotta Shavings, Black Truffle Sauce, Sage Pesto, Gorgonzola Cream Sauce, Basic Fontina Sauce with Taleggio

SAVORY HANUKKAH GNOCCHI

/ serves 6 as a first course

I dedicate these gnocchi — a cross between potato gnocchi and canederli, the bread gnocchi of northern Italy — to all who celebrate Hanukkah. Made with matzo meal instead of stale bread, shaped into small balls, cooked, and then deep-fried, these gnocchi can be eaten as a savory first course or a sweet dessert with fruit and cream. Some of the easiest gnocchi to make, they have a creamy center and a crisp, crunchy crust. I love them any time of year. To get the creamiest center, I suggest you cook the gnocchi one day in advance and fry them just before serving. I prefer serving these gnocchi with Parmigiano-Reggiano Cream Sauce, page 183, but other sauces also can be used.

1 pound Yukon Gold potatoes

¼ cup matzo meal

1 tablespoon finely minced fresh chives
   or thyme, optional

½ teaspoon kosher salt

3 large eggs, separated, whites reserved

Freshly ground black pepper

Reserved egg whites

1 cup matzo meal

Sunflower or canola oil for frying

Fresh shavings of Parmigiano-Reggiano
   from a wedge

Thyme sprigs for garnish

Bake the potatoes at 400°F, or microwave them on high, until tender. Allow to cool just enough to handle them. Peel while still warm and pass them through the fine disk of a food mill or potato ricer into a large bowl or onto a clean counter. Cool to room temperature.

In another bowl, whisk the egg yolks, salt, and optional herbs together until just combined. With a rubber spatula, mix the egg yolks lightly into the potatoes using a cutting/folding motion. Sprinkle with the matzo meal and cut lightly into the potatoes to form a uniform dough. Do not overmix.

Using a ¾-inch scoop, form small, equal-sized balls, lightly rolling them in your hands to smooth the surface of the dough. Place the finished gnocchi close together, but not touching, on a lightly floured tray.

Bring a very large, deep pot of water — no less than 1 gallon — to a simmer. Add 1 to 2 tablespoons salt and drop in the gnocchi. Stir a couple of times with a wooden spoon so the gnocchi move gently. The water should remain at a simmer.

Cook for 4 to 5 minutes, then test by breaking one open. It should be firm and fully cooked inside. If not, continue cooking another minute or two.

Remove with a slotted spoon, drain and place the balls close together on a tray. Cover with plastic wrap and refrigerate for a day. When you are ready to serve the gnocchi, prepare your chosen sauce and keep it warm.

Fill a heavy, deep-sided pot with enough oil cooking oil to reach 1 inch up the sides. Heat the oil to 375°F. (When a wooden skewer is inserted into the pot, the oil will bubble around the stick when it is hot enough.)

Beat the 3 reserved egg whites until frothy. Put about 1 cup matzo meal in a shallow bowl. Coat each gnocco in egg white and roll evenly in the matzo meal. Return the balls to the tray until all the gnocchi have been prepared in the same way.

Slowly immerse about 12 to 15 gnocchi at a time into the hot oil and fry until golden brown. Do not overload the pot or the temperature of the oil will drop significantly. Remove with a slotted spoon to a paper towel to drain while you finish the remaining gnocchi.

Have warmed serving bowls ready. Spoon some prepared sauce into the bottom of each bowl and top with the gnocchi. Scatter with fresh shavings of Parmigiano-Reggiano and garnish with a sprig of thyme.

Serve immediately.

These gnocchi can be frozen for up to two weeks after forming. See Freezer Notes, page 250.

POTATO-CARROT GNOCCHI

/ serves 8

Slightly sweet, tender and finely textured, these carrot and potato gnocchi are one of the more traditional gnocchi made in Italy. Not as sweet or dense as the sweet potato version, I love their pale orange color and their ability to pair well with a large variety of sauces. Be sure to bake the carrots instead of boiling them to intensify their delicate flavor and to keep the purée as dry as possible.

2 pounds Yukon Gold potatoes, skin pricked 5-6 times with a fork

8 medium carrots, peeled, ends trimmed, cut into ½-inch pieces

2 tablespoons extra-virgin olive oil

2 large egg yolks

1 whole egg

1 teaspoon kosher salt

Pinch freshly grated nutmeg

2 teaspoons fresh thyme leaves, minced (optional)

1¼–1½ cups unbleached all-purpose flour + more for forming

Preheat the oven to 400°F. In a bowl, toss the carrot pieces with the extra-virgin olive oil and place on a parchment- or foil-lined baking sheet. Roast until tender and beginning to brown, about 30 minutes. Watch carefully as they can quickly overcook and turn black. Remove from oven and let cool. Roughly chop, then purée in a food processor until creamy but dry. Measure 1 cup into a large bowl and save the rest for another use.

Bake the potatoes with the carrots at 400°F, or microwave on high, until tender when deeply pierced with a small knife. Allow to cool just enough to handle. Peel while still warm and pass through the fine disk of a food mill or potato ricer into the bowl with the carrots. Toss the two together until you get an almost uniform dough. Cool to room temperature.

In a small bowl whisk the eggs, salt, nutmeg, and optional thyme together until just combined. With a rubber spatula or a flexible curved plastic bowl scraper, mix the eggs lightly into the potato-carrot mixture using a cutting/folding motion similar to mixing a cake. Sprinkle with all but ¼ cup of the flour, and cut lightly into the potatoes. Do not overmix or gnocchi will be tough.

Gather the dough into a smooth ball and place it on a lightly floured board. Take a walnut-sized portion of dough, roll it into a 2-inch log, and cut the log into thirds. Test cook the three gnocchi in a small deep saucepan of simmering water until they rise to the surface. Check the texture and add more flour to the dough if necessary — ⅛ cup at a time — until the additional tests indicate you've reached the desired consistency. The gnocchi should hold together when cooked without being gummy.

Divide the remaining dough into four to six pieces and roll each piece into a finger-thick rope on a lightly floured board. Cut each rope into ¾-inch pieces. You can press each piece over a wooden gnocchi or butter paddle or the reversed tines of a fork to create the small pockets and ridges that help the sauce cling to the gnocchi — or simply cut the ropes and leave the gnocchi unshaped. Place the finished gnocchi close together, but not touching, on a lightly floured tray. Set aside or refrigerate up to an hour while making the sauce.

Bring a very large, deep pot of water — no less than 1 gallon — to a simmer. Add 1 to 2 tablespoons salt and drop in the gnocchi, cooking no more than half the batch at a time. Stir a couple of times with a wooden spoon so the gnocchi move gently. The water should remain at a simmer rather than a rolling boil.

Have ready warmed serving bowls and a large mixing bowl with half your chosen sauce portioned into it. As the gnocchi rise to the surface, remove them with a slotted spoon, toss with the sauce, garnish as desired, and serve immediately. Repeat with the remaining gnocchi and sauce.

Alternatively, you can cook all the gnocchi at the same time in two separate pots and toss them all together in a large serving bowl with the appropriate amount of sauce.

These gnocchi can be frozen for up to two weeks after forming. See Freezer Notes, page 250.

Sauce Suggestions: Lemon & Garlic Sauce, Fennel Pollen-Cream Sauce, Creamy Leek Sauce, Pancetta-Orange Sauce, Lemon, Thyme & Scamorza Sauce, Poppy Seed-Mint Butter Sauce, Savory Zabaglione with Horseradish Cream Sauce

STRANGOLAPRETI (SPINACH & POTATO GNOCCHI FROM TUSCANY)

/ serves 6 to 8

In Italy, recipes with the same name often will be interpreted differently in different regions. This version of strangolapreti *(or priest stranglers) from Italy's central region of Tuscany is made using potato rather than stale bread, which is more commonly used in regions of northern Italy. (There's a recipe for the bread-based version in the canederli chapter.)*

There are a number of stories about how this gnocchi became known as the "priest strangler," all going back to medieval Italy. My favorite tale springs from the custom of priests making the rounds of various homes in the community, where they would be fed for free — a burden for the poorer inhabitants. Serving these gnocchi as a first course became a way to satiate the priests' appetites before the second course arrived, so they would not eat as much of the precious meat the household was obligated to offer. Strangolapreti were also said to be so filling and delicious that priests often ate them too quickly, almost strangling in the process.

Use fresh spinach rather than frozen for these gnocchi — the color is better and the flavor is superior. Bunched fresh spinach can be full of sand, so wash it carefully. If you want to avoid this step, substitute the already-cleaned packaged fresh spinach available in grocery stores. Baby spinach is sweeter and more tender than older leaves.

1½ pounds fresh spinach OR 1 pound prepackaged, cleaned spinach leaves

2 pounds Yukon Gold potatoes, skin pricked 5 to 6 times

1 egg

½ cup finely grated fresh Parmigiano-Reggiano

1 teaspoon kosher salt

1-1½ cups unbleached all-purpose flour
  + more for shaping the gnocchi

⅛ teaspoon freshly grated nutmeg

Trim any tough stems from the spinach and thoroughly wash it. If using prepackaged, cleaned spinach leaves, skip this step. Put the spinach in a pot with a tablespoon or two of water, just enough to prevent it from scorching. Cover the pot and cook over medium heat until very tender. Younger leaves will take less time

Drain and cool the spinach enough to handle. Squeeze all the liquid out by twisting it in a dry towel. This is a very important step — any excess liquid will require more flour in the dough and result in a tough gnocchi. Chop the spinach very fine with a knife. Do not use a food processor as it will liquefy the spinach. Set aside.

Bake the potatoes at 400°F, or microwave them on high, until tender when deeply pierced with a small knife. Allow to cool just enough to handle them comfortably. Peel while still warm and pass them through the fine disk of a food mill or potato ricer into a large bowl or onto a clean counter. Cool to room temperature.

Gently mix the potato and chopped spinach together. Beat the egg with the salt and nutmeg until just combined. With a rubber spatula or a flexible curved plastic bowl scraper, mix the egg lightly into the potatoes using a cutting/folding motion similar to mixing a cake. Sprinkle with the finely grated fresh Parmigiano-Reggiano and all but ¼ cup of the flour. Cut lightly into the potatoes. Do not overmix or gnocchi will be tough.

Gather the dough into a smooth ball and place it on a lightly floured board. Take a walnut-sized portion of dough, roll it into a 2-inch log, and cut the log into thirds. Test cook the three gnocchi in a small, deep saucepan of simmering water until they rise to the surface. Check the texture and add more flour to the dough if necessary — ⅛ cup at a time — until the additional tests indicate you've reached the desired consistency. The gnocchi should hold together when cooked without being gummy.

Divide the remaining dough into four to six pieces and roll each piece into a finger-thick rope on a lightly floured board. Cut each rope into ¾-inch pieces. You can press each piece over a wooden gnocchi or butter paddle or the reversed tines of a fork to create the small pockets and ridges that help the sauce cling to the gnocchi — or simply cut the ropes and leave the gnocchi unshaped. Place the finished gnocchi close together, but not touching, on a lightly floured tray. Set aside or refrigerate up to an hour while making the sauce.

Bring a very large, deep pot of water — no less than 1 gallon — to a simmer. Add 1 to 2 tablespoons salt and drop in the gnocchi, cooking no more than half the batch at a time. Stir a couple of times with a wooden spoon so the gnocchi move gently. The water should remain at a simmer rather than a rolling boil.

Have ready a large bowl with half the warmed sauce of your choice portioned into it. As the gnocchi rise to the surface, remove them with a slotted spoon, toss with the sauce, garnish as desired, and serve immediately. Repeat with the remaining gnocchi and sauce.

Alternatively, you can cook all the gnocchi at the same time in two separate pots and toss them all together in a large serving bowl with the appropriate amount of sauce.

These gnocchi can be frozen for up to two weeks after forming. See Freezer Notes, page 250.

Sauce Suggestions: Basic Tomato Sauce with Basil, Sage-Butter Sauce, Thyme-Garlic Butter Sauce, Roasted Red Pepper Purée, Gorgonzola Cream Sauce

SWEET POTATO GNOCCHI

/ serves 6

Sweet potatoes, although not traditionally used in the Italian cuisine, are becoming more popular and easier to find in Italy. In this recipe they are used as a partial replacement for Yukon Golds, adding a slight sweetness and gorgeous color, to the gnocchi. Be sure to use the coppery-skinned and orange-fleshed variety of sweet potato as they are soft, creamy, and fluffy when cooked. Because they naturally contain more moisture than other potato varieties, it's important not to add too much flour or overwork the dough.

1¼ pounds Yukon Gold potatoes, skin pricked 5 to 6 times

¾ pound sweet potato

½ cup cake flour

1 cup unbleached all-purpose flour
    + more for shaping the gnocchi

1 large egg

½ teaspoon freshly grated nutmeg

1 teaspoon kosher salt

½ teaspoon freshly ground white pepper

⅓ cup finely grated fresh Parmigiano-Reggiano
    + more for serving

Bake all the potatoes at 400°F until tender. Allow to cool just enough to handle them comfortably. Peel while still warm and pass them through the fine disk of a food mill into a large bowl or onto a clean counter. Cool to room temperature.

Whisk the two flours together in a small bowl. Beat the egg with the nutmeg, salt, and pepper until just combined.

Sprinkle the freshly grated Parmigiano-Reggiano over the potatoes. With a rubber spatula or a flexible curved plastic bowl scraper, mix it lightly into the potatoes using a cutting/folding motion similar to mixing a cake. Add the beaten egg and, using the same motion, lightly mix the egg into the potatoes. Do not overmix. You should still see streaks of egg in the dough. Sprinkle with all but ¼ cup of the flour mixture, and cut lightly into the potatoes. Bits of sweet potato in the dough will only add to the gnocchi's appearance. Do not be tempted to overmix or the gnocchi will be tough.

Gather the dough into a smooth ball and place it on a lightly floured board. Take a walnut-sized portion of dough, roll it into a 2-inch log, and cut the log into thirds. Test cook the three gnocchi in a small, deep saucepan of simmering water until they rise to the surface. Check the texture and add more flour to the dough if necessary — ⅛ cup at a time — until the additional tests indicate you've reached the desired consistency. The gnocchi should hold together when cooked without being gummy.

Divide the remaining dough into four to six pieces and roll each piece into a finger-thick rope on a lightly floured board. Cut each rope into ¾-inch pieces. You can press each piece over a wooden gnocchi or butter paddle or the reversed tines of a fork to create the small pockets and ridges that help the sauce cling to the gnocchi — or simply cut the ropes and leave the gnocchi unshaped. Place the finished gnocchi close together, but not touching, on a lightly floured tray. Set aside or refrigerate up to an hour while making the sauce.

Bring a very large, deep pot of water — no less than 1 gallon — to a simmer. Add 1 to 2 tablespoons salt and drop in the gnocchi, cooking no more than half the batch at a time. Stir a couple of times with a wooden spoon so the gnocchi move gently. The water should remain at a simmer rather than a rolling boil.

Have ready warmed serving bowls and a large mixing bowl with half your chosen sauce portioned into it. As the gnocchi rise to the surface, remove them with a slotted spoon, toss with the sauce, garnish as desired, and serve immediately. Repeat with the remaining gnocchi and sauce.

Alternatively, you can cook all the gnocchi at the same time in two separate pots and toss them all together in a large serving bowl with the appropriate amount of sauce. These gnocchi can be frozen for up to two weeks after forming. See Freezer Notes, page 250.

Sauce Suggestions: Browned Butter & Preserved Lemon Sauce with Ricotta, Pestos, Herbed Brown Butters, Sage-Butter Sauce, Smoked Ricotta Shavings with Cinnamon and Toasted Hazelnuts, Fresh Fava Bean & Pancetta Sauce; avoid heavy tomato or ragù sauces that overpower the delicate flavor of the sweet potato.

Potato gnocchi, the most well-known kind in the U.S., are not only often gummy, they are also the most difficult gnocchi to make well.

GNOCCHI WITHOUT POTATO

To many, "gnocchi" means potato gnocchi, but, after traveling extensively throughout Italy, I quickly learned that gnocchi vary as widely as the terrain and its inhabitants, reflecting the history and agriculture of each region. The recipes for the different types of gnocchi weave a rich tapestry from which to learn about and experience the Italian culture.

I've included a wide range of recipes in this chapter with hopes of engaging those who may have decided they don't like gnocchi — and expanding the repertoire of those who already enjoy them. I recommend these easy recipes that include bread, cheese, polenta, and vegetable-based gnocchi variations to both novice and experienced gnocchi-makers alike.

/ CANEDERLI

Canederli reminds me of the stuffing my mother cooked inside the turkey — wonderfully soft and moderately seasoned cubes of bread that almost, but not quite, melted in my mouth — a favorite comfort food.

I vividly remember my first bowl of canederli after a morning's strenuous hike in the mountainous Dolomite region of Italy where I spend a week or two every year. It was a sunny day, and we stopped for lunch at a *rifugio* — a refuge that in Italy usually serves lunch and sometimes offers lodging, where one can usually find simple menu choices. Curious, I ordered the local dish of canederli with *verza*, or Savoy cabbage. Served in broth, and showered with Parmigiano-Reggiano, the gnocchi were the perfect lunch. Returning home, I searched old Italian cookbooks for a variety of recipes and began making my own.

Historically older than the potato variety, canederli are bread-based gnocchi found in the northeastern regions of Italy — Trentino-Alto Adige, Friuli, and parts of Veneto — as well as other southeastern European countries. The word itself derives from the German and Austrian *knödel*, or dumplings.

Canederli are a perfect example of *la cucina povera*, where everything edible is used and nothing is wasted — including stale bread. They can be plain and simple, as small as walnuts or as large as baseballs, bound together with just milk and eggs. Or they can be made more hearty and flavorful with the addition of various meats and cheeses — even elevated to a dish worthy of fine restaurants. You can serve them as a first course, as a entrée, or as an accompaniment to meat stews and roasts, sauced with a hearty ragù. They can even be sweetened and served as dessert.

I've included some of my favorite recipes, representing a wide range of possibilities for canederli, in this chapter. Although many of the recipes may seem very similar, they vary enough to warrant separate instructions because of the way the different ingredients affect the dough. Read each recipe carefully and follow it closely.

CANEDERLI TIPS

There are very few tricks to making canederli: they do not require a lot of kitchen experience or uncommon tools. I've found that hands are best for mixing the dough. Unlike potato gnocchi, the dough is simple to make and easy to form. You can always adjust liquid or breadcrumbs as needed without sacrificing the quality of the final product. I sometimes change things up by adding a few heaping tablespoons of whole milk ricotta to the dough.

If you care to experiment on your own, I suggest you pick a recipe you like and substitute some of the specified ingredients, such as a different cheese, vegetable, meat, or fish, taking into consideration the texture and flavor of the original. Once you've made canederli a few times, you will find it easy to put your own touch on them.

/ ABOUT THE BREAD

These recipes are based on the common Italian crusty white loaf or a light whole-wheat bread that does not contain enriching ingredients like eggs, fat, honey, or dough conditioners that extend its shelf life. In the U.S., a good farmer's loaf or other large round crusty bread works well. Traditionally, northern Italy, unlike other regions of the country, offers a much wider variety of grains for making bread. The canederli recipes can be easily modified by replacing the type of bread used, so search your local bakery shelves for interesting possibilities and read the labels to be sure there are no added ingredients that would affect the taste and texture.

What's most important is that the bread you use be stale, with enough moisture left in it to allow light packing when compressed into a measuring cup. If you need to make stale bread, break up the loaf and put it in a 250°F oven for 30 to 45 minutes, or leave it at room temperature overnight. Check for consistency and extend the drying time if needed. Do not substitute fine dry commercial breadcrumbs for the stale bread unless specifically stated in the recipe or the recipe will not work. Use dry breadcrumbs only as needed to tighten the dough.

/ TESTING CANEDERLI

Some of the recipes suggest testing a few canederli before forming the remaining dough and others do not. The canederli dough needs to be wet enough to hold together in simmering water. If in doubt, test before forming all of the canederli and add more liquid or fine dry crumbs as needed. I keep some fine dry breadcrumbs on hand to add to the dough if it needs tightening, as additional flour tends to leaden the texture of the finished gnocchi. I also keep stale crumbs in my freezer to use when I feel inspired.

/ MEASURING THE INGREDIENTS

I use volume rather than weight measurements for canederli with no inconsistencies in the results.

/ STUFFING CANEDERLI

These bread-based gnocchi are perfect candidates for stuffing. Any of the fillings suggested on pages 157 will also work for canederli. You can easily vary the size of the finished gnocco. It's not unusual to find baseball-sized canederli with golf-ball sized filling! One serving can make an entire meal.

/ COOKING CANEDERLI

Cook canederli in lightly simmering water rather than at a rolling boil. Canederli tend to flake when cooking, losing a few small pieces here and there; don't be alarmed unless they actually fall apart.

Bread-based gnocchi take longer to cook than other types of gnocchi and are not done when they rise to the surface. Note variations in cooking times in individual recipes, take their size into account, and adjust cooking time accordingly. Most 1 to 1½-inch canederli will be done in 5 to 6 minutes once they rise to the surface, while baseball-sized canederli will take more than 20 minutes. Fortunately, it's difficult to overcook canederli.

Once cooked, you can brown canederli in butter to crisp the exterior. This touch is particularly wonderful when serving atop vegetables.

/ FREEZING CANEDERLI

I generally don't recommend freezing canederli as some of the doughs tend to suffer freezer damage and break apart when cooked. Baseball-sized canederli in particular will deteriorate when frozen, so I don't recommend it with any gnocchi larger than 1½ inches in diameter. In a few cases, I've noted recipes that have had good results when frozen. If you do freeze your canederli, do not thaw them before cooking. Increase the recommended cooking time by two to four minutes and test for doneness.

/ SERVING CANEDERLI

When serving in the traditional manner, presented in a shallow bowl of broth, it's best to cook the canederli in water first, then dish them into the hot broth so the broth remains clear rather than speckled with pieces of bread. And it's imperative to use a really good broth. Make your favorite or follow one of the recommended recipes on pages 223-224.

ARTICHOKE CANEDERLI

/ serves 6 to 8

Combine bread-based canederli from northern Italy with artichokes from southern Italy, add some goat cheese, and you have a wonderful combination of textures and flavors that can be served in the traditional way — in a good, wholesome broth — or with a sauce. I love these either way.

Fresh artichokes are not quick to prepare, but I prefer them to the canned or frozen variety, which are not nearly as tasty and usually contain additives that affect the flavor, although you can use them if fresh artichokes are not available. Just be sure to squeeze any excess liquid out of them before chopping or processing.

A simple white bread will allow the delicate artichoke and goat cheese flavors to dominate. Sauces containing herbs such as mint, thyme, sage, and parsley, as well as sausage, smoked meats, citrus, garlic, capers, and butter will complement the artichoke and goat cheese.

8-10 medium artichokes

OR 2 (14-ounce) cans artichoke hearts or bottoms packed in water (not oil)

OR enough frozen artichoke hearts or bottoms to make 2 cups very finely chopped artichoke purée

2 lemons, quartered

2 cups unbleached all-purpose flour

2 cups crustless, coarsely crumbled, stale white breadcrumbs, lightly packed

2 large eggs

⅔ cup (5 ounces) soft goat cheese, at room temperature

1 teaspoon fresh thyme, chopped (optional)

½ teaspoon salt

Freshly ground black pepper to taste

If using fresh artichokes, wash them under cold water. Cut the stems from the artichokes at the base and set aside. Trim about 1 inch from the tip of the artichokes and place them tips down in a deep pot large enough to hold all the chokes in a single layer. Add the reserved stems. Fill the pot with enough water to cover the artichokes, add the quartered lemons, and bring to a boil. Cook, covered, over medium heat until the outer leaves pull off easily, about 30 to 45 minutes. Drain, discard the lemon, and chill in ice water to stop the cooking.

When cool enough to handle, drain and squeeze all excess water from the artichokes. Remove and discard the leaves. Using a melon scoop or spoon, scrape the flesh from the bottom of the leaves and put it into a small bowl. When you reach the center of the artichoke, remove the fibrous choke and other stringy parts, chop the hearts

coarsely, and put into the bowl with the other artichoke pieces. Repeat until all the artichokes are prepared. Peel the stems, coarsely chop and add them to the bowl. Finely chop all the pieces by hand or in a food processor. Reserve 2 cups and set aside any extra for another use.

If using canned artichokes, drain well, squeeze dry, and finely chop by hand or in a food processor. Reserve 2 cups and set aside any extra for another use.

If using frozen artichoke hearts, cook according to instructions, cool, drain well, squeeze dry, and finely chop by hand or in a food processor. Reserve 2 cups and set aside any extra for another use.

In a large bowl, beat the eggs with the goat cheese, optional thyme, salt, and freshly ground black pepper until the texture is smooth and uniform. Add the finely chopped artichoke and mix well. Sprinkle with the flour and breadcrumbs and mix lightly just until combined. Cover and let rest at least 30 minutes to allow the breadcrumbs to soak up all the liquid.

With dampened hands or a scoop, form 1½-inch balls, rolling the dough lightly between your hands to smooth the surface. Place the finished canederli close together, but not touching, on a lightly floured tray. Set aside or refrigerate up to two hours while you're making the sauce.

Bring a very large, deep pot of water — no less than 1 gallon — to a simmer. Add 1 to 2 tablespoons salt and drop in the canederli, cooking no more than half the batch at a time. Stir a couple of times with a wooden spoon so the gnocchi move gently. The water should remain at a simmer rather than a rolling boil.

After the canederli rise to the surface, cook them for another 5 to 6 minutes. Test for doneness; they should be firm with no raw taste when completely cooked. If not done, increase the cooking time another 2 minutes and test again. Remove with a slotted spoon and keep warm while cooking the remaining canederli. Toss with your chosen sauce, garnish as desired, and serve immediately.

Alternately, you can cook all the canederli at the same time in two separate pots and toss them all together in a large bowl of sauce.

If you plan to serve the canederli in broth, use your favorite rich homemade stock or follow the recipe for Italian Brodo on page 224. Serve with fresh shavings of Parmigiano-Reggiano and chopped fresh parsley or thyme.

You can make the dough up to 24 hours in advance and keep it refrigerated until ready to use. You can also shape the balls and freeze them no longer than two weeks. See Freezer Notes, page 250, for more information. Do not thaw the canederli before cooking. Time them as they rise to the surface, making adjustments as needed. You will need to increase the cooking time of frozen canederli by 2 to 4 minutes depending on their size.

Sauce Suggestions: Creamy Lemon, Peas & Prosciutto Sauce, Lemon & Garlic Sauce, Thyme-Garlic Butter Sauce, Browned Butter & Preserved Lemon Sauce, Creamy Leek Sauce

BEET CANEDERLI

/ serves 4 to 6

Any variety of beet can be used for these canederli, although the reddest ones that produce the deepest flavor and most colorful gnocchi are my favorite. I suggest a plain whole wheat or white bread for these so the beets' delicate sweetness remains prominent. A touch of cinnamon or nutmeg, even some grated orange rind, is a nice addition to the dough. These moist and tender canederli are really wonderful served in a spinach soup, a simple broth, or with any of the sauces suggested below.

1 pound beets, red, yellow, or striped Chioggia, scrubbed, root ends removed

5 cups crustless, coarsely crumbled stale white breadcrumbs, lightly packed

½ cup whole milk

4 tablespoons extra-virgin olive oil, divided

1 small onion, minced (about ⅔ cup)

1 clove garlic, minced

½ cup finely grated ricotta salata, Parmigiano-Reggiano, aged Asiago, or Gorgonzola

 Piccante

2 large eggs

1 teaspoon kosher salt

Freshly ground black pepper to taste

¼ cup finely chopped parsley, thyme, or basil (optional)

¼ cup all-purpose flour + more for shaping

Preheat the oven to 400°F. Brush the beets with 2 tablespoons olive oil, place snuggly in a baking dish with trimmed ends down, and season lightly with salt and freshly ground black pepper. Add enough water to cover beets by about ¼ inch and cover tightly with foil. Bake about 1 to 1½ hours, or until tender when pierced with a knife. Add more water to the pan if necessary during baking to keep the beets moist.

In a medium bowl, cover the breadcrumbs with the milk, stir to combine, and set aside to soak while the beets are roasting.

Remove the cooked beets from the oven, uncover and let cool completely. Peel and coarsely grate, then roughly chop them. You should have 2 cups. Squeeze any excess moisture from the beets and set aside.

The beets can be prepared a few days in advance and refrigerated until ready to use.

Meanwhile, in a small frying pan over medium heat, sauté the onion in the remaining 2 tablespoons olive oil until soft and beginning to color. Add the garlic and continue to cook, stirring, for another minute. Remove from heat and set aside.

Work the breadcrumbs between your fingers to create a thick, even-textured mass, squeezing out any extra moisture. Add the prepared beets, beaten egg, salt, grated cheese, and onion mixture to the breadcrumbs and mix well. Sprinkle with the flour and some grindings of black pepper and mix again to form a dough. Let rest for 10 minutes or refrigerate up to 2 hours.

With dampened hands or a scoop, form 1½-inch balls, rolling the dough between your hands to lightly compact and smooth the surface of the canederli. If the dough is too wet and canederli won't hold together, add up to ¼ cup fine dry breadcrumbs, a bit at a time, to firm up the dough. Place the finished canederli close together, but not touching, on a lightly floured tray. Set aside or refrigerate up to 2 hours while making the sauce.

When ready to cook the canederli, bring a very large, deep pot of water — no less than 1 gallon — to a simmer. Add 1 to 2 tablespoons salt and drop in the canederli, cooking no more than half the batch at a time. Stir a couple of times with a wooden spoon so the gnocchi move gently. The water should remain at a simmer rather than a rolling boil.

After the canederli rise to the surface, cook them for another 5 to 6 minutes. Test for doneness: they should be firm with no raw taste when completely cooked. If not done, increase the cooking time another 2 minutes and test again. Remove with a slotted spoon and keep warm while cooking the remaining canederli. Toss with your chosen sauce, garnish as desired, and serve immediately.

Alternately, you can cook all the canederli at the same time in two separate pots and toss them all together in a large bowl of sauce.

If you plan to serve the canederli in broth, use your favorite, rich homemade stock or follow the recipe for Italian Brodo on page 224. Serve with fresh shavings of Parmigiano-Reggiano and chopped fresh parsley or thyme.

You can make the dough up to 24 hours in advance and keep it refrigerated until ready to use. You can also shape the balls and freeze them no longer than two weeks. See Freezer Notes, page 250, for more information. Do not thaw the canederli before cooking. Time them as they rise to the surface, making adjustments as needed. You will need to increase the cooking time of frozen canederli by 2 to 4 minutes depending on their size.

Sauce Suggestions: Poppy Seed-Mint Butter Sauce, Savory Zabaglione with Horseradish Cream Sauce, Sage-Butter Sauce, Creamy Leek Sauce, Pancetta-Orange Sauce, Gorgonzola Cream Sauce

CABBAGE & SPECK CANEDERLI

/ serves 4 to 6

This recipe comes closest to duplicating the first canederli I tasted, which propelled me to learn how to make delicious bread gnocchi. They easily stand on their own served simply with melted butter or in your favorite homemade broth.

5 cups crustless, coarsely crumbled stale breadcrumbs from a dark or light bread, lightly packed

1 cup whole milk

2 cups finely sliced and chopped green cabbage (Savoy is best)

¼ pound unsalted butter, divided

2 ounces thinly sliced, finely chopped speck or prosciutto

3 large leeks, white part only, thinly sliced, washed, and finely chopped (about ¾ cup)

1 large whole egg and 1 large egg yolk

¼ cup finely chopped fresh Italian parsley leaves

1 teaspoon cumin seeds, crushed in a mortar

Pinch freshly grated nutmeg

½ teaspoon kosher salt

½ teaspoon freshly ground black pepper

⅞ cup unbleached all-purpose flour + more for shaping

Finely grated fresh Parmigiano-Reggiano for serving

Put the breadcrumbs in a medium bowl and pour the milk over them. Set aside to soak 20 to 30 minutes while preparing the cabbage. Lightly beat the eggs with the parsley, cumin, nutmeg, salt, and pepper. Set aside.

In a medium sauté pan over medium-high heat, melt 2 tablespoons butter. Add the cabbage, speck, and finely chopped leeks. Turn heat to low and cook, stirring frequently, about 10 to 15 minutes, or until the speck and leeks are soft. Drain any extra liquid from the cabbage mixture and set aside.

Squeeze the breadcrumbs to remove excess milk. In a medium bowl, fold the breadcrumbs and the drained cabbage together. Lightly incorporate the egg mixture. Sprinkle with the flour and mix to a uniform consistency.

With damp hands or a scoop, form 1½-inch balls. Place the finished canederli close together on a lightly floured tray. Set aside or refrigerate up to 2 hours if desired.

When ready to cook the canederli, bring a large, deep pot of water — no less than 1 gallon — to a simmer. Add 1 to 2 tablespoons salt and drop in the canederli, cooking only half the batch at a time. Stir a couple of times with a wooden spoon so the gnocchi move gently. The water should remain at a simmer rather than a rolling boil. Melt the remaining 6 tablespoons butter and keep warm.

After the canederli rise to the surface, cook another 5 to 6 minutes and test for doneness. They should be firm with no raw taste when completely cooked. If not done, increase the cooking time another 2 minutes and test again. Remove canederli with a slotted spoon and keep warm while cooking the remaining canederli. Alternatively, you can cook all the canederli at the same time in two separate pots.

Divide canederli among individual serving dishes and dribble with melted butter. Sprinkle with freshly grated Parmigiano and serve immediately.

You can make the dough up to 24 hours in advance and keep it refrigerated until ready to use. You can also shape the balls and freeze them no longer than two weeks. See Freezer Notes, page 250, for more information. Do not thaw the canederli before cooking. Time them as they rise to the surface, making adjustments as needed. You will need to increase the cooking time of frozen canederli by 2 to 4 minutes depending on their size.

Additional Sauce Suggestions: Thyme-Garlic Butter Sauce, Fonduta, Basic Tomato Sauce, Porcini Mushroom Sauce, Creamy Leek Sauce

CANEDERLI WITH LIVER

/ serves 4 to 6

This traditional canederli with a delicate liver flavor is a perfect example of la cucina povera, *where nothing is wasted. An American-born friend whose family comes from northern Italy tells me he can remember eating a similar "liver dumpling" that his* nonna *(grandmother) made — and he liked them!*

I suggest searching for lardo (a lightly seasoned and cured pork fat) if you live near an Italian market as the flavor is undeniably rich and distinctive. If lardo is not available, a high-quality, naturally processed lard is a reasonable substitute. You can use olive oil or unsalted butter if you're opposed to lard, but you will sacrifice some flavor.

Smaller-sized liver canederli are exceptionally good served in your favorite rich onion soup; larger balls can be served on a bed of caramelized onions with bacon or pancetta bits scattered on top. You can substitute equal amounts of chicken livers for the calf or pork if you like, and experiment with the optional herbs. Lemon rind can be substituted for the orange or the citrus can be completely eliminated.

5 cups crustless, coarsely crumbled stale breadcrumbs
  from a dark or light loaf, lightly packed

1½ cups whole milk

¾ pound pork or calves liver

¼ cup lardo or other pork fat

1 clove garlic, minced

1 medium onion, finely chopped

1 whole egg

1 egg yolk

1 tablespoon finely zested orange rind (optional)

1 tablespoon marjoram leaves, chopped

½ cup chopped chives

Salt and freshly ground black pepper to taste

½ cup fine semolina flour

/ OPTIONAL GARNISHES:

Finely chopped and sautéed bacon or pancetta

Caramelized onions

Lightly toasted and chopped hazelnuts

Soak liver in ½ cup milk in a small bowl for about 20 minutes. Remove the liver and discard the milk. Pat liver dry and finely chop. Set aside.

Meanwhile, in a small sauté pan over medium heat, melt the lardo or other fat with the onion and minced garlic and sauté until the onion is soft but not brown, about 5 minutes. Set aside.

In a medium bowl, beat 1 cup milk with the whole egg and additional egg yolk. Add orange zest, marjoram, and chives. Add the liver, breadcrumbs, and the onion mixture and mix well with hands until well combined. Add salt and pepper to taste. Sprinkle with the flour and mix again to form a uniform dough. Set aside to rest 30 minutes.

Bring a small, deep saucepan of lightly salted water to a simmer. Measuring about 1 heaping tablespoon of dough each, form a few canederli into balls, compress the dough, and drop them into simmering water. Cook until they rise to the surface. Continue cooking another 5 to 6 minutes and test for doneness. The inside should be firm, not raw. Add a few tablespoons of fine dry breadcrumbs if the canederli are too soft or a tablespoon or two of milk if too dry. Retest if necessary.

With dampened hands or a scoop, form 1½-inch balls, rolling the dough between your hands to lightly compact and smooth the surface of the canederli. Place the finished canederli close together, but not touching, on a lightly floured tray. Set aside or refrigerate up to 2 hours while making the sauce.

When ready to cook the canederli, bring a very large, deep pot of water — no less than 1 gallon — to a simmer. Add 1 to 2 tablespoons salt and drop in the canederli, cooking no more than half the batch at a time. Stir a couple of times with a wooden spoon so the gnocchi move gently. The water should remain at a simmer rather than a rolling boil.

After the canederli rise to the surface, cook them for another 5 to 6 minutes. Test for doneness: they should be firm with no raw taste when completely cooked. If not done, increase the cooking time another 2 minutes and test again. Remove with a slotted spoon and keep warm while cooking the remaining canederli.

Alternatively, you can cook all the canederli at the same time in two separate pots.

Have warmed, shallow bowls ready with the hot sauce or soup portioned into each one. Remove canederli with a slotted spoon when done and divide among prepared bowls. Garnish as desired and serve immediately.

You can make the dough up to 24 hours in advance and keep it refrigerated until ready to use. You can also shape the balls and freeze them no longer than two weeks. See Freezer Notes, page 250, for more information. Do not thaw the canederli before cooking. Time them as they rise to the surface, making adjustments as needed. You will need to increase the cooking time of frozen canederli by 2 to 4 minutes depending on their size.

Sauce Suggestions: Pancetta-Orange Sauce, Creamy Leek Sauce, Lemon & Garlic Sauce, Garlic Scape Pesto (thinned with olive oil), Pancetta, Radicchio, Pine Nut & Rosemary Sauce, Cabbage & Apple Sauce

STRANGOLAPRETI (BREAD & SWISS CHARD CANEDERLI)

/ serves 4 to 6

This is one of the more traditional canederli from the northeastern regions of Italy. Many variations on this theme are also served in restaurants and homes in the mountainous areas south of Austria. I've eaten them big and small, in sauce and broth, and with a variety of greens and cheeses. All are wonderful. Some of my favorites were in a small restaurant near San Martino di Castrozza, where they were as big as baseballs and swam in a pool of melted butter. As with other bread-based gnocchi, they're also easy to make.

Strangolapreti vary greatly from region to region, and the name, which means priest strangler, has as many tales of origin as there are recipes. (My favorite story is on page 52, with a recipe for potato-spinach gnocchi by the same name.) In some regions strangolapreti refers to a thick pasta instead of a bread-based gnocchi.

Be sure to weigh the Swiss chard after it's cleaned of stems and tough parts. Other hard grating cheeses from the region, such as an aged Asagio or Piave, can be substituted for the Pamigiano-Reggiano or Grana Padano. If you're making canederli larger than 1 inch in diameter, try pressing ¼-inch cubes of fontina, Taleggio, La Tur or other melting cheese into the center. It's absolutely divine!

5 cups crustless, coarsely crumbled, stale white
  breadcrumbs, lightly packed

1 cup whole milk

2 tablespoons extra-virgin olive oil

2 shallots, finely chopped

2½ pounds Swiss chard leaves, washed, stems and
  tough parts removed, shredded to make 2 pounds

2 large eggs, lightly beaten

1 teaspoon kosher salt

1 cup finely grated fresh Parmigiano-Reggiano
  OR Grana Padano

½ to ¾ cup unbleached all-purpose flour
  + additional flour for shaping

Freshly ground black pepper

Freshly grated Parmigiano-Reggiano, aged Asiago
  or Piave cheese for serving

In a bowl, soak the bread in the milk for about 30 minutes. Squeeze out any excess milk, crumble the bread into a large bowl and set aside.

Put the olive oil and shallots in a small sauté pan and cook over medium heat until transparent. Add to the crumbled bread and mix lightly.

Bring a very large pot of water — no less than 1 gallon — to a boil. Add 1 to 2 tablespoons salt and the Swiss chard and cook until tender, about 5 minutes. Remove to a strainer with a slotted spoon and allow to cool enough to handle. Squeeze the chard until very dry. You should have 2 cups.

Beat the eggs lightly with the salt. Finely chop the cooled Swiss chard and add to the bowl of bread along with the

egg mixture, grated cheese, and a few grindings of black pepper. Mix lightly, then sprinkle with ½ cup flour and mix again with your hands to form a uniform dough.

Form a tablespoon of dough into a ball and drop into the simmering water. Cook until it rises to the surface. For 1½-inch balls, continue cooking another 5 minutes and test for doneness. The inside should be firm, not raw. Add a few tablespoons of fine dry breadcrumbs if the strangolapreti are too soft, or a tablespoon or two of milk if too dry. Retest if necessary.

With damp hands or a scoop, shape the remaining dough into balls of your desired size and place the finished strangolapreti close together, but not touching, on a lightly floured tray. Set aside or refrigerate up to 2 hours while making the sauce.

When ready to cook, carefully drop the strangolapreti into the reheated salted water, cooking no more than half the batch at a time. Stir a couple of times with a wooden spoon so the strangolapreti move gently. The water should remain at a simmer rather than a rolling boil. Note that the cooking time of the strangolapreti will vary considerably depending on the size. Start testing for doneness 5 minutes after they rise to the surface for 1½-inch balls. Strangolapreti as large as baseballs will take 20 minutes or more.

When done, remove the strangolapreti with a slotted spoon and sauce as desired. Divide among heated serving bowls and serve with freshly grated cheese on the side.

Alternately, you can cook all the strangolapreti at the same time in two separate pots and toss them all together in a large bowl of sauce.

You can make the dough up to 24 hours in advance and keep it refrigerated until ready to use. You can also shape the balls and freeze them no longer than two weeks. See Freezer Notes, page 250, for more information. Do not thaw the strangolapreti before cooking. Time them as they rise to the surface, making adjustments as needed. You will need to increase the cooking time of frozen strangolapreti by 2 to 4 minutes depending on their size.

Suggested Sauces: Homemade Broth, Sage-Butter Sauce, Thyme-Garlic Butter Sauce, Lemon & Garlic Sauce, Basic Tomato Sauce, Roasted Red Pepper Purée, Oven-Roasted Cherry Tomatoes

CHICKEN & PROSCIUTTO CANEDERLI

/ serves 4 to 6

These canederli make a wonderful main course, especially when served on a bed of sautéed greens, with a chunky tomato sauce, or atop a pool of a fontina-based cheese sauce, then drizzled with olive oil and showered with freshly grated Parmigiano-Reggiano. I prefer them large — as big as baseballs — but they are equally good made smaller and served in the more traditional manner.

5 cups crustless, coarsely crumbled stale white
   breadcrumbs, lightly packed

1 cup whole milk

12 ounces skinless chicken breast, finely chopped
   (about 1 whole large skinless breast)

4 ounces prosciutto, finely chopped, including fat

1 medium red onion, finely chopped

3 tablespoons unsalted butter

Salt and freshly ground black pepper to taste

⅜ cup finely grated fresh Parmigiano-Reggiano

1 large egg, beaten

½ cup whole milk ricotta (does not need to be drained)

2 tablespoons chopped thyme, marjoram or sage

⅜-½ cup unbleached all-purpose flour

In a medium bowl, soak the bread in the milk for about 30 minutes. Mean-while, melt the butter in a sauté pan over medium heat. Add the chicken, onion, and prosciutto and cook, stirring, until barely browned. Season lightly with salt and freshly ground black pepper.

Squeeze any excess milk from the breadcrumbs and crumble into a large bowl. Add the chicken mixture, beaten egg, ricotta, grated Parmigiano-Reggiano and herb of choice. Mix well. Sprinkle with ⅜ cup of the flour and mix again with hands to form a uniform dough.

Bring a small deep saucepan of lightly salted water to a simmer. Measuring about 1 heaping tablespoon of dough each, form a couple of canederli into balls, compressing the dough, and drop them into simmering water. Cook until they rise to the surface. Continue cooking another 4 to 6 minutes, then test for doneness. The inside should be firm, not raw. Add a few tablespoons of fine dry breadcrumbs if the canederli are too soft or a tablespoon or two of milk if too dry.

With damp hands or a scoop, shape the dough into balls of desired size and place the finished canederli close together, but not touching, on a lightly floured tray. Set aside or refrigerate up to 2 hours while preparing the sauce.

When ready to cook the canederli, bring a very large, deep pot of water — no less than 1 gallon — to a simmer. Add 1 to 2 tablespoons salt and drop in the canederli, cooking no more than half the batch at a time. Stir a couple of times

with a wooden spoon so the gnocchi move gently. The water should remain at a simmer rather than a rolling boil.

Start timing when the gnocchi rise to the surface. Note that the cooking time of the canederli will vary considerably depending on the size. For baseball-size canederli, allow 20 minutes versus the 4 to 6 minutes for smaller balls. Test for doneness and increase cooking time another 2 minutes if necessary. Alternatively, you can cook all the canederli at the same time in two separate pots.

Have warmed, shallow bowls ready with hot sauce portioned into each one. Remove canederli with a slotted spoon when done and divide among prepared bowls. Add a drizzle of olive oil and a dusting of the freshly grated Parmigiano-Reggiano, or serve in a pool of your chosen sauce.

You can make the dough up to 24 hours in advance and keep it refrigerated until ready to use. You can also shape the balls and freeze them no longer than two weeks. See Freezer Notes, page 250. Do not thaw the canederli before cooking. Time them as they rise to the surface. You will need to increase the cooking time of frozen canederli 2 to 4 minutes depending on their size.

Sauce Suggestions: Roasted Red Pepper Purée, Parmigiano-Reggiano Cream Sauce, Lemon, Thyme & Scamorza Sauce, Thyme-Garlic Butter Sauce, Sage-Butter Sauce, Oven-Roasted Cherry Tomatoes

FISH CANEDERLI

/ serves 4

Canederli made with fish is more common than you might think; although I've not found it on many mountain restaurant menus, it's often served at home. The fish used is typically a tender variety from one of the many northern Italian lakes, often caught by an enthusiastic local fisherman, perhaps a member of the family. Any lightly flavored and tender fish — such as such as flounder, sole, red snapper, tilapia, lake trout, or lake whitefish — can be used. I love the buttery flavor of these canederli, most appreciated when they're on the small side, 1 to 2 inches in diameter. If you choose to serve them with a lemon and garlic sauce, omit the lemon zest in the dough.

8 ounces mild, finely textured fish fillet of choice

3 cups crustless, finely crumbled stale white
    breadcrumbs, lightly packed

⅔ cup whole milk

2 tablespoons unsalted butter, cut into small pieces
    and brought to room temperature

2 large eggs

½ lemon, finely zested (about 1½ tablespoons)

Finely chopped parsley or thyme to taste

Salt and freshly ground black pepper to taste

⅜ cup unbleached all-purpose flour

In a medium bowl, soak the breadcrumbs in milk for about 30 minutes. Hard-boil one of the eggs. When cooked, finely chop it, along with the fish, and set aside.

Add the softened butter, chopped egg and fish, lemon zest, remaining egg, and parsley to the breadcrumbs and mix with hands until well combined. Add salt and pepper to taste. Sprinkle with the flour and mix again to form a uniform dough.

Bring a small deep saucepan of lightly salted water to a simmer.

Measuring 1 heaping tablespoon of dough each, form a couple of canederli into balls, compressing the dough, and drop them into the simmering water. Cook until they rise to the surface. Continue cooking another 4 to 6 minutes and test for doneness. The inside should be firm, not raw. Add a few tablespoons of fine dry breadcrumbs if canederli are too soft or a tablespoon of milk if too dry. Retest if necessary.

With dampened hands or a scoop, form 1- to 2-inch balls, rolling the dough between your hands to lightly compact and smooth the surface of the canederli. If the dough is too wet and canederli won't hold together, add up to ¼ cup fine dry breadcrumbs, a bit at a time, to firm up the dough. Place the finished canederli close together, but not touching, on a lightly floured tray. Set aside or refrigerate up to 2 hours while making the sauce.

When ready to cook the canederli, bring a very large deep pot of water to simmer — no less than 1 gallon — add 1-2 tablespoons of salt. Drop in the canederli, cooking no more than half the batch at a time. Stir a couple of times with a wooden spoon so the gnocchi move gently. The water should remain at a simmer rather than a rolling boil.

After the canederli rise to the surface, cook them for another 5 to 6 minutes. Test for doneness: they should be firm with no raw taste when completely cooked. If not done, increase the cooking time another 2 minutes and test again. Remove with a slotted spoon and keep warm while cooking the remaining canederli. Alternately, you can cook all the canederli at the same time in two separate pots.

Have shallow bowls ready with hot sauce portioned into each one. Remove canederli with a slotted spoon and divide among prepared bowls. Add a drizzle of olive oil.

You can make the dough up to 24 hours in advance and keep it refrigerated until ready to use. You can also shape the balls and freeze them no longer than two weeks. Do not thaw the canederli before cooking. Time them as they rise to the surface, making adjustments as needed. You will need to increase the cooking time of frozen canederli by 2 to 4 minutes depending on their size.

Sauce Suggestions: Lemon & Garlic Sauce, Uncooked Fresh Tomato Sauce, Thyme-Garlic Butter Sauce, Olive-Mint Pesto, Fish or Vegetable Broth

SAVORY RICOTTA CANEDERLI

/ serves 4 to 6

Canederli, the traditional gnocchi from northern Italy, are usually made with a base of breadcrumbs. These canederli, however, are made with ricotta and just enough breadcrumbs, Parmigiano-Reggiano cheese, and egg to hold them together. As a result, they're softer and richer than other savory canederli found in the mountainous regions of Italy. Served with browned butter and an additional dusting of Parmigiano-Reggiano, they're superb as either a first or main course. If you can find ricotta di bufala (buffalo milk) or pecora (sheep's milk) ricotta, the subtle difference in flavor will make the search worthwhile.

2 cups fresh whole milk ricotta OR a 15-ounce
    container, placed in a cheesecloth-lined colander
    set in a bowl and drained for 30 minutes before using

4 eggs, beaten

½ teaspoon kosher salt

½ cup unbleached all-purpose flour

⅔ cup finely grated fresh Parmigiano-Reggiano

⅜ cup fine dry breadcrumbs, untoasted

½ cup unsalted butter

Additional finely grated fresh Parmigiano-Reggiano
    for the table

Dash of ground cinnamon (optional)

Fill a large pot with about 6 quarts water, add 1 tablespoon salt, and bring to a boil.

Put the butter in a large skillet and melt it over very low heat. Set aside and keep warm.

In a medium bowl, lightly blend the ricotta with the eggs and salt.

Mix the dry ingredients together in another bowl until well combined and sprinkle over the ricotta mixture. Fold together just until incorporated. Do not overmix or canederli will be tough. The dough will be stiff and somewhat sticky.

With dampened hands or a scoop, form 1½-inch balls, rolling the dough between your hands to lightly compact and smooth the surface of the canederli. If the dough is too wet and canederli won't hold together, add up to ¼ cup fine dry breadcrumbs, a bit at a time, to firm up the dough. Place the finished canederli close together, but not touching, on a lightly floured tray. Set aside or refrigerate up to 2 hours while making the sauce.

Bring a very large deep pot of water to simmer — no less than 1 gallon — add 1-2 tablespoons of salt. Drop the shaped canederli into the simmering salted water, cooking no more than half a batch at a time.

After the canederli rise to the surface, cook another 5 to 6 minutes and test for doneness. They should be firm with no raw taste when completely cooked. If not done, increase the cooking time another 2 minutes and test again. Alternatively, you can cook all the canederli at the same time in two separate pots.

Meanwhile, rewarm the butter, allowing it to lightly brown. Remove the canederli from the pot with a large slotted spoon and drain for a few seconds. Gently place the canederli in the browned butter and roll them around a bit to firm them up and completely coat them. Add a dash of ground cinnamon if desired. Serve immediately in warm shallow bowls, passing additional freshly grated Parmigiano-Reggiano at the table.

You can make the dough up to 24 hours in advance and keep it refrigerated until ready to use. You can also shape the balls and freeze them no longer than two weeks. See Freezer Notes, page 250, for more information. Do not thaw the canederli before cooking. Time them as they rise to the surface, making adjustments as needed. You will need to increase the cooking time of frozen canederli by 2 to 4 minutes depending on their size.

Additional Sauce Suggestions: Basic Tomato Sauce, Sage or Thyme Butter Sauce, Poppy Seed-Mint Butter Sauce, Pine Nut-Butter Sauce, Lemon & Garlic Sauce, Sage Pesto

WHOLE GRAIN-BUCKWHEAT CANEDERLI

/ serves 6 to 8

The rich, deep, wholegrain flavor of these canederli lends itself to a hearty meal on a cold winter night. I prefer to serve them with a regional cheese sauce, such as fontina, or in a soup showered with some shavings of Parmigiano-Reggiano. The dark color and shape reminds me of meatballs.

6 cups crustless, coarsely crumbled stale breadcrumbs from a dark whole-wheat or rye loaf, lightly packed

1 tablespoon olive oil

¼ pound speck or prosciutto, thinly sliced and coarsely chopped

3 large leeks, white part only, cleaned and finely minced (about 1 cup)

2 garlic cloves, minced

¼ cup finely chopped fresh Italian parsley

½ cup finely grated fresh Parmigiano-Reggiano

2 large eggs, lightly beaten with 1 teaspoon salt

1¼ cups whole milk

½ cup finely milled buckwheat flour

¼-½ finely milled whole-wheat flour

   + more for shaping

Freshly ground black pepper to taste

Place the crumbled bread in a large bowl.

Coat the bottom of a sauté pan with the olive oil and toss in the speck, leek, and garlic. Cook over medium heat, stirring constantly, until the leeks are wilted and speck or prosciutto is soft, about 5 minutes. Add the grated Parmigiano-Reggiano and stir again. Lightly beat the eggs and milk together, add to the bread mixture and mix well, squeezing with your hands to make a uniform dough.

Mix the buckwheat flour and ¼ cup whole-wheat flour together. Sprinkle over the bread and mix with your hands until well incorporated. The mixture should be just firm enough to hold its shape when formed into balls. If too wet, add the remaining whole-wheat flour. If too dry, add milk, 2 tablespoons at a time, until desired consistency is reached. Set aside for 20 to 30 minutes.

With damp hands or a scoop, compress and shape the dough into balls of desired size and place the finished canederli close together, but not touching, on a lightly floured tray. Set aside or refrigerate up to 2 hours while making the sauce.

When ready to cook the canederli, bring a very large, deep pot of water — no less than 1 gallon — to a simmer. Add 1 to 2 tablespoons salt and drop in the canederli, cooking no more than half the batch at a time. Stir a couple of

times with a wooden spoon so the canederli move gently. The water should remain at a simmer rather than a rolling boil.

After the canederli rise to the surface, cook them for another 5 to 6 minutes. Test for doneness; they should be firm with no raw taste when completely cooked. If not done, increase the cooking time another 2 minutes and test again. Remove canederli with a slotted spoon and toss with your preferred sauce. Serve immediately, garnished with shavings of Parmigiano-Reggiano and chopped parsley. Repeat with the remaining canederli and sauce.

Alternatively, you can cook all the canederli at the same time in two separate pots and toss them all together in a large bowl of sauce.

Although these canederli do not freeze well, you can make the dough up to 24 hours in advance and keep it refrigerated until ready to use.

Sauce Suggestions: Savory Zabaglione with Horseradish Cream Sauce, Parmigiano-Reggiano Cream Sauce, Basic Tomato Sauce, Garden Paté, Fennel Pollen-Cream Sauce, Cabbage & Apple Sauce, Fonduta

LEEK & CHEESE CANEDERLI
WITH CHANTERELLE MUSHROOMS, WALNUTS & BLACK TRUFFLE

/ serves 4 to 6

Cinzia Ubaldi, a longtime Perugian chef/friend, shared this recipe with me years ago when I first started research for this book. At the time, she owned one of my favorite go-to restaurants in Perugia, La Locanda degli Artisti, where we often shared Sunday lunch with her family; I feel fortunate to have watched her children grow from birth to adulthood. Her parents, who lived nearby in Assisi, would often be present on Sunday, and one of my cherished memories is when her mother Argenta asked me one fall day, as I was preparing to depart for Santa Fe, when I would be returning to Perugia. I responded that I would be back around the first of May. She smiled and said, "Perfetto — arrivi con le ciliegie!" Perfect — you arrive with the cherries. I learned a great about Italian food and family life from those experiences, and cherish the moments Cinzia and I spent cooking together.

The Italian finferli *or* gallinacci *(chanterelle) mushrooms and black truffles in the sauce, along with the young pecorino cheese in the dough, gives this dish an Umbrian twist. The dried chanterelles have a nice chewy texture; the fresh ones less so. If you substitute other mushrooms, avoid strong-flavored ones like porcini as they will overwhelm the truffle. The sauce itself is thin and soup-like, and makes an elegant presentation worthy of an upscale restaurant. It's also good with simple potato or ricotta gnocchi. Absolutely delicious!*

/ FOR THE CANEDERLI

2 medium leeks, white part only, separated, rinsed
   well, and finely chopped

3 tablespoons unsalted butter

½ cup fresh pecorino cut into ⅛-inch dice (another
   semi-soft, distinctly flavored cheese such as Asiago
   or provolone can be substituted)

5 cups crustless, coarsely crumbled, stale white
   breadcrumbs, lightly packed

½ teaspoon salt

½ teaspoon freshly ground black pepper or to taste

2 whole eggs

1 cup whole milk

⅜ cup unbleached all-purpose flour + more for shaping

3 scallions, minced

2 tablespoons finely chopped fresh parsley leaves

/ FOR THE SAUCE

2 tablespoons extra-virgin olive oil

1 medium shallot, minced

1 large garlic clove, minced

¾ pound fresh finferli (chanterelle) mushrooms,
   or other mushrooms, cleaned and thinly sliced
   OR 2 ounces reconstituted dry finferli can
   be substituted

Salt and freshly ground black pepper to taste

1-1½-cups low-sodium chicken broth,
   preferably homemade

½ cup toasted walnuts, chopped

1 tablespoon minced parsley

2 black truffles, thinly sliced

Truffle oil for garnish

In a medium sauté pan, melt the butter over medium heat. Add the chopped leeks and cook until soft, about 3 minutes. Remove from heat and set aside.

In a medium bowl, beat milk and eggs together. Add the cheese, breadcrumbs, salt, and pepper. Mix well with your hands and allow to rest 30 minutes. Mix again, breaking apart any larger pieces of bread. Sprinkle with ⅜ cup flour, the scallions and minced parsley, and mix again lightly to form a uniform dough.

With dampened hands or a scoop, form 1½-inch balls, rolling the dough between your hands to lightly compact and smooth the surface of the canederli. If the dough is too wet and canederli won't hold together, add up to ¼ cup fine dry breadcrumbs, a bit at a time, to firm up the dough. Place the finished canederli close together, but not touching, on a lightly floured tray. Set aside or refrigerate up to 2 hours while making the sauce.

/ MAKE THE MUSHROOM SAUCE

If using dried mushrooms, cover with hot tap water and soak for 30 minutes. Using a fine sieve or cheesecloth, drain well, reserving the liquid. Coarsely chop the mushrooms.

In a medium sauté pan, heat the olive oil, shallot, and garlic together over medium heat until aromatic. Add the fresh mushrooms and cook until they release most of their liquid and the mushrooms are tender, about 5 minutes.

If using dried mushrooms, simmer them along with the reserved soaking liquid until tender, about 10 minutes, making sure they don't dry out.

Add 1 cup chicken broth, bring to a boil and reduce the liquid to make a light, stew-like sauce. You may add more broth if desired. Add salt and pepper to taste. Remove from heat and keep warm. Add the toasted walnut pieces and parsley just before serving.

/ WHEN READY TO SERVE

Bring a very large, deep pot of water to a simmer. Add 1 to 2 tablespoons salt and drop in the canederli, cooking half the batch at a time. Stir a couple of times with a wooden spoon. The water should remain at a simmer. After the canederli rise to the surface, cook 5 to 6 minutes. If needed, increse the cooking time for 2 more minutes.

Remove the canederli with a slotted spoon and add to half the mushroom sauce. Alternativly, you can cook all the canederli at the same time in two separate pots.

Serve immediately in shallow heated bowls. Garnish with thinly sliced black truffles and dribbles of truffle oil.

You can make the dough up to 24 hours in advance and keep it refrigerated until ready to use. You can also shape the balls and freeze them no longer than two weeks. See Freezer Notes, page 250, for more information. Do not thaw the canederli before cooking and adjust the timing as they rise to the surface accordingly. You will need to increase the cooking time of frozen canederli by 2 to 4 minutes, depending on their size.

Adapted recipe from Cinzia Ubaldi, friend/chef/sommelier from Perugia, Italy

PORCINI CANEDERLI

/ serves 4 to 6

The deep woodsy flavor of porcini that is typical of the northern and central regions of Italy is particularly prominent in these tasty canederli. I love them simply served in broth or with melted butter, but mild cheese sauces, such as fontina, will complement rather than overwhelm the earthy porcini flavor. Many fresh porcini found in the U.S. are milder than those in Italy, so I prefer the imported dried mushrooms to those I find in the mountains of Santa Fe. Other wild mushrooms can be substituted in this recipe, in equal amounts, but the flavor will not be as pronounced.

5 cups crustless, coarsely crumbled, stale white breadcrumbs, lightly packed

½ cup heavy cream

3 large eggs, lightly beaten

½ pound fresh porcini OR 2 ounces dried porcini, free of any residual dirt

2 tablespoons grappa, optional

¼ cup unsalted butter

1 clove garlic, minced

½ cup minced red onion

¼ cup minced parsley

Salt and freshly ground black pepper to taste

¼ cup all-purpose unbleached flour + more for shaping

½ cup unsalted butter, melted

Freshly grated Parmigiano-Reggiano to taste

Lightly toasted and chopped walnuts

If using dried porcini, put them in a small bowl, add enough hot water to barely cover them, and allow to soak for 30 to 45 minutes. Using a fine sieve or cheesecloth, drain well, reserving the liquid. Finely chop and set aside.

If using fresh porcini, clean them well and finely chop. Set aside.

In a medium bowl, beat the eggs with the heavy cream, add the breadcrumbs, and mix well with your hands. Let rest for 30 minutes.

In a sauté pan, melt the butter over medium heat along with the minced onion, the garlic, and the fresh porcini, if using. Sauté, stirring constantly, until the porcini are soft, about 5 minutes. Add the optional grappa and cook, stirring, until nearly all liquid has evaporated.

If using dried porcini, sauté the onion and garlic together about 3 minutes. Add the chopped, softened porcini along with their soaking liquid and optional grappa. Cook, stirring, until nearly all liquid has evaporated.

Add the cooked porcini, the chopped parsley, and salt and pepper to taste to the soaked breadcrumbs and mix well with your hands. Sprinkle with the flour and mix again to form a uniform dough.

Measuring about 1 heaping tablespoon of dough each, form a couple of canederli into 1-inch balls, compressing the dough, and drop into the simmering water. Cook until they rise to the surface. Continue cooking another 4 to 6 minutes and test for doneness. The inside should be firm, not raw. Add a few tablespoons of fine dry breadcrumbs if the canederli are too soft, or a tablespoon or two of cream if too dry. Retest if necessary.

With damp hands or a scoop, compress and shape the remaining dough into balls of your desired size and place them close together, but not touching, on a lightly floured tray. Set aside or refrigerate up to 2 hours while making the sauce.

When ready to cook the canederli, bring a very large, deep pot of water — no less than 1 gallon — to a simmer. Add 1 to 2 tablespoons salt and drop in the canederli, cooking no more than half the batch at a time. Stir a couple of times with a wooden spoon so the gnocchi move gently. The water should remain at a simmer rather than a rolling boil.

After the canederli rise to the surface, cook them for another 5 to 6 minutes. Note that the cooking time of the canederli will vary considerably depending on the size. For baseball-size canederli, allow 20 minutes. The gnocchi should be firm with no raw taste when completely cooked. If not done, increase the cooking time another 2 minutes and test again. Remove with a slotted spoon and keep warm while cooking the remaining canederli.

Alternatively, you can cook all the canederli at the same time in two separate pots.

Have warm shallow bowls ready with the melted butter portioned into each one. Remove canederli with a slotted spoon when done and divide among prepared bowls. Add a dusting of the freshly grated Parmigiano-Reggiano and some chopped toasted walnuts as desired, or toss with your chosen sauce, garnish as desired, and serve immediately.

You can make the dough up to 24 hours in advance and keep it refrigerated until ready to use. You can also shape the balls and freeze them no longer than two weeks. See Freezer Notes, page 250, for more information. Do not thaw the canederli before cooking. Time them as they rise to the surface, making adjustments as needed. You will need to increase the cooking time of frozen canederli by 2 to 4 minutes depending on their size.

Additional Sauce Suggestions: Mascarpone Cream Sauce, Pine Nut-Butter Sauce, Sagrantino Cream Sauce, Porcini Mushroom Sauce (for hardcore porcini lovers)

PRUNE CANEDERLI WITH PORK & MARSALA

/ serves 4 to 6

Canederli are often stuffed with prunes. In the following recipe the dried plums are chopped and added to the canederli dough instead, then paired with pork in the sauce. A bit of broth along with cooked, shredded Tuscan kale or other greens makes a satisfying combination for a main course. I suggest using pork tenderloin as it's lean and flavorful, but pork loin can be substituted. Ground pork contains too much fat and has the wrong texture for this dish.

1 cup whole milk

2 large eggs, lightly beaten

5 cups crustless, coarsely crumbled stale white
    breadcrumbs, lightly packed

2 tablespoons unbleached all-purpose flour

Salt and freshly ground black pepper to taste

2 tablespoons extra-virgin olive oil

1 medium shallot, finely chopped

1 cup pitted prunes, chopped into ¼-inch pieces

4 tablespoons unsalted butter

½ cup Marsala, divided

8 ounces pork tenderloin, finely chopped

1 cup finely shredded Tuscan kale
    OR hearty green of choice

2 cups homemade chicken broth or low-sodium
    canned broth

Freshly grated semi-aged pecorino cheese, optional

In a large mixing bowl, beat eggs with milk until combined. Add breadcrumbs, mix well with your hands, and let rest until liquid is absorbed and bread is soft, about 30 minutes.

Meanwhile, melt 2 tablespoons olive oil over medium heat, add shallot and cook 2 minutes. Stir in the chopped prunes and 2 tablespoons Marsala. Cook until liquid has evaporated, remove from heat and cool to room temperature.

Sprinkle flour over bread mixture and mix, breaking apart any bread lumps. Add prunes, salt, and pepper to taste, and mix well with hands to form a dough. With damp hands or a scoop, form about 30 (1½-inch) balls. Place the finished canederli close together on a lightly floured tray. Set aside or refrigerate up to 2 hours while making the sauce.

Add pork to skillet, stirring, over medium-high heat until well browned. Add remaining Marsala and stir well, scraping up the brown bits from the bottom of pan. Add finely shredded kale and chicken broth and bring to a boil. Turn off the heat, cover, and keep warm while finishing the canederli.

When ready to cook the canederli, bring no less than 1 gallon of water to a simmer. Add 1 to 2 tablespoons salt and drop in the canederli, cooking half the batch at a time.

Stir a couple of times with a wooden spoon so the gnocchi move gently. The water should remain at a simmer.

After the canederli rise to the surface, cook another 5 to 6 minutes and test for doneness. They should be firm with no raw taste when completely cooked. If not done, increase the cooking time another 2 minutes and test again. Transfer cooked canederli to a large plate with a slotted spoon.

Alternatively, you can cook all the canederli at the same time in two separate pots.

In a large skillet, melt butter over medium-high heat. Add cooked canederli in a single layer and brown on all sides, about 5 minutes. Divide canederli and sauce among warmed serving bowls. Serve immediately, passing optional grated pecorino at table.

You can make the dough up to 24 hours in advance and keep it refrigerated until ready to use. You can also shape the balls and freeze them no longer than two weeks. See Freezer Notes, page 250, for more information. Do not thaw the canederli before cooking. Time them as they rise to the surface, making adjustments as needed. You will need to increase the cooking time of frozen canederli by 2 to 4 minutes depending on their size.

Recipe inspired by November 2011 edition of Cucina Italiana

SAUSAGE CANEDERLI WITH CABBAGE & APPLE

/ serves 4 to 6

Memories of mountain hikes in the Dolomites return when I prepare and eat these delicious canederli. They make a perfect lunch at a rifugio — *a mountain cabin for hikers — a welcome supper at a restaurant after walking forested trails, or an evening meal with friends on a chilly evening. Eliminate the meats in the recipe, replace them with an equal amount of minced and lightly sautéed vegetables that complement the sauce, and you have a substantial vegetarian meal. I like to save any leftover sauce to serve next to grilled or roasted pork.*

5 cups crustless, coarsely crumbled, stale white
    breadcrumbs, lightly packed
Freshly ground black pepper to taste
1 cup whole milk
1 whole egg
1 egg yolk

4 ounces pancetta or smoked bacon, thinly sliced
    and finely chopped
4 ounces Italian sausage, crumbled OR finely
    chopped cured salami such as Genoa or Sopressata
½ cup finely chopped chives
⅜ cup unbleached all-purpose flour + more for shaping

Put the breadcrumbs in a medium bowl. In a small bowl, beat the milk and egg together until well combined. Pour the egg mixture over the breadcrumbs and sprinkle with freshly ground black pepper to taste. Mix lightly with hands and allow to rest 30 minutes. Do not overmix.

In a medium sauté pan, cook the meats until they render their fat. Remove from heat and set aside. With your hands, break apart any large pieces of bread. Lightly fold in the cooked meats and chopped chives. (If using vegetables instead of meats, add salt to taste.) Sprinkle with ⅜ cup flour and mix lightly to form a uniform dough. Bring a small deep saucepan of lightly salted water to a simmer.

Measuring about 1 heaping tablespoon of dough each, form a few canederli into balls, compressing the dough, and drop them into simmering water. Cook the gnocchi until they rise to the surface. Continue cooking another 4 to 6 minutes, then test. The inside should be firm. Add a few tablespoons of fine, dry breadcrumbs if the canederli are too soft or a tablespoon or two of milk if too dry.

With damp hands or a scoop, compress and shape the dough into balls of desired size and place the finished canederli close together, but not touching, on a lightly floured tray. Set aside or refrigerate up to 2 hours, if desired, while preparing the sauce.

When ready to cook the canederli, bring no less than 1 gallon of water to a simmer. Add 1 to 2 tablespoons salt

and drop in the canederli, cooking half the batch at a time. Stir with a wooden spoon so the canederli move gently. The water should remain at a simmer.

Start timing when the canederli rise to the surface. Note that the cooking time of the canederli will vary considerably depending on their size. For baseball-size canederli, allow 20 minutes versus the 4 to 6 minutes for smaller balls. Test and increase cooking time another 2 minutes if necessary. Alternately, you can cook all the canederli at the same time in two separate pots.

Have warmed bowls ready with hot sauce portioned into each one. Remove the canederli with a slotted spoon and divide among the prepared bowls.

You can make the dough up to 24 hours in advance and keep it refrigerated until ready to use. You can also shape the balls and freeze them no longer than two weeks. See Freezer Notes, page 250. Do not thaw the canederli before cooking. Time them as they rise to the surface, making adjustments as needed. You will need to increase the cooking time of frozen canederli by 2 to 4 minutes depending on their size.

Additional Sauce Suggestions: Creamy Leek Sauce, Cabbage & Cheese Sauce, Tomato & Olive Sauce, Mushroom Sauce, Gorgonzola Cream Sauce

/ POLENTA GNOCCHI

Polenta is typically found in the alla Romana disk-shaped versions of gnocchi on page 133. The following two recipes are variations of the classic polenta gnocchi. Prepared and shaped in alternative ways, one version starts with cold, cooked polenta formed into balls and fried; the other uses a pastry bag to drop freshly cooked polenta into a boiling liquid, forming small, elongated gnocchi.

Follow the recipes and proportions as written or the gnocchi will not hold their shape. For more information and a basic recipe for cooked polenta, see page 222.

HERBED POLENTA GNOCCHI WITH LARDO, PECORINO & TRUFFLE

/ serves 6

This is a perfect recipe to celebrate some of Italy's finest ingredients — and a great way to use leftover cold polenta. The very soft dough is easy to form with the use of a pastry bag or a Ziploc bag with the corner cut to the desired size. The gnocchi are rich and creamy, sauced with lardo instead of butter, and garnished with optional truffle.

Lardo is cured Italian pork back fat, prized in Tuscany and often eaten as an appetizer, very thinly sliced, on bruschette. The texture is meltingly delicate and creamy, while the flavor is slightly sweet. It's available via mail order from various Italian import companies. The truffles suggested here are the black ones from Norcia that have a deep earthy flavor. You can use bottled truffles if fresh are not available, but they lose some potency in the packing process. Be sure to shave the truffles very thinly. I like to finish the dish with a few drops of black truffle oil.

3 cups cooked, cold, basic firm polenta (page 222), preferably taragna polenta made with buckwheat and corn OR another non-instant, medium-grain polenta of your choice

4 large eggs, beaten

¼ cup cornstarch

⅔ cup unbleached all-purpose flour

½ cup semi-aged pecorino or fresh Parmigiano-Reggiano, finely grated + more for garnish

1 tablespoon finely chopped fresh chives

2 tablespoons extra-virgin olive oil

/ FOR THE SAUCE

⅔ cup very finely chopped lardo OR unsalted butter

2 small shallots, finely chopped

6 fresh rosemary stems, tips set aside for garnish

8-10 black truffles, very thinly shaved

Black truffle oil (optional)

In a medium bowl, mix all the gnocchi ingredients together, breaking up any lumps of polenta to form a uniform dough. Refrigerate for 20 to 30 minutes.

Oil a baking dish large enough to hold all the gnocchi in a single layer and set aside.

Bring a very large, deep pot of water — no less than 1 gallon — to a simmer. Add 1 to 2 tablespoons salt. Tightly tie a piece of dental floss or fine string from one handle to the other across the top of the pot.

Fill a pastry bag fitted with a large, ½-inch plain tip (or a Ziploc bag with a corner clipped) with some of the polenta mixture. Carefully shake the bag to condense the dough and eliminate air bubbles. Gently pressing the bag, use the string to cut the gnocchi into ¾-inch segments, letting the gnocchi fall gently into the pot of simmering water. Cook 5 minutes.

Test for doneness and remove with a slotted spoon to the oiled baking dish. Keep warm in a preheated 250°F oven while preparing the sauce. You can also refrigerate the cooked gnocchi up to 2 days and reheat in simmering water just until they rise to the surface.

In a medium sauté pan, heat the lardo, shallot, and rosemary together until the lardo is melted, the shallot softened, and the rosemary begins to sizzle. Remove the rosemary.

Divide the gnocchi among six warm, shallow bowls. Drizzle with the lardo, shower with grated cheese, and garnish with shaved truffle and a rosemary tip. Add a few drops of black truffle oil if desired.

Do not freeze.

Additional Sauce Suggestions: Fresh Fava Bean & Pancetta Sauce, Garlic Scape Pesto, Thyme-Garlic Butter Sauce, Basic Tomato Sauce, Mixed Mushroom & Sausage Sauce

POLENTA GNOCCHI IN BROTH

/ serves 4

These tasty gnocchi are made from polenta, a traditional food of the northern Italian regions. Wonderful in your favorite broth, they also are delicious served with browned butter or a sauce. Shaped into balls and sautéed rather than simmered, these gnocchi are very tender, with a cheesy, cornmeal richness like no other.

I've made these gnocchi with both medium and fine polenta with equal success. The finer polenta produces a creamier center that contrasts with the crispy, fried exterior. Using milk rather than water also results in a richer dough. I sometimes add ¼ pound of very finely chopped speck or prosciutto for variety; some chopped herbs such as rosemary, sage, or thyme also add flavor. If you're using fine polenta, the gnocchi can be simmered directly in the broth, although you will miss the rich buttery sautéed flavor.

1½ cups water

1 cup whole milk

4-5 tablespoons unsalted butter

½ teaspoon kosher salt

1¼ cups fine polenta

2 large egg yolks

½ cup finely grated fresh Parmigiano-Reggiano
or Grana Padano

2 tablespoons roughly chopped flat-leaf parsley,
fresh rosemary, or sage

4 cups chicken or vegetable broth (homemade or
high-quality, low-sodium, store-bought)

Thinly sliced fresh chives (optional)

Additional freshly grated Parmigiano-Reggiano
or Grana Padano (optional)

Combine water, milk, and salt in a large, deep saucepan. Bring to a boil over high heat. Slowly whisk in polenta, reduce heat to medium and cook, whisking constantly, for 2 minutes. Reduce heat to low and cook, stirring frequently with a wooden spoon, 35 to 40 minutes, or until polenta is smooth and very stiff, like cold mashed potatoes. Do not be tempted to shorten the cooking time, or the gnocchi will not hold their shape.

Remove polenta from the heat; stir in the egg yolks, 2 tablespoons of the butter, the cheese, and herbs. Let stand until cool, 15 minutes or more.

Line a baking sheet with waxed or parchment paper. With damp hands or a small scoop, form into approximately 36 (1-inch) balls. Place the finished gnocchi close together, but not touching, on the lined sheet.

Set aside or refrigerate up to 2 hours while making the sauce.

When ready to cook, heat the remaining butter in a large nonstick skillet over medium-high heat. Cook the gnocchi in two batches, turning and shaking the pan gently, until browned on all sides, 6 to 8 minutes per batch. Keep warm while finishing the second batch, adding more butter to the pan if necessary.

Meanwhile, heat the broth.

Divide the gnocchi among four warm bowls and ladle 1 cup hot prepared broth over the top of each or serve immediately with one of the suggested sauces. Garnish with thinly sliced chives and freshly grated Parmigiano-Reggiano if desired.

Do not freeze.

Sauce Suggestions: Poppy Seed-Mint Butter Sauce, Simple Tomato Sauces, Ragùs, Wild Mushroom & Blueberry Sauce, Radish & Turnip Pesto, Black Truffle Sauce

/ RICOTTA & OTHER CHEESE GNOCCHI

Gnocchi made with ricotta and other cheeses are not the first to come mind when one thinks of gnocchi — but they're one of my favorite varieties to make and to teach. The dough, which comes together very quickly, is one of the more forgiving gnocchi doughs, making the recipes in this chapter perfect for the gnocchi novice. Basic ricotta dough is soft, pliable and perfect for stuffing. The addition of various vegetables, meats, and other flours produces a beautifully textured gnocchi. From traditional recipes to more contemporary variations, cheese-based gnocchi are complemented by a large choice of sauces and are a welcome addition to any meal as a first or main course.

A short discussion of ricotta cheese before you begin to work with any of the recipes is helpful. As with potato gnocchi, it's extremely important that all the ingredients for cheese gnocchi contain as little liquid as possible. In Italy, ricotta cheese — always made from whole milk of various kinds — is sold by weight and is rarely prepackaged as it is in the U.S. If it is pre-packed, it's usually sold in a double container that allows extra whey to drain from the cheese. When cooking with commercially produced ricotta in the U.S., it's imperative to follow the instructions to drain the ricotta for at least 30 minutes before proceeding with the recipe. You can also drain your ricotta overnight (or even longer) and save it for future use.

Most ricotta cheese produced in the U.S. also contains additives of various kinds that make it difficult to drain and give it a grainy texture that will affect the gnocchi. Read the labels and search for ricotta that contains only whole milk, salt, and a coagulating agent, such as Trader Joe's whole-milk brand. Better yet, make your own ricotta following the recipe on page 225 to insure the finest results. Always use whole milk when making your own cheese, never part-skimmed.

Refer to the notes on page 235-236 for more information about ricotta and the other cheeses used in these recipes. You'll also find suggestions for appropriate substitutions there. To maintain the integrity of the recipe, it's extremely important to use cheeses with a similar consistency.

BASIC RICOTTA GNOCCHI

/ serves 6

This is my go-to recipe for ricotta gnocchi. They come together quickly, are extremely versatile, and freeze consistently well. Other hard grating cheeses can be substituted for those specified here; finely chopped herbs are another easy addition. One of my favorite variations is to add a tablespoon or two of white truffle oil to the dough and serve the gnocchi with browned butter, dribbled with more truffle oil and garnished with a shaving of fresh truffles. It's the perfect first course for an elegant dinner or a light meal with close friends.

These are also my favorite gnocchi for stuffing as the dough is easier to work with than potato-based dough. If you plan to stuff your ricotta gnocchi, you may need to work in a bit more flour as you shape them. See the Stuffed Gnocchi chapter for specific recipes.

2 cups whole milk ricotta OR a 15-ounce container, placed in a cheesecloth-lined colander set in a bowl and drained at least 30 minutes before using

1-1¼ cups unbleached all-purpose flour + more for shaping

2 egg yolks

½ cup finely grated fresh Parmigiano-Reggiano OR ricotta salata cheese

1 teaspoon salt

Place the drained ricotta, grated cheese, egg, and salt in a bowl and whisk until smooth. Add 1 cup of the flour and mix lightly with a spatula using a cutting motion. Add only as much additional flour as you need to create a soft, workable dough. Be careful not to overwork or gnocchi will be tough.

Gather the dough into a smooth ball and place it on a lightly floured board. Take a walnut-sized portion of dough, roll it into a 2-inch log, and cut the log into thirds. Test cook the three gnocchi in a small, deep saucepan of simmering water until they rise to the surface. Check the texture and add more flour to the dough if necessary — ⅛ cup at a time — until the additional tests indicate you've reached the desired consistency. The gnocchi should hold together when cooked without being gummy.

Shape immediately or cover and refrigerate the dough for up to 2 hours, then proceed with shaping as follows:

Divide the remaining dough into four to six pieces and roll each piece into a finger-thick rope on a lightly floured board. Cut each rope into ¾-inch pieces. You can press each piece over a wooden gnocchi or butter paddle or the reversed tines of a fork to create the small pockets and ridges that help the sauce cling to the gnocchi — or simply cut the ropes and leave the gnocchi unshaped. Place the

finished gnocchi close together, but not touching, on a lightly floured tray. If not using immediately, place in the refrigerator for up to 1 hour.

Bring a very large, deep pot of water — no less than 1 gallon — to a simmer. Add 1 to 2 tablespoons salt and drop in the gnocchi, cooking no more than half the batch at a time. Stir a couple of times with a wooden spoon so the gnocchi move gently. The water should remain at a simmer rather than a rolling boil.

Have ready warmed serving bowls and a large mixing bowl with half your chosen sauce portioned into it. As the gnocchi rise to the surface, remove them with a slotted spoon, toss with the sauce, garnish as desired, and serve immediately. Repeat with the remaining gnocchi and sauce.

Alternatively, you can cook all the gnocchi at the same time in two separate pots and toss them all together in a large serving bowl with the appropriate amount of sauce.

These gnocchi can be frozen for up to two weeks after forming. See Freezer Notes, page 250.

Sauce Suggestions: All savory sauces will work with these gnocchi

FOUR-CHEESE GNOCCHI WITH MELTED BUTTER

/ serves 4 to 6

Mouth-wateringly rich with cheese and butter, I prefer to present these simple gnocchi as a second course. Served with a mixed green salad and a hunk of crusty bread, they are ethereal!

½ pound Emmental or Gruyère cheese, finely grated

½ pound provolone cheese, finely grated

¼ pound (½ cup) whole-milk ricotta, placed in a cheesecloth-lined colander set in a bowl, and drained at least 30 minutes before using

⅔ cup finely grated fresh Parmigiano-Reggiano

2 large eggs, beaten

⅞ cup unbleached all-purpose flour
   + more for shaping the gnocchi

⅓ cup unsalted butter

Salt to taste

Freshly ground black pepper

Ground cinnamon

In a small saucepan, melt the butter with salt and freshly ground pepper; add a touch of cinnamon and set aside while making the gnocchi.

Finely grate the Emmental and provolone cheeses into a large bowl. Add the grated Parmigiano-Reggiano, the ricotta, and the beaten eggs. Mix lightly with a spatula or wooden spoon, using a cutting motion. Sprinkle with the flour and mix again to make a uniform dough.

Gather the dough into a smooth ball and place it on a lightly floured board. Take a walnut-sized portion of dough, roll it into a 2-inch log, and cut the log into thirds. Test cook the three gnocchi in a small deep saucepan of simmering water until they rise to the surface. Check the texture and add more flour to the dough if necessary — ⅛ cup at a time — until the additional tests indicate you've reached the desired consistency. The gnocchi should hold together when cooked without being gummy.

Divide the remaining dough into four to six pieces and roll each piece into a finger-thick rope on a lightly floured board. Cut each rope into ¾-inch pieces. You can press each piece over a wooden gnocchi or butter paddle or the reversed tines of a fork to create the small pockets and ridges that help the sauce cling to the gnocchi — or simply cut the ropes and leave the gnocchi unshaped. Place the finished gnocchi close together, but not touching, on a lightly floured tray.

Bring a very large, deep pot of water — no less than 1 gallon — to a simmer. Add 1 to 2 tablespoons salt and drop in the gnocchi, cooking no more than half the batch at a time. Stir a couple of times with a wooden spoon so the gnocchi move gently. The water should remain at a simmer rather than a rolling boil.

Alternatively, you can cook all the gnocchi at the same time in two separate pots and toss them all together in a large serving bowl with the appropriate amount of sauce.

Have ready warmed serving bowls and a large mixing bowl with half the melted butter, or your chosen sauce, portioned into it. As the gnocchi rise to the surface, remove with a slotted spoon, toss with the butter or sauce, and serve immediately. Repeat with the remaining gnocchi and sauce.

Alternately, you can heat the butter in a large frying pan and sauté the cooked gnocchi until lightly browned before serving.

These gnocchi can be frozen for up to two weeks after forming. See Freezer Notes, page 250.

Sauce Suggestions: Pestos, Tomato Sauces, Herbed Butters, Ragùs; avoid most creamy cheese sauces as they will compete with the flavor of the gnocchi

SPINACH & CHEESE GNOCCHI

/ serves 6

Using puréed rather than chopped spinach makes a wonderfully tender gnocchi that is also easier to shape into traditional small logs with ridges. Served with some halved, sautéed cherry tomatoes and fresh basil in a white bowl, it's a beautiful presentation that reflects the colors of the Italian flag. Although spinach is often used to make green gnocchi, other soft greens can partially replace the spinach. The addition of ricotta affumicata (smoked) or salata (salted) adds a different flavor dimension to the dough — one I'm particularly fond of. Just don't mix ricotta salata with ricotta affumicata in the same dough.

1½ pounds fresh baby spinach (OR a mix of spinach, watercress and/or arugula to equal 1½ pounds)

¼ cup finely grated fresh Parmigiano-Reggiano, Grana Padano or aged Asiago

½ cup finely grated ricotta salata or ricotta affumicata

2 large eggs, lightly beaten

½ cup high quality, very dry, fine white unseasoned breadcrumbs or panko

Large pinch freshly grated nutmeg

Kosher salt and freshly ground black pepper to taste ⅓ cup unbleached all-purpose flour + more for shaping

Shaved or freshly grated cheese of choice for serving

In a large pot, bring 2 quarts of salted water to a boil. Blanch the greens until tender. Remove with a slotted spoon to a strainer and let rest until cool enough to handle. Drain, squeezing the greens really well. Transfer the greens to a blender or use a blending wand to process to a thick, smooth purée.

Measure 1⅓ cups of the spinach purée into a medium bowl, reserving any leftover for another use. Beat the eggs with the nutmeg and ½ teaspoon each kosher salt and freshly ground black pepper, and mix into the purée.

Combine the grated cheeses and breadcrumbs with ⅓ cup of the flour and sprinkle over it the spinach mixture. Mix lightly and thoroughly to form a soft dough. Let rest 20 minutes.

Gather the dough into a smooth ball and place it on a lightly floured board. Take a walnut-sized portion of dough, roll it into a 2-inch log, and cut the log into thirds. Test cook the three gnocchi in a small deep saucepan of simmering water until they rise to the surface. Check the texture and add more flour to the dough if necessary. The gnocchi should hold together when cooked without being gummy.

Divide the remaining dough into four to six pieces and roll each piece into a finger-thick rope on a lightly floured board. Cut each rope into ¾-inch pieces. You can press

each piece over a wooden gnocchi paddle to create the small pockets and ridges. Place the finished gnocchi close together, but not touching, on a lightly floured tray.

Bring a very large, deep pot of water — no less than 1 gallon — to a simmer. Add 1 to 2 tablespoons salt and drop in the gnocchi, cooking no more than half the batch at a time. Stir a couple of times with a wooden spoon so the gnocchi move gently. The water should remain at a simmer rather than a rolling boil. Have ready warmed serving bowls and a large mixing bowl with half your chosen sauce.

After the gnocchi rise to the surface, cook them for another 2 to 3 minutes. Test for doneness. Remove with a slotted spoon, toss with your chosen sauce, garnish as desired and serve immediately. Repeat with the remaining gnocchi and sauce.

Alternatively, you can cook all the gnocchi at the same time in two separate pots.

These gnocchi can be frozen for up to two weeks after forming. See Freezer Notes, page 250.

Sauce Suggestions: Tomato Sauces, Oven-Roasted Cherry Tomatoes with Basil, Ragús, Savory Zabaglione with Horseradish Cream Sauce, Browned Butter & Preserved Lemon Sauce, Roasted Red Pepper Purée, Lemon, Thyme & Scamorza

RICOTTA-BEET GNOCCHI

/ serves 6 to 8

I wasn't a fan of beets because I grew up with the canned variety. I avoided them for years until I roasted them and discovered how rich, sweet, and wonderful they can be. Then, a few years back, one of my favorite contadine *(female farmers) at the local market in Perugia turned me on to using raw beets in salads or grated and simply seasoned with extra-virgin olive oil, salt, pepper, and a touch of mint. I quickly became a fan of* barbabietola *(beetroot) in all its varieties and varied preparations — including these meltingly soft gnocchi. They lend themselves to many sauces and are a breathtakingly rich, red color in the serving bowl. If you substitute Italian heirloom Chiogga beets, they will be pink; yellow beets will make them golden. Not a fan of beets? You'll quickly change your mind.*

1 pound small/medium red beets, scrubbed,
   root ends removed

2 tablespoons extra-virgin olive oil for brushing

Salt and freshly ground black pepper

1 cup whole-milk ricotta, placed in a cheesecloth-lined
   colander set in a bowl, and drained for 30 minutes
   before using

1 large egg

Pinch freshly grated nutmeg

1 teaspoon kosher salt

½ cup finely grated fresh Parmigiano-Reggiano
   OR semi-aged pecorino cheese

1¾-2 cups unbleached all-purpose flour
   + more for shaping

2 tablespoons unsalted butter

2 tablespoons extra-virgin olive oil

Preheat the oven to 400°F. Brush the beets with olive oil, place snuggly in a baking dish trimmed ends down, and season lightly with salt and freshly ground black pepper. Add enough water to cover beets by about ¼ inch and cover tightly with foil. Bake the beets 1 to 1½ hours, or until tender when pierced with a knife. Add more water to the pan if necessary during baking to keep the beets moist. Remove from the oven, uncover, and cool completely.

Trim and peel the beets and cut them into ½-inch pieces. Using a blender or food processor, process the beets, scraping the bowl often to make a smooth purée. Set aside 1¼ cups of the beet purée, saving any extra for another use. (The beets can be prepared a few days in advance and refrigerated until ready to use.)

In a medium bowl, whisk the egg with the salt and nutmeg. Add the drained ricotta and the grated cheese and mix until smooth. Add the beet purée and continue mixing just until well combined. Sprinkle with 1¾ cups of the flour. With a rubber spatula or a flexible curved plastic bowl scraper, combine the ingredients using a cutting/ folding motion similar to mixing a cake. Do not overmix or gnocchi will be tough.

Scrape the dough onto a floured work surface and knead gently until the dough is smooth and forms a ball. Take a walnut-size portion of dough, roll into a 2-inch log, and cut into thirds. Test cook the three gnocchi for consistency in a small, deep saucepan pan of simmering water until the gnocchi rise to the surface. Check the texture and add more flour — ⅛ cup at a time — if necessary, until the desired consistency is reached. This is a very soft and smooth gnocchi dough; it should be barely firm enough to hold its shape when formed against the paddle. Don't be tempted to add more flour than necessary.

Line a baking sheet with waxed or parchment paper and lightly dust with flour. On a barely floured surface, divide the dough into 4 to 6 pieces and roll into finger-thick ropes. If the surface has too much flour, this soft dough will not roll easily. Cut into ¾-inch pieces, sprinkle lightly with flour, and press each over the reversed tines of a fork or a butter or wooden gnocchi paddle, or simply cut and leave unshaped. Place the finished gnocchi close together, but not touching, on the lightly floured tray. Sprinkle sparingly with more flour. Refrigerate while making your sauce.

Put the unsalted butter and 2 tablespoons extra-virgin olive oil in a large skillet. Keep warm while you cook the gnocchi. Or, if you've chosen a different sauce, put it in a large bowl.

Bring a very large, deep pot of water — no less than 1 gallon — to a simmer. Add 1 to 2 tablespoons salt and drop in the gnocchi. Stir a couple of times with a wooden spoon so the gnocchi move gently. The water should remain at a simmer rather than a rolling boil. Cook the gnocchi until they rise to the surface, then simmer 1 minute longer to cook them through.

Transfer the cooked gnocchi to the skillet, tossing and heating gently for 1 to 2 minutes. You may need to use 2 skillets to contain all the gnocchi.

Alternatively, you can cook all the gnocchi at the same time in two separate pots and toss them all together in a large serving bowl with the appropriate amount of sauce.

These gnocchi can be frozen for up to two weeks after forming. See Freezer Notes, page 250.

Sauce Suggestions: Sage-Butter Sauce, Poppy Seed-Mint Butter Sauce, Fennel Pollen-Cream Sauce, Pancetta-Orange Sauce, Savory Zabaglione with Horseradish Cream Sauce, Dollops of Gorgonzola or Goat Cheese with Mint & Toasted Walnuts

RICOTTA-CHESTNUT GNOCCHI

/ serves 6

This is one of my favorite gnocchi. Its earthiness reminds me of crisp Italian fall days when street vendors sell snack-size bags of freshly roasted chestnuts. I walk the street slowly, peeling and munching on the sweet morsels while their heat warms my hands and the crisp air lifts my spirits.

Use whole boiled chestnuts, fresh or jarred, for this recipe; canned chestnut paste has sugar added. Whole chestnuts are difficult to pass through the food mill — and a ricer absolutely will not work — but I find the slightly grainy texture superior to using finely milled chestnut flour to make the dough. I prefer these gnocchi tossed in Browned Butter & Sage Sauce, sprinkled with a hint of cinnamon, and garnished with shavings of smoked ricotta. The combination of sweet and smoky is heavenly. You can order smoked ricotta online or by mail, or make your own with a stovetop smoker. See the Ricotta notes on page 236 for more information.

2 cups whole milk ricotta OR a 15-ounce container,
    placed in a cheesecloth-lined colander set in a bowl,
    and drained for 30 minutes before using

1 whole egg

1 egg yolk

1 teaspoon kosher salt

12 ounces whole boiled chestnuts, canned or fresh

½ cup unbleached all-purpose flour
    + more for shaping the gnocchi

Pinch of freshly grated nutmeg

Freshly ground black pepper to taste

In a medium bowl, beat the egg and yolk together with the salt. Whisk in the drained ricotta. Pass the chestnuts through the disk of a food mill and add to the ricotta, mixing lightly. Sprinkle with the flour, nutmeg, and black pepper. With a spatula mix the flour lightly into the ricotta using a cutting/folding motion similar to mixing a cake. Do not overmix or gnocchi will be tough.

Gather the dough into a ball and place it on a lightly floured board. Take a walnut-sized portion of dough, roll it into a 2-inch log, and cut the log into thirds. Test cook three gnocchi in a saucepan of simmering water until they rise to the surface. Check the texture and add more flour to the dough if necessary — ⅛ cup at a time — until the additional tests indicate you've reached the desired consistency. The gnocchi should hold together when cooked without being gummy.

Divide the remaining dough into four to six pieces and roll each piece into a finger-thick rope on a lightly floured board. Cut each rope into ¾-inch pieces. Press each piece over a wooden gnocchi paddle or the reversed tines of a fork to create the small pockets and ridges, or simply cut the ropes and leave the gnocchi unshaped. Place the finished gnocchi close together, but not touching, on a lightly floured tray.

When ready to serve the gnocchi, bring a very large, deep pot of water — no less than 1 gallon — to a simmer. Add 1 to 2 tablespoons salt and drop in the gnocchi, cooking no more than half the batch at a time. Stir a couple of times with a wooden spoon so the gnocchi move gently. The water should remain at a simmer rather than a rolling boil.

Have ready warmed serving bowls and a large mixing bowl with half your chosen sauce portioned into it. As the gnocchi rise to the surface, remove them with a slotted spoon, toss with the sauce, garnish as desired, and serve immediately. Repeat with the remaining gnocchi and sauce. Alternatively, you can cook all the gnocchi at the same time in two separate pots and toss them all together in a large serving bowl with the appropriate amount of sauce.

These gnocchi can be frozen for up to two weeks after forming. See Freezer Notes, page 250.

Sauce Suggestions: Fontina or other mild-flavored cheese sauces, Mushroom Sauces, Pancetta, Radicchio, Pine-nut & Rosemary Sauce, Sage-Butter Sauce with Smoked Ricotta, Cinnamon & Sugar, Pestos, Chicken Sausage & Fennel Sauce

RICOTTA-ZUCCHINI FLOWER GNOCCHI

/ serves 4 to 6

The addition of lightly sautéed zucchini flowers adds color and texture to a simple ricotta gnocchi; add a touch of fresh basil and the gnocchi reach a different level. This dough is more tender and softer than basic ricotta gnocchi and produces a softer gnocchi when shaped into small balls. I prefer a scoop no larger than 1 inch. The gnocchi can also be formed in the traditional log shape and cut to the length desired. If you plan to serve these gnocchi with the Zucchini Pesto on page 191, leave the basil out of the dough so the flavor won't be overwhelming. These gnocchi are equally good with a simple tomato sauce or some of the other sauce suggestions below.

30-40 freshly-picked zucchini flowers

1 tablespoon extra-virgin olive oil

¾ teaspoon kosher salt

Freshly ground black pepper to taste

2 cups whole milk ricotta (OR a 15-ounce container),
   placed in a cheesecloth-lined colander set in a bowl,
   and drained at least 30 minutes before using

1 large egg, lightly beaten

¼ cup finely grated ricotta salata

1 heaping tablespoon chopped fresh basil

¾-1 cup unbleached all-purpose flour

Finely grated fresh Parmigiano-Reggiano
   OR ricotta salata for garnish

Remove the stems and pistils from the zucchini flowers, rinse well, and squeeze dry. Coarsely chop and set aside.

Put the olive oil, chopped zucchini flowers, salt, and freshly ground pepper into a sauté pan. Stirring continually, slowly sauté over low heat until the zucchini flowers are dry, but not browned, about 5 minutes. Remove from heat and set aside to cool.

In a medium bowl, mix the drained ricotta, beaten egg, ricotta salata, zucchini flowers, and chopped basil with a wooden spoon until smooth. Sprinkle with ¾ cup of the flour and mix lightly with a spatula, using a cutting/folding motion similar to mixing a cake, until the flour is well integrated. Set aside.

Bring a very large, deep pot of water — no less than 1 gallon — to a simmer and add 1 to 2 tablespoons salt. Using a small scoop (about 1 inch), form a few balls, drop them into the simmering water, and cook for 6 minutes after they rise to the surface. If forming into logs, cook for only 2 minutes. Check the texture and add more flour if necessary — ⅛ cup at a time — until the desired consistency is reached. The gnocchi should hold together without being gummy.

Continue shaping the gnocchi. Place them close together, but not touching, on a lightly floured tray. If not using immediately, place in the refrigerator for up to 1 hour.

When ready to serve, drop in the gnocchi, cooking no more than half the batch at a time. Stir a couple of times with a wooden spoon so the gnocchi move gently. The water should remain at a simmer rather than a rolling boil.

Have ready warmed serving bowls and a large mixing bowl with half your chosen sauce portioned into it. As the gnocchi rise to the surface, remove them with a slotted spoon, toss with the sauce, garnish as desired, and serve immediately. Repeat with the remaining gnocchi and sauce.

Alternatively, you can cook all the gnocchi at the same time in two separate pots and toss them all together in a large serving bowl with the appropriate amount of sauce.

These gnocchi can be frozen for up to two weeks after forming. See Freezer Notes, page 250.

Sauce Suggestions: Zucchini Pesto, Tomato Sauces, Sun-Dried Tomato and Olive Pesto, Garlic-Scape Pesto, Lemon & Garlic Sauce, Browned Butter & Preserved Lemon Sauce

RICOTTA, CREAM CHEESE & YOGURT GNOCCHI

/ serves 4

This is an unusual gnocchi recipe, and one that I adore because of its tangy flavor, versatility, and ease of preparation. But — cream cheese in Italy? Yes. And they call it "Philadelphia," its brand name. Funny how that happens with language.

This is a wonderful gnocchi for beginners, creamy and delicious with just melted butter, toasted breadcrumbs and a scattering of finely chopped parsley. Semolina flour adds a touch of golden color while the fat content of whole milk Greek-style yogurt and cream cheese keep the gnocchi meltingly soft. It's one of my "go to" doughs for stuffing because it's pliable and forgiving.

6 ounces full fat cream cheese, at room temperature

½ cup whole milk Greek-style yogurt

½ cup whole milk ricotta

1 cup finely grated fresh Parmigiano-Reggiano

Pinch salt

2 large egg yolks

¾ cup unbleached all-purpose flour

¼ cup finely ground semolina flour + more for shaping

In a small bowl, whisk the cream cheese with the yogurt until smooth. In a medium bowl, lightly beat the egg yolks and salt until combined. Add the ricotta to the eggs and mix well with a wooden spoon. Add the cream cheese and the freshly grated Parmigiano to the eggs and continue to mix until you get a uniform consistency.

Whisk the two flours together in a small bowl. Sprinkle with all but ⅛ cup of the flour, and cut lightly into the cheese mixture until completely incorporated.

Gather the dough into a smooth ball and place on a lightly floured board. Knead lightly to form a soft, uniform dough. Take a walnut-size portion of dough, roll into a 2-inch log, and cut into thirds. Test cook the three gnocchi in a small, deep saucepan of simmering water until the gnocchi rise to the surface. Cook another 2 minutes. Check for texture and doneness, making sure the inside is completely cooked. Increase cooking time and add more flour — ⅛ cup at a time — if necessary, until the desired consistency is reached. The gnocchi should hold together without being gummy.

Divide the dough into 4 to 6 pieces and roll into finger-thick ropes on a lightly floured board. Cut into ¾-inch pieces and press each over the reversed tines of a fork, or a wooden gnocchi or butter paddle — or simply cut and leave the gnocchi unshaped. Place the finished gnocchi close together, but not touching, on a lightly floured tray. Refrigerate while making your sauce.

When ready to serve the gnocchi, bring a very large, deep pot of water — no less than 1 gallon — to a simmer. Add 1 to 2 tablespoons salt and drop in the gnocchi, cooking no more than half the batch at a time. Stir a couple of times with a wooden spoon so the gnocchi move gently. The water should remain at a simmer rather than a rolling boil.

Have ready warmed serving bowls and a large mixing bowl with half your chosen sauce portioned into it. As the gnocchi rise to the surface, remove them with a slotted spoon, toss with the sauce, garnish as desired, and serve immediately. Repeat with the remaining gnocchi and sauce.

Alternatively, you can cook all the gnocchi at the same time in two separate pots and toss them all together in a large serving bowl with the appropriate amount of sauce.

These gnocchi can be frozen for up to two weeks after forming. See Freezer Notes, page 250.

Sauce Suggestions: Cabbage & Cheese Sauce, Sage-Butter Sauce, Sagrantino Cream Sauce, Umbrian Herbed Pesto, Savory Fig Sauce, Artichoke & Sausage Sauce; avoid sweet sauces, cheese sauces, and cheese stuffings

RICOTTA-GARBANZO BEAN FLOUR GNOCCHI

/ serves 4 to 6

Ceci, *the Italian word for garbanzo beans, have been a staple of Italian and other Mediterranean cuisines since ancient times. Commonly used in Italian pasta dishes, soups, and* cecina *or* farinata — *the very thin Tuscan focaccia made out of chickpea flour, water, and olive oil — here combines wonderfully with ricotta cheese to make delicious gnocchi. Using the chickpea flour commonly available at natural food stores — rather than puréed beans — produces a more desirable, somewhat cake-like texture. Note that you can substitute buckwheat flour for the garbanzo flour with equally good results.*

This is one of the quickest and easiest gnocchi to assemble and cook, and it's good as a first course, side dish, or in soups. You're highly unlikely to find these gnocchi on any restaurant menu, so I encourage you to experiment and enjoy these at home.

1 cup whole milk ricotta cheese, placed in a
    cheesecloth-lined colander set in a bowl, and
    drained for 30 minutes before using
2 whole eggs
¼ cup lightly packed flat-leaf parsley leaves,
    very finely chopped (optional)

1 teaspoon kosher salt
½ teaspoon freshly grated nutmeg
1 cup garbanzo bean flour
¼ cup finely grated fresh Parmigiano-Reggiano
    OR aged pecorino
All-purpose flour for shaping the gnocchi

Choose and prepare a sauce before you make the gnocchi.

In a medium bowl, mix the drained ricotta, eggs, salt, optional parsley, and nutmeg together. Sprinkle the garbanzo flour and grated cheese over the mixture. With a rubber spatula or a flexible curved plastic bowl scraper, mix lightly into the ricotta using a cutting/folding motion similar to mixing a cake. Do not overmix.

With floured hands or a small scoop, form a few small portions of dough into ¾-inch spheres. Alternately, you can shape the gnocchi using the traditional rope technique on page 26. Do not compress the dough or the gnocchi will be dense rather than tender.

Test cook a few gnocchi in a small saucepan full of simmering water. Start timing once the gnocchi rise to the surface. Check the texture after 3 minutes by breaking one open to make sure the center is firm. If the center is still undone, cook a minute more. Larger gnocchi will take a bit longer to cook.

Continue to form the gnocchi as desired and place the finished gnocchi close together, but not touching, on a lightly floured or parchment-lined tray.

Cook the formed gnocchi immediately. Bring a very large, deep pot of water — no less than 1 gallon — to a simmer. Add 1 to 2 tablespoons salt and drop in the gnocchi, cooking no more than half the batch at a time. Stir a couple of times with a wooden spoon so the gnocchi move gently. The water should remain at a simmer rather than a rolling boil.

Have ready warmed serving bowls and a large mixing bowl with half your chosen sauce portioned into it. As the gnocchi rise to the surface, remove them with a slotted spoon, toss with the sauce, garnish as desired, and serve immediately. Repeat with the remaining gnocchi and sauce.

Alternatively, you can cook all the gnocchi at the same time in two separate pots and toss them all together in a large serving bowl with the appropriate amount of sauce.

Do not freeze.

Sauce Suggestions: Italian Brodo or Cream Soups, Thyme-Garlic Butter Sauce, Light Cream Sauces, Wild Mushroom Sauce, Creamy Lemon, Peas & Prosciutto Sauce, Cabbage & Cheese Sauce

RICOTTA-GOAT CHEESE GNOCCHI

/ serves 6

These are very tender gnocchi with a somewhat intense goat-cheese flavor. The Roasted Red Pepper Purée on page 215 subdues the rich flavor of the cheese; the more traditional browned butter sauce with rosemary or sage enhances it. Be sure to start with the ingredients at room temperature to insure an evenly mixed dough.

11 ounces fresh soft goat cheese, at room temperature

2 cups whole milk ricotta OR a 15-ounce container, placed in a cheesecloth-lined colander set in a bowl and drained at least 30 minutes before using

2 large eggs, lightly beaten

1 teaspoon salt

Freshly ground white pepper to taste

Pinch freshly grated nutmeg

¾-1 cup all-purpose flour + more for shaping the gnocchi

2 tablespoons extra-virgin olive oil

In a large mixing bowl, whisk together the goat cheese, ricotta, eggs, salt, and nutmeg until smooth. Gently fold in ¾ cup of flour until the dough begins to form a ball. Add more flour, 1 tablespoon at a time if needed, to make a soft, smooth dough. Do not overwork the dough or the gnocchi will be tough. Cover the bowl with plastic wrap and refrigerate 30 to 45 minutes.

Gather the dough into a smooth ball and place it on a lightly floured board. Take a walnut-sized portion of dough, roll it into a 2-inch log, and cut the log into thirds. Test cook the three gnocchi in a small deep saucepan of simmering water until they rise to the surface. Check the texture and add more flour to the dough if necessary — ⅛ cup at a time — until the tests indicate you've reached the desired consistency. The gnocchi should hold together when cooked without being gummy.

Divide the remaining dough into four to six pieces and roll each piece into a finger-thick rope on a lightly floured board. Cut each rope into ¾-inch pieces. You can press each piece over a wooden gnocchi or butter paddle or the reversed tines of a fork to create the small pockets and ridges that help the sauce cling to the gnocchi — or simply cut the ropes and leave the gnocchi unshaped. Place the finished gnocchi close together, but not touching, on a lightly floured tray.

When ready to serve the gnocchi, bring a very large, deep pot of water — no less than 1 gallon — to a simmer. Add 1 to 2 tablespoons salt and drop in the gnocchi, cooking no more than half the batch at a time. Stir a couple of times with a wooden spoon so the gnocchi move gently. The water should remain at a simmer rather than a rolling boil.

Have ready warmed serving bowls and a large mixing bowl with half your chosen sauce portioned into it. As the gnocchi rise to the surface, remove them with a slotted spoon, toss with the sauce, garnish as desired, and serve immediately. Repeat with the remaining gnocchi and sauce.

Alternatively, you can cook all the gnocchi at the same time in two separate pots and toss them all together in a large serving bowl with the appropriate amount of sauce.

You can also lightly brown the cooked, drained gnocchi over medium-high heat in a large sauté pan coated lightly with olive oil, tossing while cooking to brown all sides.

These gnocchi can be frozen for up to two weeks after forming. See Freezer Notes, page 250.

Sauce Suggestions: Roasted Red Pepper Purée Sauce, Sage-Butter Sauce, Green Olive Cream Sauce, Sun-Dried Tomato & Olive Pesto, Pancetta-Orange Sauce

RICOTTA-MILLET GNOCCHI

/ serves 4 to 6

Millet is an ancient grain that's staging a comeback with those who choose a gluten-free diet. I found this traditional recipe for gnocchi using millet flour years ago when I began searching every Italian publication on the subject, and set it aside as a possible addition to this book. With today's dietary interests, I felt compelled to experiment with the recipe and I now urge everyone to try it. Toasting the millet flour — available at many natural foods stores or online — with the butter adds a sweet, nutty flavor and removes any raw taste from the millet. These gnocchi don't freeze well, but the dough can be prepared up to 4 hours in advance and cooked at the last minute.

1 cup whole milk ricotta cheese, placed in a
    cheesecloth-lined colander set in a bowl, and
    drained for 30 minutes before using
¼ cup unsalted butter
1½ cups millet flour
½ cup finely grated fresh Parmigiano-Reggiano
    OR other hard grating cheese

2 large eggs, beaten
Large pinch freshly grated nutmeg
1 tablespoon chopped fresh thyme (optional)
Kosher salt and freshly ground black pepper to taste
All-purpose flour for shaping the gnocchi

In a medium sauté pan over medium heat, melt the butter until foamy. Add the millet flour and cook about 5 minutes, stirring occasionally, until the millet begins to give off a toasty aroma. Stir well to break up any lumps and set aside.

In a medium bowl, mix the ricotta, eggs, grated cheese, nutmeg, optional thyme, about ½ teaspoon salt, and a few grindings of pepper. Add the toasted millet flour and mix well, breaking up any lumps. Cover lightly and set aside at room temperature for at least 30 minutes, or up to 4 hours.

When ready to finish the gnocchi, bring 1 gallon of water to a simmer. Add 1 to 2 tablespoons salt and drop in the gnocchi, cooking half the batch at a time. Stir a couple of times with a wooden spoon so the gnocchi move gently. The water should remain at a simmer rather than a rolling boil.

Test a few gnocchi. With a small scoop, form a few ½-inch balls of dough, dropping them into the simmering water. When the gnocchi rise to the surface, cook for another 3 minutes to be sure the center is evenly firm. If the gnocchi fall apart or are too soft, add more all-purpose flour to the dough, a few tablespoons at a time. Test again. The gnocchi should be firm enough to hold their shape.

Keep the water at a simmer while you continue forming the gnocchi, lightly rolling the balls in your hands to smooth the surface. Place the finished gnocchi close together, but not touching, on a lightly floured tray.

Add the gnocchi to the simmering water all at once; stir a couple of times with a wooden spoon so they move gently. The water should remain at a simmer rather than a rolling boil. Begin timing when the gnocchi rise to the surface.

Have ready warmed serving bowls and a large mixing bowl with half your chosen sauce portioned into it. As the gnocchi rise to the surface, remove them with a slotted spoon, toss with the sauce, garnish as desired, and serve immediately.

Alternatively, you can cook all the gnocchi at the same time in two separate pots and toss them all together in a large serving bowl with the appropriate amount of sauce.

Do not freeze.

Sauce Suggestions: Italian Brodo or Cream Soups, Thyme-Garlic Butter Sauce, Light Cream Sauces, Porcini Mushroom Sauce, Ragùs

Adapted from 100 Grandi Scuole di Cucina, *2000, Editore: A Tavola*

RICOTTA-PANCETTA GNOCCHI

/ serves 6

Although they are similar to bread-based canederli, these ricotta gnocchi are lighter in texture and incorporate the pancetta into the dough. They're wonderful sprinkled with toasted breadcrumbs and freshly grated Parmigiano-Reggiano — and are equally good in soups or broth as is typical of the mountainous regions of northern Italy. Other semi-aged grating cheeses, such as ricotta salata, ricotta affumicata, or pecorino can be substituted for the Parmigiano–Reggiano to finish the dish. And other fatty meats — such as naturally cured bacon, guanciale, speck, salami, or prosciutto — can replace the pancetta. Just be sure the meat you choose is finely chopped.

1¼ cups whole milk ricotta, placed in a cheesecloth-lined colander set in a bowl, and drained for 30 minutes before using

2 eggs

½ teaspoon kosher salt

Freshly ground black pepper to taste

Pinch freshly grated nutmeg

1¾ cups crustless, coarsely crumbled stale breadcrumbs from a dark or light loaf

1 cup whole milk

1 cup semolina flour

4 ounces pancetta, thinly sliced, then finely chopped

1 small onion, grated (about ½ cup)

⅓ cup unsalted butter

¼ cup dry breadcrumbs, sautéed with 2 tablespoons olive oil until lightly browned and crisp

Finely grated fresh Parmigiano-Reggiano for the table

In a bowl, soak the breadcrumbs in the milk for 30 minutes, or until the crumbs have absorbed all the milk possible.

Meanwhile, in a small sauté pan over medium heat, cook the chopped pancetta with the grated onion until the fat has been released and the pancetta is lightly browned. Drain the extra fat and set aside to cool. In a small bowl, beat the eggs with the salt, pepper, and nutmeg.

Squeeze the breadcrumbs to remove as much milk as possible. Crumble the ricotta into the breadcrumbs, add the pancetta and onion, and mix lightly to combine. Add the eggs and mix again to obtain a uniform dough. Sprinkle the semolina flour over the mixture. With a spatula mix the flour lightly into the ricotta using a cutting/folding motion similar to mixing a cake. Do not overmix. Cover with a dry towel and set aside to relax for about an hour.

Gather the dough into a ball and place on a lightly floured board. With floured hands form small portions of dough into 1-inch spheres. Place the finished gnocchi close together on a floured tray. Refrigerate up to 2 hours while preparing the sauce.

Bring a deep pot of water — no less than 1 gallon — to a simmer. Add 1 to 2 tablespoons salt and drop in the gnocchi, cooking no more than half the batch at a time. Stir a couple of times with a wooden spoon. The water should remain at a simmer. Cook for 5 to 6 minutes after they rise to the surface. They should be warm and thoroughly cooked in the center. If not, increase the cooking time by 2 minutes. In a medium sauté pan, melt the butter. Keep warm while the gnocchi finish cooking.

When the gnocchi are done, remove with a slotted spoon, toss with the melted butter, divide between warmed serving bowls and garnish with the toasted breadcrumbs and grated cheese. Serve immediately. Alternatively, you can cook all the gnocchi at the same time in two separate pots and toss them all together in a large serving bowl with the appropriate amount of sauce.

These gnocchi can be frozen for up to two weeks after forming. See Freezer Notes, page 250.

Additional Sauce Suggestions: Italian Brodo, Pine Nut-Butter Sauce, Fennel Pollen-Cream Sauce, Lemon Thyme & Scamorza Sauce, Zucchini Pesto, Garden Purée

RICOTTA-SEMOLINA GNOCCHI PIEMONTESE

/ serves 6 to 8

Reminiscent of Gnocchi alla Romana (page 132) and made from the same semolina flour used for dried pasta in southern Italy, these gnocchi from Piemonte are a bit softer than the original because of the ricotta added to the dough. They have a very soft, slightly sandy texture due to the grainy semolina; a rich, almost buttery flavor; a gorgeous golden color; and are less tricky to make than potato gnocchi. The dough is softer than most, but don't be tempted to add too much flour or the gnocchi will be gummy. Instead, coat the work surface with enough semolina to prevent sticking while rolling and cutting the dough into small pieces — then cook as is, without ridging with a fork or gnocchi paddle. Be sure to use finely ground semolina or the gnocchi will have a tendency to fall apart when cooked. These are among my favorite go-to gnocchi and can be matched with a wide variety of savory sauces.

3 cups whole milk

1 teaspoon kosher salt

Large pinch freshly grated nutmeg

1 cup fine semolina flour + more for shaping

2 whole eggs

3 egg yolks

⅔ cup whole milk ricotta, placed in a cheesecloth-lined colander set in a bowl, and drained at least 30 minutes before using

¾ cup finely grated fresh Parmigiano-Reggiano or other hard grating cheese + more for serving if desired

In a bowl, whisk the yolks and whole eggs together with the drained ricotta and grated Parmigiano until smooth. Set aside. In a large saucepan heat the milk, salt, and nutmeg. As soon as the milk begins to simmer, add the semolina flour in a slow steady stream, stirring constantly with a wooden spoon to prevent lumps. Lower the heat and continue stirring until the mixture is well thickened. It should resemble cold mashed potatoes.

Remove from heat, add the egg mixture and stir until well blended. The dough will be very soft and somewhat sticky, but will hold its shape. Turn out onto a well-floured work surface and lightly knead in enough additional semolina to make a soft, but workable, dough. Form into a ball and place in a floured bowl. Cover and refrigerate until well chilled, about 2 hours.

Remove the dough from the refrigerator and place on a floured board. Take a walnut-size portion of dough, roll into a 2-inch log, and cut into thirds. Test cook the three gnocchi in a small, deep saucepan of simmering water until the gnocchi rise to the surface. Check the texture and add more flour if necessary — ⅛ cup at a time — until the desired consistency is reached. The gnocchi should hold together without being gummy. Divide the dough into 4 to 6 pieces and roll into finger-thick ropes on a lightly floured board. Cut into ¾-inch pieces. Place the finished gnocchi close together on a lightly floured tray.

Bring a very large, deep pot of water — no less than 1 gallon — to a simmer. Add 1 to 2 tablespoons salt and drop in the gnocchi, cooking no more than half the batch at a time. Stir a couple of times with a wooden spoon so the gnocchi move gently. The water should remain at a simmer rather than a rolling boil.

Have ready warmed serving bowls and a large mixing bowl with half your sauce portioned into it. As the gnocchi rise, check for doneness. If not fully cooked, continue simmering 2 minutes. When done, remove them with a slotted spoon, toss with the sauce, garnish as desired, and serve immediately. Repeat and serve immediately. Alternatively, you can cook all the gnocchi at the same time in two separate pots and toss them all together in a large serving bowl with the appropriate amount of sauce.

Variation: To serve as an appetizer or soup garnish, coat the cooked, drained, and cooled gnocchi with beaten egg white, dip in semolina, fry until golden, and garnish with a dusting of freshly grated Parmigiano-Reggiano.

These gnocchi can be frozen for up to two weeks after forming. See Freezer Notes, page 250.

Any of the savory sauce suggestions on pages 174-204 will compliment these gnocchi.

RICOTTA-SPINACH GNOCCHI (MALFATTI)

/ serves 4 to 6

Gnudi, meaning nude, refers to a filling used to make ravioli that is cooked without being enclosed in pasta and is, thus, naked. Another name for the same gnocchi, depending on the region of Italy you're in, is malfatti, *or poorly made, which refers to their irregular shape. A favored gnocchi in many regions, these gnudi are rich and creamy — and one of the easier gnocchi to make. Swiss chard or other greens can be substituted for the spinach, but the hardier greens need to be cooked until very tender, up to 20 minutes, before proceeding with the recipe. For an alternative way to serve these gnocchi, see the recipe for Malfatti Caprese on page 146.*

1 pound clean baby spinach leaves

2 cups whole milk ricotta OR a 15-ounce container, placed in a cheesecloth-lined colander set in a bowl and drained at least 30 minutes before using

2 whole eggs

1 egg yolk

1-1¼ cups all-purpose unbleached flour
    + more for shaping the gnocchi

½ cup finely grated fresh Parmigiano-Reggiano
    + more for serving

Pinch of freshly ground nutmeg

Salt and freshly ground black pepper to taste

In a medium saucepan, cook the spinach in just enough water to wilt it, stirring constantly.

Drain and squeeze out all excess water. Finely chop and squeeze thoroughly once more.

Place the spinach, ricotta, eggs, Parmigiano-Reggiano, nutmeg, salt, and pepper in a mixing bowl and combine lightly. Add all but 2 tablespoons of the flour and mix well.

Bring a very large, deep pot of water — no less than 1 gallon — to a simmer. Add 1 to 2 tablespoons salt. With floured hands, or a 1¼-inch scoop, take one walnut-sized piece of dough and lightly roll to coat it with a little flour. Drop into the simmering water. After it floats to the top, cook an additional 2 minutes, remove and test. If it holds together and the interior is thoroughly cooked, repeat with the rest of the dough. If needed, add the remaining flour to the mixture and test again until the gnocchi hold together.

Continue shaping the rest of the dough, placing the finished gnocchi close together, but not touching, on a lightly floured tray.

When ready to cook, carefully drop the gnocchi into the simmering water, cooking half at a time. When the gnocchi float to the surface, cook an additional 2 minutes, then remove with a slotted spoon and toss gently in a large bowl with half the sauce of your choice. Serve immediately, passing finely grated fresh Parmigiano-Reggiano at the table. Repeat with the remaining gnocchi and sauce.

Alternatively, you can cook all the gnocchi at the same time in two separate pots and toss them all together in a large serving bowl with the appropriate amount of sauce.

These gnocchi are best cooked as soon as you shape them, but you can mix the ingredients together and refrigerate them a few hours until needed.

These gnocchi can be frozen for up to two weeks after forming. See Freezer Notes, page 250.

Sauce Suggestions: Basic Tomato Sauce, Oven-Roasted Cherry Tomato Sauce, Lemon & Garlic Sauce, Wild Mushroom Sauce, Tomato, Sausage & Leek Sauce

RICOTTA-SWEET POTATO GNOCCHI

/ serves 6

These earthy, naturally sweet gnocchi are tasty any time of year; spiced with cinnamon and nutmeg, they are particularly special during the fall and holiday season. The use of ricotta cheese rather than potato results in a creamier, richer gnocchi suitable for a number of sauces as suggested below. Until recently, sweet potatoes (called patate americane*), were very difficult to find in Italian markets, but they are becoming more available as cooking trends change. Because of the high water content of both the potatoes and the ricotta, bake or microwave the potatoes rather than boiling them. This will keep the amount of added flour to a minimum and produce a more tender gnocchi.*

2 pounds sweet potatoes, coppery-skinned orange-fleshed variety

1 cup fresh whole milk ricotta cheese, placed in a cheesecloth-lined colander set in a bowl, and drained for 30 minutes before using

1 large egg yolk

1 teaspoon kosher salt

½ teaspoon freshly ground black pepper

Pinch freshly grated nutmeg

¼ teaspoon cinnamon

1-1½ cups all-purpose flour + more for shaping

Pierce the sweet potatoes with a fork and bake at 400°F for about an hour, or until they are tender when deeply pierced with a small knife. Alternatively, they can be microwaved on high. Cool just enough to handle. Peel while still warm and pass through the fine disk of a food mill or potato ricer into a large bowl or onto a clean counter. Cool to room temperature. In a small bowl, beat the ricotta with the egg yolk, salt, black pepper, nutmeg, and cinamon until just combined.

With a spatula, mix the ricotta into the potatoes using a cutting/folding motion. Do not overmix; there should still be streaks of ricotta in the dough. Sprinkle with all but ¼ cup of the flour and cut into the potatoes until combined.

Gather the dough into a smooth ball and place it on a floured board. Take a walnut-sized portion of dough, roll it into a 2-inch log, and cut the log into thirds. Test cook the three gnocchi until they rise to the surface. Check the texture and add more flour to the dough if necessary. The gnocchi should hold together when cooked without being gummy.

Divide the remaining dough into four to six pieces and roll each piece into a finger-thick rope on a floured board. Cut each rope into ¾-inch pieces. Press each piece over a wooden gnocchi paddle or the reversed tines of a fork to create the small pockets and ridges — or simply cut the ropes and leave the gnocchi unshaped. Place the finished gnocchi close together on a floured tray. Set aside or refrigerate up to 2 hours while making the sauce.

Bring a very large, deep pot of water — no less than 1 gallon — to a simmer. Add 1 to 2 tablespoons salt and drop in the gnocchi, cooking no more than half the batch at a time. Stir a couple of times with a wooden spoon so the gnocchi move gently. The water should remain at a simmer rather than a rolling boil. Have ready warmed serving bowls and a large mixing bowl with half your chosen sauce portioned into it.

After the gnocchi rise to the surface, cook them for another 2 to 3 minutes. Test for doneness. Remove with a slotted spoon, toss with your chosen sauce, garnish as desired and serve immediately. Repeat with the remaining gnocchi and sauce.

Alternatively, you can cook all the gnocchi at the same time in two separate pots and toss them all together in a large serving bowl with the appropriate amount of sauce.

These gnocchi can be frozen for up to two weeks after forming. See Freezer Notes, page 250.

Sauce Suggestions: Pancetta-Orange Sauce, Browned Butter & Preserved Lemon Sauce, Cavolo Nero & Horseradish Pesto, Sage-Butter Sauce with Toasted Pecans or Roasted Chestnuts; avoid tomato, ragù or heavy cheese sauces as they will overwhelm the delicate sweet potato

/ VEGETABLE GNOCCHI

Traditionally shaped gnocchi made with vegetable purée and no potato has a unique texture. Because they are frequently denser than plain potato gnocchi, these gnocchi often spark a negative reaction. But there are two recipes for vegetable-based gnocchi that I've favored over the years — one made with roasted squash, the other with parsnips — that can be kept reasonably light by roasting the vegetables to caramelize their sugars and eliminate any extra moisture. As noted in the Gnocchi Tips section, extra water means extra flour, which in turn means overworking the dough, which ultimately results in heavy, gummy gnocchi. Once you have that tendency to overdo licked, the following two recipes may also join your list of favorites.

PARSNIP GNOCCHI

/ serves 4

Although they were commonly eaten in ancient times, parsnips are rarely found in modern Italian cuisine. They are still cultivated as far south as the Emilia-Romagna region, where they are most often fed to the pigs that produce the famed prosciutto di Parma, contributing a particularly wonderful flavor to the prized dry-cured ham. Further north in the Dolomites, however, parsnips are still found on local tables, often used in soups, paired with apples, or even made into gnocchi. Their subtle, sweet flavor is akin to that of carrots.

These gnocchi are denser than some others because of the texture of the parsnips, so you need to handle the dough delicately. A favorite at any time, these gnocchi are a particularly good match for a pork roast when served with any of the buttery sauces suggested below.

1 pound parsnips

½ cup mascarpone

½ cup unbleached all-purpose flour + more for forming

½ cup finely grated fresh grated Parmigiano-Reggiano or other semi-aged grating cheese

½ teaspoon salt

Freshly ground black pepper to taste

Freshly grated nutmeg to taste

2 tablespoons finely chopped parsley, thyme, or mint

Preheat oven to 400° F. Steam parsnips until tender, about 15 minutes. Transfer to a baking sheet and roast for 45 minutes. Purée parsnips in a food processor. It's OK if a few small pieces remain in the purée. Put the parsnips into a medium bowl, mix in the mascarpone, and set aside.

In a small bowl, mix the flour with the finely grated fresh Parmigiano-Reggiano, salt, pepper, nutmeg, and herbs. Add to the parsnip purée, gradually working the flour mixture in with your fingertips, using the same method you would use to form pastry dough. Do not overmix.

Gather the dough into a ball and place on a floured board. Take a walnut-size portion of dough, roll into a 2-inch log, and cut into thirds. Test cook the three gnocchi in a small saucepan full of simmering water until they rise to the surface. Check the texture and add more flour if necessary — ⅛ cup at a time — until the desired consistency is reached. The gnocchi should hold together without being gummy.

Divide the dough into 4 to 6 pieces and roll into finger-thick ropes. Cut into ¾-inch pieces and press each over the reversed tines of a fork or a wooden gnocchi paddle. Place the finished gnocchi close together, but not touching, on a lightly floured tray.

Bring a very large, deep pot of water — no less than 1 gallon — to a simmer. Add 1 to 2 tablespoons salt and drop in the gnocchi, cooking no more than half the batch at a time. Stir a couple of times with a wooden spoon so the gnocchi move gently. The water should remain at a simmer rather than a rolling boil.

Have ready warmed serving bowls and a large mixing bowl with half your chosen sauce portioned into it. As the gnocchi rise to the surface, remove them with a slotted spoon, toss with the sauce, garnish as desired, and serve immediately. Repeat with the remaining gnocchi and sauce. Serve immediately.

Alternatively, you can cook all the gnocchi at the same time in two separate pots and toss them all together in a large serving bowl with the appropriate amount of sauce.

These gnocchi can be frozen for up to two weeks after forming. See Freezer Notes, page 250.

Sauce Suggestions: Lemon & Garlic Sauce, Thyme-Garlic Butter Sauce, Browned Butter & Preserved Lemon Sauce, Mascarpone Cream Sauce, Chestnut, Pancetta & Sage Sauce

PUMPKIN-SQUASH GNOCCHI

/ serves 6

As fall approaches in Italy, large, beautifully colored Hubbard-type squash, or zucca, *begin to appear in the markets. Because of their size, typically 8 to 20 pounds, they are cut to order and sold by the kilo. They have a beautiful yellow-orange flesh that is high in sugar, which make them suitable for purée — and for gnocchi. When making pumpkin gnocchi in the U.S., I usually choose the widely available kabocha squash because of its size — about 2 to 3 pounds — and its sweet, dry, dense flesh.*

2 pounds peeled, seeded, and cubed kabocha,
    butternut, or other fine-grained winter squash
    to make 2 cups purée

2 tablespoons extra-virgin olive oil

1 teaspoon kosher salt

Freshly ground black pepper to taste

1 egg, lightly beaten

Finely grated zest of 1 lemon

¼ teaspoon freshly grated nutmeg

1-1¼ cups unbleached flour

Finely grated fresh Parmigiano-Reggiano for serving

Preheat the oven to 400°F. Toss the squash with the olive oil in a large bowl and season with salt and pepper. Arrange the coated squash on a baking sheet and roast in the preheated oven until the squash is tender and lightly browned, 20 to 30 minutes. Combine the beaten egg with nutmeg and lemon zest. Set aside.

While still warm, pass the squash through a ricer into a medium-size bowl. With a rubber spatula or a flexible curved plastic bowl scraper, mix the egg lightly into the squash using a cutting/folding motion similar to mixing a cake. Sprinkle with 1 cup of the flour and cut lightly into the squash. Do not overmix or gnocchi will be tough.

Gather the dough into a ball and place on a lightly floured board. Take a walnut-size portion of dough, roll into a 2-inch log, and cut into thirds. Test cook the three gnocchi in a small saucepan full of simmering water until they rise to the surface. Check the texture and add more flour if necessary — ⅛ cup at a time — until the desired consistency is reached. The gnocchi should hold together without being gummy.

Divide the dough into 4 to 6 pieces and roll into finger-thick ropes. Cut into ¾-inch pieces and place the finished gnocchi close together, but not touching, on a lightly floured tray.

Bring a very large, deep pot of water — no less than 1 gallon — to a simmer. Add 1 to 2 tablespoons salt and drop in the gnocchi, cooking no more than half the batch at a time. Stir a couple of times with a wooden spoon so the gnocchi move gently. The water should remain at a simmer rather than a rolling boil.

Have ready warmed serving bowls and a large mixing bowl with half your chosen sauce portioned into it. As the gnocchi rise to the surface, remove them with a slotted spoon, toss with the sauce, garnish as desired, and serve immediately. Repeat with the remaining gnocchi and sauce. Pass freshly grated Parmigiano-Reggiano at the table.

These gnocchi can be frozen for up to two weeks after forming. See Freezer Notes, page 250.

Note: Sweet potatoes may be substituted for the squash by following the roasting directions above, but they tend to produce a heavier gnocchi.

Sauce Suggestions: Sage-Butter Sauce with Hazelnuts, Savory Fig Sauce, White Truffle & Cream Sauce, Chestnut, Pancetta & Sage Sauce, Umbrian Herbed Pesto

Italians love both sweet and savory gnocchi, and sometimes even eat slightly sweet variations as a first course.

SWEET GNOCCHI

"Sweet dessert gnocchi" may strike you as an oxymoron. Often, gnocchi are more commonly thought of as a savory dish suitable for a first or main course, not a dessert. Gnocchi, however, can be made from a variety of ingredients and prepared both savory and sweet.

You can choose how you will serve your gnocchi, but don't be shy about trying any of the recipes in this chapter. I've noted a few favorites that I often prepare to surprise my dinner guests.

CHOCOLATE-RICOTTA GNOCCHI WITH ORANGE WATER

/ serves 8 to 10

This recipe for sweet gnocchi is traditionally made with amaretti — *small, round, almond-paste cookies that originated in Venice during the Renaissance. Amaretti are still popular today, and can be found in specialty food stores in the U.S., most often during the Christmas holidays. Try this "Americanized" chocolate version of the fritters, or replace the chocolate wafers with an equal amount of amaretti. For an even crisper crust, substitute lightly toasted panko breadcrumbs for the fine, dry variety. Whichever way you make them, these gnocchi are a divine dessert.*

15 ounces whole milk ricotta, placed in a
   cheesecloth-lined colander set in a bowl,
   and drained at least 30 minutes before using

1 cup unbleached all-purpose flour

⅓ cup granulated sugar

4 ounces dark-chocolate wafer cookies (about 20),
   preferably the Famous brand, very finely crushed
   to make 1 cup

2 large eggs

1 large egg yolk

Finely grated zest of 1 small orange
   OR lemon, about 2 tablespoons

2 teaspoons orange water
   (OR rose water if using lemon zest)

½-1 cup unbleached all-purpose flour

3 large eggs

About 2 cups unseasoned fine breadcrumbs,
   lightly toasted, preferably homemade

3 cups canola or sunflower oil

Granulated or confectioners' sugar for dusting

Mascarpone Cream, optional (see recipe on page 206)

Place drained ricotta in a bowl, add the sugar and the flour and beat well with a wooden spoon. Add the chocolate cookie crumbs along with the eggs, egg yolk, grated lemon or orange peel, and the orange or rose water. Mix very well to form a very smooth, thick dough. It will be very soft.

Using a teaspoon or a scoop, form ¾-inch balls and lightly roll in flour. Keep them small or the center won't cook. Place finished balls close together on a parchment-lined baking sheet and refrigerate for 1 hour. Bring to room temperature 30 minutes before frying. When ready to fry, lightly beat the eggs in a small bowl. Put the breadcrumbs in another bowl.

Heat the oil in a skillet over medium heat. When the oil reaches 350°F. — hot enough to make a wooden skewer sizzle when inserted into the oil — dip each ball in the beaten egg, then roll it in the breadcrumbs. Fry until golden all over, 2 to 3 minutes. Break one gnocco open to test. The fritters should be very crusty on the outside and

warm and creamy on the inside. Do not cook more than six at a time or the oil temperature will fall too quickly. Should some of the dough break through the outer crust, simply break it off before serving.

Transfer the cooked balls to a serving platter lined with paper towels and sprinkle with some granulated or confectioners' sugar. Serve hot, with Mascarpone Cream or another sweet sauce of your choice.

Note: You can also fry the fritters without dipping them in egg and crumbs. The result is a thin, crusty, chocolate outer layer. Do not freeze.

Additional Sauce Suggestions: Any of the Sweet Sauces starting on page 205

RICOTTA & CINNAMON-BREAD GNOCCHI FRITTERS

/ serves 6 to 8

While searching for bread to make canederli, I spied a wonderfully rich loaf of cinnamon bread that struck my fancy. I purchased it figuring I'd find a use for it — if not for gnocchi, then to enjoy for breakfast. It's not uncommon to find cinnamon used in Italian sweets, and, even though I had not found a recipe for a sweet gnocchi with cinnamon, I experimented with the bread and came up with this wonderful rendition of a sweet gnocchi fritter.

Because the cinnamon bread is naturally rich and the crumbs are used fresh instead of stale, you will need to use less milk to prepare the dough and soak the crumbs just long enough for the bread to absorb the milk. The resulting interior is soft and creamy. Dipped in dry crumbs and gently fried, they're a perfect centerpiece for fresh fruit and Mascarpone Cream (page 206). If you want to add yet another taste dimension, stuff each gnocchi with a piece of melting cheese such as Taleggio, a whole blueberry, or small chocolate bits that will melt in your mouth with the first bite. Mi prendono in cielo! *(They take me to heaven!)*

2 cups lightly packed crumbled or chopped crustless, fresh cinnamon bread

⅓ cup whole milk

1 cup whole milk ricotta placed in a cheesecloth-lined colander set in a bowl, and drained at least 30 minutes before using

1½ cups plain, fine, dry breadcrumbs, preferably panko, divided

¾ cup sugar, divided

Pinch kosher salt

2 large egg yolks

1 teaspoon finely grated orange zest (optional)

4 cups canola or sunflower oil for frying

½ teaspoon ground cinnamon

Powdered sugar for dusting (optional)

Soak the bread in the milk for 5 minutes, then squeeze dry and place in a large bowl. Stir in the ricotta, ¼ cup of the sugar, ½ cup of the dry breadcrumbs, egg yolks, salt, and optional orange zest. Cover with plastic wrap and refrigerate 1 to 12 hours.

When ready to serve, heat the oil in a deep 10-inch pan to 350°F., or until it is hot enough to make a wooden skewer sizzle when inserted into the oil. Put the remaining breadcrumbs in a medium bowl.

Mix the remaining sugar with the ground cinnamon and place in a shallow dish.

Using a small scoop or teaspoon, drop 1-1½-inch balls of the ricotta mixture into the breadcrumbs and toss to evenly coat. Transfer to the hot oil and fry 8 or 10 gnocchi at a time, turning once, about 3 minutes per side, until a golden

brown all over. Remove with a slotted spoon to a plate lined with paper towels and drain well. Continue in the same manner with the remaining ricotta mixture, maintaining the temperature of the oil.

Serve the fritters hot, rolled in the remaining sugar and ground cinnamon if desired.

Do not freeze.

Additional Sauce Suggestions: Saba, Chocolate Sauce, Sweet Seared Fresh Fig Sauce, Marmalade, Fresh Plum Sauce, Rosemary-Orange Syrup

ROMAN-STYLE MILK GNOCCHI

/   serves 4 to 6

This is a Roman-style, lightly sweet dessert gnocchi that I enjoy serving with fresh berries or any of the dessert sauces included in this book. The recipe is based on one I discovered buried in an old Italian cookbook and revised to fit a more contemporary menu. My favorite part is the crispy topping that forms as the Parmigiano melts under the broiler. This gnocchi can also make an unusual (and delicious) savory appetizer with a spoonful of pesto on the side. Try it both ways: you won't be disappointed!

6 large egg yolks

5 tablespoons unbleached all-purpose flour

4 tablespoons cornstarch

1 tablespoons sugar

¼ teaspoon salt

2 cups whole milk

½ teaspoon of freshly ground nutmeg

6 tablespoons finely grated fresh Parmigiano-Reggiano

1½ teaspoons cinnamon

¼ cup butter, melted and divided

Fresh berries, fruit, or sweet sauce (optional)

Lightly oil an 8-inch square deep-sided pan and set aside.

In a medium saucepan, mix together egg yolks, flour, cornstarch, sugar, and salt and whisk until smooth. Very gradually add the milk and nutmeg, whisking until well blended.

Place the pan over low heat and cook, whisking continuously, until mixture is very thick and smooth. At first it will thicken very slowly, then move more quickly as it reaches the boiling point. It should be as thick as cold mashed potatoes.

Just before the liquid comes to a boil, quickly remove it from the heat and scrape it into the oiled pan. Using a small, wet metal spatula, smooth the mixture evenly in the pan and refrigerate, covered with plastic wrap, until chilled. You can leave the mixture refrigerated up to 1 day before finishing the recipe.

When ready to finish the gnocchi, preheat the oven to 375°F.

Butter a shallow baking dish with some of the melted butter. Cut the refrigerated dough into small squares, about 1½-inches, and overlap them in the prepared baking dish. Sprinkle with grated cheese, cinnamon, and remaining butter.

Bake about 20 minutes, or until bubbly and golden in color. Broil lightly to crisp the top.

Serve immediately with fruit or a sweet sauce if desired.

Do not freeze.

Sauce Suggestions: Any sauce from the Sweet Sauce chapter (page 205-207).

Recipe revised from The Talisman Italian Cookbook, *Ada Boni, Crown Publishers, 1950*

THREE-CHEESE CANEDERLI WITH GRAPPA–RASPBERRY SAUCE

/ serves 6 to 8

The flavor of these sweet canederli, a favorite of mine, is reminiscent of the best New York City cheesecake. And, because they're rolled in crisp, spiced breadcrumbs to finish, they have a crunchy crust. They're great for a dinner party because the canederli, cooking water, raspberry-grappa sauce, and spiced breadcrumbs can all be prepared up to a day in advance.

/ FOR THE CANEDERLI

2 tablespoons unsalted butter, at room temperature

2 large eggs, lightly beaten

⅓ cup fine granulated sugar

1 cup whole-milk ricotta, placed in a cheese cloth-lined colander set in a bowl, and drained 30 minutes

½ cup mascarpone cheese

4 cups lightly packed, crustless, white country breadcrumbs

1 cup cake flour + more for shaping

1 cup finely grated fresh Parmigiano-Reggiano

2 teaspoon finely grated lemon zest

2 teaspoons finely grated orange zest

/ FOR THE COOKING WATER

½ cup sugar

3-inch strip lemon peel

3-inch strip orange peel

5 whole cloves

3-inch cinnamon stick

/ FOR THE SPICED BREADCRUMBS

5 tablespoons unsalted butter

2 teaspoons ground cinnamon

¼ cup fine granulated sugar

/ FOR THE GRAPPA-RASPBERRY SAUCE

2 pints raspberries, 1 pint reserved for garnish

¼ cup grappa or sweet Moscato wine

2 tablespoons sugar

Fresh mint leaves for garnish

½ cup heavy cream, whipped with 2 tablespoons confectioners' sugar (optional)

In a medium bowl, beat the butter, eggs, sugar, mascarpone, and ricotta together until smooth. Add 1½ cups of the breadcrumbs, the flour, grated Parmigiano-Reggiano, lemon and orange zests, and mix well. Cover and refrigerate 2 hours.

Using a 1½-inch scoop, form the dough into balls and place close together on a lightly floured tray lined with parchment paper. Cover with plastic wrap and refrigerate overnight. For the Grappa-Raspberry Sauce, combine 1 pint raspberries, sugar, and grappa in a food processor or blender. Purée until smooth. Strain through a fine sieve into a bowl and set aside. The sauce will keep in a jar, refrigerated, for two weeks.

For the cooking water, combine the sugar, citrus peels, and spices in a deep pot. Add 2 quarts water. Bring to a boil, turn heat to low and simmer for 5 minutes. Cover and set aside. Reheat to a simmer when ready to cook the canederli.

In a medium sauté pan, toast the remaining 1½ cups breadcrumbs over medium heat until golden. Remove from heat and add the cinnamon and sugar. Cover and set aside.

When ready to cook, drop the gnocchi into the simmering flavored cooking water and cook for 6 to 8 minutes. Check after 6 minutes for doneness. They should be hot and firm in the center. If not, cook another 2 minutes. When done, remove them with a slotted spoon, and roll in the reserved spiced breadcrumbs.

Divide the sauce between 6 to 8 shallow dessert dishes. Top with a serving of canederli, and garnish with fresh raspberries and mint. Add a dollop of whipped cream. Serve immediately.

These gnocchi can be frozen for up to two weeks after forming. See Freezer Notes, page 250.

Inspired by a recipe in La Cucina Italiana *June, 2001*

SWEET FRIED POLENTA GNOCCHI

/ serves 6 to 8

The town of Spello, about one hour from my home in Perugia, traditionally prepares these sweet, fried polenta-based gnocchi during the celebration of Carnevale and the Festa di San Giuseppe, a religious holiday on March 19 that honors Joseph, the husband of the Virgin Mary. These gnocchi make a grand presentation at the end of a meal, or set on a buffet table where guests can serve themselves. Alternately, they can be served in small bowls drizzled with any of the sauces recommended below.

5 cups water

1 teaspoon salt

2⅓ cups fine polenta or corn flour + more if needed

½ cup sultana raisins

¼ cup rum

⅞ cup granulated sugar

4 large eggs

¼ cup pine nuts, lightly toasted

1 lemon, finely zested

1 tablespoon unsalted butter

2 teaspoons vanilla extract

Ground cinnamon and confectioners' sugar for garnish

3 cups canola or sunflower oil for frying

In a large saucepan, bring 5 cups of water to boil over high heat; add 1 teaspoon salt. Add the polenta in a stream, whisking constantly. Immediately reduce heat to low and cook, stirring vigorously every few minutes, until the polenta is thick and pulls away from the sides of the pan, about 30 to 45 minutes. Remove pan from the heat and cool to room temperature.

When cool, whisk in the eggs, one at a time, until well incorporated. Add the sugar, butter, rum, raisins, pine nuts, lemon zest, and vanilla. Mix well. If dough doesn't hold its shape, add a little more fine polenta or corn flour.

With a scoop or floured hands, form the dough into balls no larger than 1½ inches and place close together, but not touching, on a parchment-lined tray. Refrigerate for 1 to 2 hours, or cook immediately.

When ready to fry the gnocchi, line another tray with paper towels.

In a deep pot, heat the cooking oil to 350°F — or hot enough to make a wooden skewer sizzle when inserted into the oil. Frying no more than 6 gnocchi at a time, cook the gnocchi until golden brown. Test for doneness; they should be hot and solid in the center. If not, continue cooking another minute or two. Remove with a slotted spoon to the paper towel-lined tray. Fry the remaining gnocchi.

Make a pyramid of the gnocchi on a large, round platter, building up from the bottom and sprinkling each layer with confectioners' sugar and a dash of ground cinnamon.

Do not freeze.

Sauce Suggestions: Saba, Rosemary-Orange Syrup, Sweet Mascarpone Cream, Sweet Seared Fresh Fig Sauce

Adapted from a recipe in La Cucina Umbra *by Amelia Valli, Newton & Compton 2003*

SWEET SWEET-POTATO GNOCCHI STUFFED WITH CHESTNUT PURÉE

/ serves 6 to 8

Stuffed or not, this is a perfect dish for autumn. This recipe is grouped with dessert gnocchi, but can easily become a first course by eliminating the sugar in the dough and serving the gnocchi with a savory rather than sweet sauce and a savory filling, such as bits of cooked pancetta. Here the gnocchi are stuffed with chestnut purée and paired with a wonderful sweet amaretto sauce — but I encourage you to experiment with other combinations.

Sweet potatoes are not botanically related to potatoes and respond to the gnocchi-making process differently than regular potatoes. Often confused with or labeled yams — which are rarely available in the U.S. — they tend to make a denser, but still tender gnocchi. If the sweet potatoes are boiled, you will need to add too much flour to the dough and the resulting gnocchi will be gummy — so bake or microwave the sweet potatoes and make sure the final purée is dry. If need be, you can carefully remove some of the moisture by stirring the purée over low heat on top of the stove; the texture should be like very stiff mashed potatoes.

2 pounds coppery-skinned, orange-fleshed
   sweet potatoes

¼ cup fine granulated sugar

½ cup almond flour OR very finely ground almonds

2 large egg yolks

1 teaspoon kosher salt

½ teaspoon ground cinnamon

1-1¼ cups unbleached all-purpose flour
   + more for shaping

About 1 cup sweet chestnut purée from a 15-ounce
   can (or follow recipe on page 227)

½ cup amaretto (almond liqueur)

¼ pound unsalted butter

¾ cup golden raisins, roughly chopped

½ cup sliced almonds, toasted

In a small saucepan, warm the amaretto and raisins over low heat until hot and steamy. Do not boil. Set aside.

Bake at 400°F, or microwave the sweet potatoes on high, until tender when deeply pierced with a small knife. Slice open lengthwise to cool. Peel the potatoes while still warm and pass through the fine disk of a food mill or potato ricer into a medium saucepan. Cook the potatoes over medium heat, stirring constantly to remove extra moisture, until they are stiff and dry, about 5 to 10 minutes. Cool to room temperature and turn into in a medium mixing bowl.

Whisk the sugar and ground almonds or almond flour together in a small bowl. In another bowl, whisk the egg yolks, salt, and cinnamon together until just combined. With a rubber spatula or a flexible curved plastic bowl scraper, mix the eggs lightly into the potatoes using a cutting/folding motion similar to mixing a cake. Add the sugar and almonds and mix again until nearly uniform. Sprinkle with all but ¼ cup of the flour, and cut lightly

into the potatoes to make a soft, but workable, dough. Do not overmix or gnocchi will be tough.

Gather the dough into a smooth ball and place on a lightly floured board. Take a walnut-size portion of dough, roll into a 2-inch log, and cut into thirds. Test cook the three gnocchi in a small, deep saucepan of simmering water until they rise to the surface. Check the texture and add more flour if necessary — ⅛ cup at a time — until the desired consistency is reached. The gnocchi should hold together without being gummy.

With well-floured hands, break off a 1-inch piece of dough and roll into a ball. Place the ball in the palm of one hand, flatten slightly, and make an indentation in the middle of the gnocco with the forefinger of your other hand. Fill with about 1 teaspoon of the chestnut purée, and close the dough around the filling, reshaping the gnocchi into balls or ovals. Place the finished gnocchi close together, but not touching, on a lightly floured tray. Refrigerate up to

2 hours while preparing the sauce. In a large sauté pan, melt the butter over medium-low heat until it turns golden. Add the amaretto and raisin mixture, combine well, and remove half the sauce to a small bowl.

Bring a very large, deep pot of water — no less than 1 gallon — to a simmer. Add 1 to 2 tablespoons salt and drop in the gnocchi, cooking no more than half the batch at a time. Stir a couple of times with a wooden spoon so the gnocchi move gently. The water should remain at a simmer rather than a rolling boil.

As the gnocchi rise to the surface, remove with a slotted spoon to the sauté pan. Toss gently over medium-high heat until well coated and golden. Divide among heated serving bowls and garnish with the toasted almonds. Serve immediately. Repeat with the remaining gnocchi and sauce.

Alternatively, you can cook all the gnocchi at the same time in two separate pots and toss them all together in 1 large sauté pan of sauce.

These gnocchi can be frozen for up to two weeks after forming. See Freezer Notes, page 250.

Variations: Refer to the Stuffed Savory Gnocchi notes (page 157) for more detailed information about stuffed gnocchi. Adding ¼ cup granulated sugar to the Basic Ricotta Gnocchi dough on page 90 makes a wonderfully basic sweet gnocchi that can be stuffed with a variety of fillings. Some ideas: poppy-seed filling (preferably homemade), small pieces of semi-sweet chocolate, chopped dates and almonds mixed with honey, chocolate and hazelnut ganache (*gianduja*), chestnut purée (page 227), finely chopped, spiced and sweetened apple, small berries

Once stuffed and cooked, serve the gnocchi with your favorite sweet sauce, or coat them with olive oil and lightly sauté them over medium heat until golden before serving.

Additional Sauce Suggestions: Any sauce from the Sweet Sauce chapter (page 205-207)

SWEET POLENTA GNOCCHI DI VIGILIA

/ serves 4

"Di vigilia" means "the Eve of," and, when referring to a traditional meal on a religious holidays such as Christmas or Easter, it is usually a time when si mangia di magro, *one doesn't eat meat. But that fast doesn't preclude rich desserts like this one. An unusual combination of colorful cooked polenta squares sprinkled with nuts and chocolate that's lightly broiled to crisp and brown the top, it's a perfect way to end a light meal. That said, a scoop of gelato or mascarpone cream (page 206) is a welcome, if unnecessary, addition. If you're lucky enough to have leftovers, you can just reheat them in a well-buttered skillet until crispy-brown on the bottom. If children are helping with the holiday preparations, it's fun to let them cut the polenta using fanciful, simple cookie cutter shapes that are easy to overlap in the baking pan.*

Alchermes is a spicy, red, syrupy Italian liqueur used to make the Italian dessert zuppa inglese. *Its distinct and wonderful flavor comes from a blend of anise flowers, cinnamon, cloves, coriander, jasmine, mace, nutmeg, orange peel, sugar, and vanilla. You can substitute brandy or another liqueur of your choice, but the polenta won't be the same festive reddish-pink.*

4 cups water or milk	½ cup Alchermes or other liqueur
2¼ cups fine polenta OR corn flour	Pinch cinnamon
1 teaspoon salt	1 cup walnuts, coarsely chopped
½ cup unsalted butter, softened, divided	2 ounces bittersweet chocolate, grated
1 lemon, finely zested, or to taste	1 cup fine dry breadcrumbs, toasted
1 egg yolk	½ cup sugar

Bring the liquid and salt to a boil in a large, deep cooking pot. Slowly add the polenta, showering it over the liquid while stirring briskly with a whisk. Turn the heat to low and continue cooking and stirring until polenta is smooth and very stiff, about 35 to 40 minutes, or until it has the consistency of cold mashed potatoes. Add 2 tablespoons of the butter, the lemon zest, egg yolk, and Alchermes (or other liqueur), mixing well to create a uniform dough.

With a wet metal spatula, spread the polenta onto a large, well-oiled baking sheet or wooden board while it's still hot. Level to a thickness of ⅜-inch and chill until firm. You can prepare the polenta up to a day in advance and hold it, covered and refrigerated.

Preheat a broiler when you are ready to complete the dessert. Cut the chilled polenta into 1½- to 2-inch squares (or other shapes) and arrange them in a buttered, shallow baking dish, slightly overlapping each other. Sprinkle the chocolate, walnuts, toasted breadcrumbs, sugar, and cinnamon evenly over the top and dot with remaining butter. Broil just until lightly crisp and browned.

Do not freeze.

SWEET RICOTTA GNOCCHI

/ serves 4 to 6

These sweet, soft, and scrumptious ricotta gnocchi are browned in butter and served with fresh fruit or marmalade and whipped cream — an unexpected surprise for those who are familiar only with the savory variety. They're not difficult to make, but should be cooked and served at the last minute. A sauce of macerated fruit (page 206) can be easily prepared a few hours in advance; the rest can come together quickly if the ingredients have been prepped in advance.

Various flavorings can also be added to the dough — grated citrus peel, chopped chocolate nibs, a few finely chopped hazelnuts, a few tablespoons of cocoa, or a touch of cinnamon, for example. My favorite combination is ¼ cup cocoa nibs lightly mixed into the dough, with the finished gnocchi served with macerated raspberries, whipped cream, and a sprinkling of orange zest for garnish. A drizzle of Saba (page 205) can add yet another dimension to a dish of these sweet gnocchi.

/ FOR THE GNOCCHI

2 cups whole milk ricotta, placed in a cheesecloth-lined
   colander set in a bowl, and drained at least 30
   minutes before using

3 eggs, beaten

½ teaspoon kosher salt

¾ cup unbleached all-purpose flour

¼ cup fine dry breadcrumbs

⅛ cup sugar

¼ cup unsalted butter

/ FOR THE TOPPING

Sweet Macerated Fruit Sauce (page 206)

OR 1-2 cups marmalade or jam thinned to desired
   consistency with grappa or other liqueur of
   your choice

1 cup heavy cream

Superfine sugar and/or cinnamon for dusting

Prepare Sweet Macerated Fruit or Marmalade Sauce.

Put the butter in a large skillet and melt it over very low heat. Set aside and keep warm.

In a medium bowl, lightly blend the ricotta with the eggs and salt. In another bowl, mix the dry ingredients until well combined and sprinkle them over the ricotta mixture. Fold together just until incorporated. Do not overmix or gnocchi will be tough. The dough will be soft and somewhat sticky.

Bring a large pot of water — no less than a gallon — to a simmer and add 1 tablespoon salt.

Use your moistened hands, or an ice cream scoop if available, to form balls about 1 ½-inches in diameter. As they're shaped, drop them into the simmering, salted water. Let the gnocchi cook, without stirring, until they have risen to the surface. Simmer another 5 minutes and remove one to test. It should feel firm to the touch. If not, return it to the pot and cook all the gnocchi another 2 minutes. Test again by breaking a gnocco open to make sure the center is cooked. The outside may seem mushy but it will firm up when tossed in the butter.

Meanwhile, rewarm the butter, allowing it to lightly brown. Remove the gnocchi from the pot with a large slotted spoon, allow to drain a few seconds, and gently place them in the browned butter. Roll them around a bit to firm them up and completely coat with butter. Set aside to cool slightly.

Whip the cream to soft peaks. Serve the gnocchi immediately in shallow bowls, garnishing each serving with the fruit or marmalade sauce and a dusting of fine sugar and cinnamon to taste. Add whipped cream as desired.

Do not freeze.

Additional Sauce Suggestions: Any sauce from the Sweet Sauce Section (page 205-207)

SWEET HANUKKAH GNOCCHI

/ serves 6

Some of the easiest gnocchi to make, these have a creamy center and a crisp, crunchy crust. I suggest you cook the gnocchi a day before you plan to use them and fry them just before serving. The result is a creamier center. You can vary the garnishes with your favorite fruit, jam, or syrup.

1 pound Yukon Gold potatoes, skin pierced 5 to 6 times

1 teaspoon ground cinnamon

½ teaspoon freshly grated nutmeg

½ teaspoon kosher salt

¼ cup matzo meal

2 tablespoons fine sugar

3 large eggs, separated, whites reserved

Reserved egg whites

1 cup matzo meal

Sunflower or canola oil for frying

2 cups fresh berries OR 1 cup jam, marmalade, OR syrup of choice

1 cup whipped whole milk ricotta, heavy cream OR mascarpone for garnish

Fresh mint leaves

Bake the potatoes at 400°F, or microwave them on high, until tender. Allow to cool just enough to handle them. Peel while still warm and pass them through the fine disk of a food mill or potato ricer into a large bowl. Cool to room temperature.

In another bowl, whisk the egg yolks, salt, and spices until just combined. With a rubber spatula, mix the egg yolks lightly into the potatoes using a cutting/folding motion. Mix the matzo meal and sugar together and sprinkle over the potato mixture, cutting in lightly to form a uniform dough. Do not overmix.

Using a ¾-inch scoop, form small, equal-sized balls, lightly rolling them in your hands to smooth the surface of the dough. Place the finished gnocchi close together, but not touching, on a lightly floured tray.

Bring a very large, deep pot of water — no less than 1 gallon — to a simmer. Add 1 to 2 tablespoons salt and drop in the gnocchi, cooking no more than half the batch at a time. Stir a couple of times with a wooden spoon so the gnocchi move gently. The water should remain at a simmer rather than a rolling boil. Cook for 4 to 5 minutes, then test by breaking one open. It should be firm and fully cooked inside. If not, continue cooking another minute or two.

Remove gnocchi with a slotted spoon, drain, and place close together, but not touching, on a tray. Cover with plastic wrap and refrigerate for a day or two.

Before frying the gnocchi, have serving bowls with the fruit and garnishes of your choice ready. If you're using syrup or jam, put the desired amount into the bottom of each bowl. Fill a heavy, deep-sided pot with enough cooking oil to reach 1 inch up the sides. Heat the oil to 375°F. (When a wooden skewer is inserted into the pot, the oil will bubble around the stick when the oil is hot enough.)

Beat the 3 reserved egg whites until frothy. Put about 1 cup matzo meal in a shallow bowl. Coat each gnoccho in egg white and roll evenly in the matzo meal. Return the balls to the tray until all the gnocchi have been prepared in the same way.

Gently drop about 12 to 15 gnocchi at a time into the hot oil and fry until golden brown. Do not overload the pot or the temperature of the oil will drop significantly. Remove with a slotted spoon to a paper towel to drain while you finish the remaining gnocchi.

Divide the gnocchi into the serving bowls. Top with the sauce and/or garnishes of your choice. Serve immediately.

These gnocchi can be frozen for up to two weeks after forming. See Freezer Notes, page 250.

I've also included a few recipes in this section from Italian friends whom I consider "gnocchi masters," and who generously donated to my collection for this book.

OTHER GNOCCHI PREPARATION STYLES

Gnocchi differs widely, not only in its ingredients but also in its styles of preparation and presentation. For example, gnocchi alla Romana, considered by many the original form of gnocchi, is made from a cooked and cooled porridge that is cut into disks, sauced or layered with cheese, and reheated. Other dough preparations can be either baked or piped from a pastry bag, and — for special occasions — stuffed with savory ingredients that will win the hearts of your diners.

The leftover gnocchi you worked so hard to make can be recycled and appreciated all over again when it's used to garnish soups and salads. I sometimes fry it in a bit of butter or olive oil to crisp the exterior and give it a golden glow before finishing the presentation. I've also included a few recipes in this section from Italian friends whom I consider "gnocchi masters," and who generously donated to my collection for this book.

/ GNOCCHI ALLA ROMANA

Gnocchi originated long before the introduction of the potato to European shores. The first official recipe can be found in *De re Coquinaria, (On the Subject of Cooking)*, a Roman cookbook thought to have been published in the 4th or 5th century CE. In that work, gnocchi is described as a mixture of semolina flour combined with milk or water, then fried, and finally seasoned with honey and black pepper — a recipe similar to the contemporary version of gnocchi alla Romana popular in southern Italy made with semolina flour, a liquid, egg, cheese, and butter.

A favorite comfort food of mine, gnocchi alla Romana are easy to make at home and are extremely versatile. I've included a few basic recipes in this chapter, as well as some suggested variations noted below. The basic recipe can also be easily presented as a substantial main dish rather than a first course.

/ SUGGESTED VARIATIONS

* Add crumbled cooked sausage, extra cheese, or chopped herbs of choice to the cooked mixture before spreading it to cool.

* Add a touch of chopped fresh herbs.

* Serve on top of any meaty ragù, mushroom or tomato sauce, a béchamel, a dab of pesto, or cooked greens.

* Top with cheese such as ricotta salata, smoked ricotta, provolone, Gorgonzola, fontina, mozzarella, Taleggio, or goat cheese — then broil to melt and lightly brown the cheese.

* Serve in broth: Cut the slab of prepared polenta or semolina into small cubes and serve directly in hot, homemade broth. Shower with finely grated fresh Parmigiano-Reggiano and dribble with olive oil.

* Grill or panfry before serving with the sauce of your choice: brush lightly with olive oil before grilling over hot charcoal or in a heated fry pan, about 3 minutes per side.

* Make it a kids' project by cutting out freeform shapes or by using whatever cookie cutters you have on hand. Make sure the pieces are small enough to hold together when transferred to the baking pan.

* Gluten free: Because disk-shaped gnocchi do not require gluten to hold their shape, you can replace the semolina flour with 2¼ cups chickpea, roveja, or white bean flour for a tasty, creamier alternative to the traditional Roman gnocchi. Chickpea flour is used in Tuscany to make *farinata*, *cecina*, or *pan elle,* a thick Ligurian pancake eaten as a snack. Most natural food stores in the U.S. stock garbanzo and white bean flours. Roveja is an heirloom wild pea from Umbria, recently rediscovered and produced on a small scale. Its flavor is more like fava beans than peas. Check the internet for availability. Any of these gluten-free replacements taste much like creamy, cheesy mashed potatoes with lots of crusty bits — my favorite with a hearty ragù.

SEMOLINA GNOCCHI ALLA ROMANA

/ serves 6

This is the classic basic recipe to follow when using any of the variations suggested on page 131 that will inspire you to experiment and modify alla Romana-style gnocchi to your liking. Though traditionally eaten simply browned with butter and cheese, see the sauce suggestions below for alternative ways to present them as a main course.

½ cup unsalted butter + extra for greasing the pan

4 cups whole milk

1½ cups semolina flour

Salt to taste

2 large egg yolks, lightly beaten

¾ cup finely grated fresh Pecorino Romano
    OR Parmigiano-Reggiano

Thoroughly whisk together the semolina, milk, and salt in a 2-quart heavy saucepan and bring to a boil over moderate heat, whisking constantly. Reduce heat to low and cook, stirring frequently with a wooden spoon, until very stiff, 8 to 10 minutes. The mixture should be thick enough to leave the sides of the pan as you stir.

Let cool slightly, no more than 5 minutes, then slowly stir in the beaten egg yolks, followed by ½ cup of the grated cheese and ¼ cup of the butter. Pour the mixture onto a clean oiled counter or buttered jellyroll pan and spread it evenly to a ½-inch depth with a damp knife or offset spatula, making sure it's smooth. Sprinkle with drops of oil if needed to help smooth it out. Cool to room temperature or chill for 15 to 20 minutes, or until it holds its shape when cut.

Preheat the oven to 400°F. Lightly butter a 13-x-9-inch baking dish and set aside.

Using a 1½- or 2-inch round cookie cutter, stamp out rounds and layer them, overlapping slightly, in the prepared dish. Alternately, you can cut them into 2-inch squares. To make single servings, use individual porcelain au gratin dishes.

Sprinkle the gnocchi with some of the remaining cheese and dot with butter. Continue making layers of disks in this way until all the ingredients are used up. The scraps can be reshaped, chilled and recut to avoid waste. Bake for 15 minutes, until golden brown. They should be heated through. If not sufficiently browned, put under the broiler for a minute or two.

Do not freeze.

Sauce Suggestions: Meaty Ragùs, Mushroom Sauce, Besciamella Sauce, Tomato Sauce, a dab of Pesto, or Sautéed Greens

POLENTA GNOCCHI ALLA ROMANA

/ serves 6

Polenta makes a wonderful alternative to the traditional semolina gnocchi alla Romana, and is delicious with any of the sauces used with the proceeding recipe. Don't be tempted to use instant polenta or the precooked polenta you can find in tubes as they are inferior products. It's worth the extra effort to make it from scratch — it does not require constant stirring. The most important way to avoid lumps is to add the polenta to the water very slowly and gradually at the start. That said, Italian cooks are often judged by the smoothness of their polenta.

4 cups whole milk, chicken broth, water, or any combination

1½ cups polenta, preferably medium grind

1 teaspoon kosher salt

4 tablespoons unsalted butter, divided

3 large egg yolks

¾ cup finely grated fresh Parmigiano-Reggiano

In a large saucepan, combine liquid ingredients and the salt. Bring to a boil over high heat. Slowly shower the polenta over the water, whisking constantly. Reduce heat to medium and cook, whisking constantly, for 2 minutes. Reduce heat to low and cook, stirring frequently with a wooden spoon, until polenta is smooth and very stiff, like cold mashed potatoes, about 35 to 40 minutes. Do not be tempted to shorten the cooking time or the gnocchi will not hold their shape.

Remove the polenta from the heat and stir in the egg yolks, remaining butter, and cheese until well combined. Immediately pour the mixture onto a clean counter or buttered jellyroll pan and spread it evenly to a ½-inch depth with a damp knife or offset spatula, making sure it's smooth. Sprinkle with drops of oil if needed to help smooth it out. Cool for 15 to 20 minutes or until it holds its shape when cut. The polenta can be prepared to this point one day in advance, covered with plastic and refrigerated.

Preheat the oven to 400°F. Lightly butter a 13-x 9-inch baking dish and set aside.

Using a 1½- or 2-inch round cookie cutter, stamp out rounds and layer them, overlapping slightly, in the prepared dish. Alternately, you can cut them into 2-inch squares. Sprinkle the disks with some of the remaining cheese and dot with butter. Continue making layers of disks in this way until all the ingredients are used up. (The scraps can be reshaped, chilled, and recut to avoid waste.)

To make single servings, layer the disks in individual porcelain au gratin dishes.

Bake for 15 minutes, or until golden brown; the disks should be heated through. If not sufficiently browned, put under the broiler for a minute or two.

Do not freeze.

Sauce Suggestions: Meaty Ragùs, Mushroom Sauce, Besciamella Sauce, Tomato Sauce, a dab of Pesto, or Sautéed Greens

ROMAN-STYLE FISH GNOCCHI

/ serves 6

Giulio Piccini, aka Jarro — a culinary expert, journalist, and writer from Florence — published a recipe similar to this during the height of Florence's prominence as the artistic and intellectual center of Italy.

Prepared in the traditional alla Romana style, these gnocchi are made with a base of mild-flavored fish held together with egg and cheese. They make an exceptional first course for the traditional La Vigilia, *or Feast of the Seven Fishes, celebrated on Christmas Eve — or a light main course any time of year.*

1½ pounds filleted light-flavored fish, such as red
    snapper, cod, or halibut

4 extra-large eggs, separated

1 cup whole milk

½ cup unbleached all-purpose flour

¼ pound unsalted butter, divided

1 teaspoon kosher salt

Freshly ground black pepper to taste

1 teaspoon fresh thyme, minced

½ cup finely grated fresh Parmigiano-Reggiano, divided

1 tablespoon extra-virgin olive oil

Chop the fish by hand until very finely minced. Put into a large bowl.

Separate the eggs, reserving 4 yolks in one small bowl and 2 of the whites in another, larger bowl, preferably copper. Save the remaining 2 whites for another use. Stir the egg yolks into the fish and combine well.

Beat the egg whites with a wire whisk or an electric mixer until medium-stiff peaks form. Gently fold into the fish mixture.

Transfer the fish mixture to a medium saucepan and cook over low heat, stirring gently with a wooden spoon, until it just begins to bubble. Add ⅓ cup of the milk and then a bit of the flour, stirring to combine. Continue to alternately add the milk and flour a bit at a time until all is incorporated and the mixture is smooth.

Add 6 tablespoons of the butter and continue to cook, stirring continuously, for about 10 minutes to completely cook the flour. Remove from heat and add half the grated Parmigiano-Reggiano, along with the thyme. Season with salt and freshly ground black pepper to taste.

Pour the mixture onto a lightly oiled, clean counter or jellyroll pan and spread it evenly to a ½-inch depth with a damp knife or offset spatula, making sure it's smooth. Sprinkle with drops of oil if needed to help smooth it out. Cool to room temperature or chill for 15 to 20 minutes or until it holds its shape when cut.

Preheat the oven to 375°F. Lightly oil a 13-x-9-inch baking dish and set aside.

Using a 1½- or 2-inch round cookie cutter, stamp out rounds and layer them, overlapping slightly, in the prepared dish. Alternately, you can cut them into 2-inch squares. The scraps can be reshaped, chilled and recut to avoid waste. Shower them with some of the remaining cheese and dot with remaining butter.

Bake for 15 minutes, until golden brown. They should be heated through. If not sufficiently browned, put under the broiler for a minute or two.

Sauce Suggestions: I prefer these delicate gnocchi served without sauce, but they're also good with Garlic-Lemon Sauce, Béchamel Sauce, or Basil Pesto. Heat the sauce separately and divide it among serving dishes. Top with the cooked gnocchi. If serving with pesto, simply put a dollop alongside.

Inspired by a recipe from The Art of Fine Italian Cooking, *Giuliano Bugialli, 1977, Times Books, Random House*

/ BAKED OR PIPED GNOCCHI

Spoons are sometimes used to shape gnocchi like oval quenelles. Gnocchi dough also can
be piped through a pastry bag — and the gnocchi are not always boiled in water. Here
are a few examples of these alternate gnocchi styles; each can be prepared a few hours in
advance and finished just before serving. These gnocchi are much lighter in texture and far
less tricky to form and cook, with no need for the usual trepidation about gnocchi-making.

SOUFFLÉD POTATO GNOCCHI

/ serves 4 to 6

These gnocchi are lighter than mashed potatoes and have a crispy crust because of the butter in the dough. Terrific as a side dish with grilled or roasted meats, fish, and chicken, they can also be used as a first course. If you wish to serve them with a sauce, spoon the sauce on the plate or bowl first and place the cooked gnocchi on top.

½ cup whole milk

6 tablespoons unsalted butter, divided

½ teaspoon each salt and freshly ground black pepper

⅓ cup unbleached all-purpose flour

3 large eggs

1 pound small to medium Yukon Gold potatoes, all of equal size

¼ cup minced fresh Italian parsley

¼ cup finely grated fresh Parmigiano-Reggiano

Put the potatoes in a saucepan and cover them with 2 inches of salted water. Bring the water to a boil and simmer the potatoes, covered, until they are tender, about 20-30 minutes. Drain and let the potatoes cool until you can handle them. Peel, then force them through the fine holes of a ricer or food mill into a large bowl.

In a small bowl, mix the flour with the salt and pepper.

In a medium-sized heavy saucepan combine the milk and 4 tablespoons of the butter. Bring the milk to a boil and add the flour mixture all at once, whisking until the mixture cleans the sides of the pan, about 1 to 2 minutes. Cool the mixture, then vigorously whisk in the eggs, one at a time, beating well after each addition.

With a wooden spoon or rubber spatula, gently fold the egg mixture into the riced potatoes until combined. Do not beat or the mixture will lose volume. Stir in the minced parsley and transfer the mixture to a large pastry bag fitted with a large tip.* You can refrigerate the dough up to 12 hours at this point and pipe and bake at a later time.

When ready to complete the dish, preheat the oven to 400°F.

Pipe 1-inch mounds, barely touching each other, in a single layer in a buttered, ovenproof dish, approximately 12-x-9-inches. Sprinkle top with the grated Parmigiano-Reggiano and dot with the remaining 2 tablespoons butter. Bake for 30-35 minutes, or until puffed and golden.

Sauce Suggestions: Basic Tomato Sauce, White Truffle & Cream Sauce, Creamy Roasted Garlic & Parmigiano-Reggiano Sauce, Meyer Lemon-Butter Sauce, Mixed Mushroom & Sausage Sauce

You can substitute a pastry bag without the large tip, or use a large heavy freezer bag with the corner cut off. The finished gnocchi won't have ridges, but they will still look pretty. Make sure you fill the bag only half full so you can twist the large end closed and use it to push the potato out the tip end. Make a few practice gnocchi; the dough can be reused without negative consequences.

CARROT GNOCCHI

/ serves 4

A delicately flavored and lightly textured gnocchi shaped and cooked in the style of quenelles, this is a favorite recipe that I often serve as a side dish with pork, fish, or chicken. The dough is easy to prepare several hours in advance — then shape, cook and bake off just before serving. Alternatively, you can bring these gnocchi to the point where they are ready to bake and then refrigerate them in the baking dish for up to an hour. Bring to room temperature before finishing.

½ pound carrots, peeled, trimmed, and cut into
   1-inch pieces

3 tablespoons unsalted butter, divided

2 tablespoons finely chopped onion

3 tablespoons all-purpose flour

1 large egg yolk

½ cup finely grated fresh Parmigiano-Reggiano

Salt and freshly ground black pepper to taste

Pinch freshly grated nutmeg

Fresh sage leaves to taste

Cook the carrots in boiling salted water until tender, about 10 minutes. Drain well and allow to cool to release moisture.

In a sauté pan, melt 1 tablespoon butter over medium heat; immediately add the chopped onion and cook, stirring until it softens, about 3 minutes. Add the carrots and cook for 6 to 8 minutes, stirring occasionally. Transfer to a blender or food processor and purée until creamy and smooth. Turn the purée into a bowl and let cool completely. You may place the bowl over ice water and stir to speed the process.

When cool, add the egg yolk, ¼ cup freshly grated Parmigiano-Reggiano, nutmeg, salt and pepper to taste, and mix thoroughly. Stir in the flour until no streaks remain.

Preheat the oven to 400°F.

In a large, 3- to 4-inch deep saucepan, bring water to a simmer and add 1 to 2 tablespoons salt. Set a large bowl of ice water nearby.

Form oval-shaped gnocchi: Using 2 soup spoons, scoop a rounded portion of the carrot mixture into one of the spoons. With the spoon bowls side by side and handles in opposite directions, gently scoop the mixture into the second spoon using a sideways motion. Repeat once more to form a 3-sided, oval-shaped gnoccho. Slide the gnocchi into the simmering water. Quickly make another 5 or 6 gnocchi, adding them to the pan as they are formed, and cook about 10 seconds, until they all rise to the surface. Transfer with a slotted spoon to the ice water. Repeat the process until all the gnocchi are cooked.

Lightly butter a shallow baking dish, about 12-x 9-inches, or large enough to hold the gnocchi in a single layer.

Drain the gnocchi well and arrange them on the bottom of the buttered dish. Tear or finely shred the sage leaves and scatter them over the gnocchi. Sprinkle the gnocchi with the remaining grated Parmigiano-Reggiano and dot with the remaining butter. Bake on the upper shelf of the preheated oven for about 10 minutes.

Adapted from a recipe by Marcella Hazan

BAKED CHEESE GNOCCHI

/ serves 4 to 6

Rich and creamy with the addition of cheeses and béchamel sauce, these gnocchi are from the Marché region of Italy. Rather than being shaped like potato gnocchi and simmered, they are formed into ovals with two spoons and then baked. They are very simple to prepare and can be assembled in advance and held until you're ready to bake them — a terrific choice for a dinner party. Traditionally, this dish is paired with a simple tomato sauce poured over the gnocchi before baking. My personal preference is to top them with cherry tomatoes.

/ FOR THE GNOCCHI

1¼ cups whole-milk ricotta cheese, placed in a
    cheesecloth-lined colander set in a bowl and
    drained at least 30 minutes before using

1 pound fresh bunched spinach
    OR 12 ounces fresh baby spinach leaves

¼ cup fontina cheese, cut into ⅛-inch dice

¼ cup semi-soft Asiago, cut into ⅛-inch dice

¼ cup finely grated fresh Parmigiano-Reggiano cheese

⅜ cup fresh breadcrumbs, toasted

2 egg yolks, beaten

½ teaspoon kosher salt

/ FOR THE BÉCHAMEL SAUCE

2 tablespoons butter

2 tablespoons all-purpose flour

2 cups whole milk

1 teaspoon salt

½ teaspoon freshly grated nutmeg

/ FOR THE TOPPING

2 cups halved cherry tomatoes

2 tablespoons extra-virgin olive oil

Kosher salt to taste

1-2 tablespoons chopped fresh herbs, such as
    thyme, basil, oregano, or marjoram

Trim any tough stems from the spinach and wash it thoroughly. (If using pre-packaged cleaned spinach leaves, skip this step.) In a medium saucepan, cook the spinach in just enough water to wilt it, stirring constantly. Drain and squeeze out all the excess water. Finely chop and squeeze once more. Preheat oven to 350°F.

In a large bowl, combine the ricotta, spinach, fontina, Asiago, Parmigiano-Reggiano, breadcrumbs, ½ teaspoon salt, and egg yolks to form a uniform mixture. Chill the mixture while preparing the béchamel.

In a medium saucepan, heat the butter over low heat until melted. Add the flour and stir until smooth. Over medium heat, cook the mixture for about 5 minutes.

Meanwhile, heat the milk in a separate pan until it's just about to boil. Add the hot milk to the butter and flour mixture ½ cup at a time, whisking continuously until smooth. Bring to a boil, lower the heat and cook 5 to 8 minutes, stirring constantly. Remove from heat and season with salt and freshly grated nutmeg. To cool this sauce for later use, cover it with wax paper or pour a film of milk over it to prevent a skin from forming.

When you are ready to proceed with dish, spread the béchamel evenly in a baking dish large enough to hold the gnocchi in a single layer — about 12-x-9-inches.

Form the oval-shaped gnocchi: Using 2 soup spoons (or teaspoons for smaller gnocchi), scoop up a rounded portion of the cheese mixture into one of the spoons, and, with the spoon bowls side by side and handles in opposite directions, gently scoop the mixture into the second spoon using a sideways motion. Repeat once more to form a 3-sided, oval-shaped gnocco. Place the gnocchi close together, but not touching, on top of the béchamel in the baking dish. Bake for 15 minutes.

Meanwhile, mix the halved cherry tomatoes with olive oil and salt to taste and set aside.

Remove the gnocchi from the oven, scatter with the tomatoes, and bake about 15 minutes more, until the gnocchi are lightly browned and the sauce is bubbly.

Garnish with freshly grated Parmigiano-Reggiano and herbs of choice. Serve immediately.

/ VARIATIONS

*Substitute a simple Cooked Tomato Sauce (page 208) for the béchamel and scatter with shredded basil or other herbs and some freshly grated Parmigiano-Reggiano before serving.

*Use Swiss chard or other cooking greens instead of the spinach. Tougher greens will take longer to cook — about 20 to 30 minutes in all. Chop them fine to measure 1 cup of cooked greens.

*You can prepare the gnocchi for baking up to 2 hours in advance. Cover and refrigerate. Add 5 minutes to the oven time.

*Use all fontina or all Asiago, or replace some or part of these cheeses with provolone. It's important that the cheese you use is semi-soft.

/ ONE-DISH PRESENTATIONS & SPECIAL RECIPES FROM ITALIAN FRIENDS

Gnocchi need not be limited to a first course. Some of my favorite gnocchi dishes are those that take the center stage, are served in a creamy, puréed soup, or added to a main-dish salad. All you need is hunk of bread and the meal is complete.

Also included here are special recipes from Italian friends, a few one-dish meals I've favored over the years, and a traditional holiday dish for New Year's Eve.

ANNA MARIA'S POTATO GNOCCHI WITH TOMATO & MOZZARELLA

/ serves 6

When I asked Anna Maria Rodriquez D'Amato — my dear friend, gnocchi teacher, and the woman to whom this book is dedicated — for her favorite gnocchi recipe, she didn't hesitate to respond "a voce," out loud. "Gnocchi di patate con sugo di pomodorro e la migliore mozzarella disponibile tagliata in pezzi" — "Potato gnocchi tossed with simple tomato sauce and dimpled with torn chunks of the best fresh mozzarella you can find," she said. That's a freehand translation from the Italian. The recipe details are mine. I encourage you to try this gnocchi variation — it's wonderful!

1 recipe potato gnocchi without egg page 23

1 recipe Simple Tomato Sauce with Basil page 208

1 pound fresh whole milk mozzarella cut into ½-inch chunks, at room temperature

3-4 tablespoons fresh shredded basil for garnish

Prepare the simple tomato sauce, the fresh mozzarella, and the basil garnish. Set aside.

Make the potato gnocchi according to recipe directions.

Have ready some heated serving bowls and a large, warm bowl with half the tomato sauce portioned into it. As the gnocchi rise to the surface, remove with a slotted spoon and toss with the sauce in the large bowl. Add chunks of mozzarella and toss again to heat and distribute the cheese. Divide among the serving bowls and garnish with shredded basil. Serve immediately.

Repeat with the remaining gnocchi and sauce. Alternatively, you can cook all the gnocchi at the same time in two separate pots and toss them all together in a large bowl of sauce and cheese.

CLAUDIO BRUGALOSSI'S POTATO GNOCCHI alla Taverna Restaurant, Perugia

/ serves 6

Claudio Brugalossi, owner and chef of La Taverna, one of the most prestigious restaurants in Perugia, kindly gave me his recipe for potato gnocchi, written and executed as they do it in the restaurant. Claudio is one of the few Italian chefs I know who bake rather than boil the potatoes, and the resulting gnocchi are superb. "Make a fountain" is the Italian equivalent of "make a well" in the U.S. — which refers to mounding flour onto a work surface and forming a depression in the middle that will contain the egg as you begin forming the dough.

1 kilo potatoes

180 grams 00 Flour (180g to 200g), depends on
    the potatoes

1 egg, large

A pinch of salt

Here, everybody boils the potatoes. I prick them and bake them. You'll get less moisture inside. Peel them while warm and pass them through a fine-hole potato press. Make a fountain, add egg, flour, and salt (and, if you want color, saffron).

Work the dough and roll into tubes. Cut the gnocchi and roll them with the inside of a fork to make dents.

Boil the gnocchi in salty simmering water, and, as soon as they come up toss in a sauté pan with your choice of sauce (Gorgonzola fondue, boar ragù, ossobuco ragù, etc.).

Baci, cb

Thank you, Claudio, for the recipe and for your friendship over the years! CH

MALFATTI (GNUDI CAPRESE)

/ serves 4 to 6

Following is a recipe I've dedicated to Alessandro Alunni, a chef/restaurant owner I was fortunate to work with one summer in Castiglione del Lago, Umbria. He specialized in local Umbrian dishes and served a similar recipe at Il Falchetto, his restaurant in Perugia. I often ordered it when dining there. Variations on the theme can also be found in other regions of Italy.

Although I never procured the exact recipe, this is my Alunni–inspired version of his dish. Served in individual pots, much like traditional French onion soup, it makes a particularly special presentation that can be made ahead and reheated before serving. The result is a unique bubbly, crunchy crust.

The recipe calls for double the amount of tomato sauce normally recommended for a serving of gnocchi. You can use less, but in this dish the sauce functions like gravy in a stew, adding succulence to each and every bite of gnudo and morsel of mozzarella.

1 recipe Ricotta-Spinach Gnudi (page 106)

1 recipe Simple Tomato Sauce with Basil (page 208)

   OR 3-4 cups of your favorite meatless tomato sauce

2 cups fresh whole milk mozzarella ciliegine

3-4 tablespoons freshly shredded basil for garnish

Have ready Simple Tomato Sauce, the fresh mozzarella, and the basil garnish.

Prepare gnudi according to recipe directions. Layer cooked gnudi with the tomato sauce and mozzarella ciliegine, dividing it all among 4 to 6 individual ovenproof soup tureens or gratin dishes. Refrigerate until ready to bake, up to a day in advance.

Remove the dishes from the refrigerator and allow them to come to room temperature while you preheat the oven to 375°F.

Place the tureens on a sheet pan and bake until bubbly and crusty, about 30 minutes. Serve immediately garnished with shredded fresh basil.

Do not freeze.

GNOCCHI GRATIN WITH GREENS, SAUSAGE & CABBAGE

/ serves 6 to 8

This is a perfect first course or one-dish meal that can be varied with different kinds of greens, meat, and gnocchi. I first enjoyed this using a vegetable called pan di zucchero, *which translates as "sweet loaf," but is actually a light green member of the endive family easily found in Italy's northern mountains. It's less bitter than other endives, is slender and long like napa cabbage, and shreds easily. In the U.S., I substitute napa cabbage for this green.*

The dish is easily put together the day before you plan to serve it and can be refrigerated and baked at the last minute. If using polenta gnocchi, you do not need to cook them before assembling the dish. Prepare them through the shaping stage, forming them into balls 1 to 2 inches in diameter. All other gnocchi need to be cooked first — so this is also a great way to use leftover gnocchi.

1 recipe gnocchi of choice, preferably polenta
   (page 87 or 133)

1 pound dark greens of choice (kale, Swiss chard,
   spinach, mustard greens or chicory) large stems
   removed, leaves washed and finely shredded

½ pound cabbage of choice: green, red, Savoy,
   or napa, washed and shredded

¼ pound shredded Brussels sprouts, thinly sliced (optional)

4 tablespoons unsalted butter, divided

2 tablespoons extra-virgin olive oil

1 medium onion, thinly sliced

2-4 garlic cloves, finely chopped

½ pound ground beef or pork
   OR ¼ pound ground meat and ¼ pound pancetta

½ pound bulk Italian sausage

1 cup chicken broth, preferably homemade, or water

Kosher salt and freshly ground black pepper to taste

1 to 1½ cups Besciamella (page 223) or Fonduta
   (page 180) sauce, optional

1 cup finely grated fresh Parmigiano-Reggiano
   OR other semi-hard grating cheese

Butter a large, deep baking dish, about 13-x-9-x-2-inches, with 2 tablespoons butter and set aside.

Preheat oven to 375°F.

In a large sauté pan over medium heat, cook the remaining butter, olive oil, garlic, and onions together until the onions are soft and transparent. Turn the heat to medium-high, add the greens, cabbage, and optional Brussels sprouts, and cook, tossing constantly, for 5 minutes. Cover, turn the heat to low, and continue to cook until the vegetables are soft but not mushy, about 10 minutes. Remove from heat and transfer to a large bowl.

Using the same sauté pan, cook the ground meat and sausage together over medium heat, breaking it up with a wooden spoon, until lightly browned. Add the chicken broth or water, turn the heat to high and continue to cook until the liquid is reduced by half. Add to the cooked

vegetables and stir well to combine. Transfer to the prepared baking dish, spreading evenly.

Using a the back of a spoon, and starting from the middle of the dish, make indentations at close intervals and place a gnocco in each one. Leave a border of vegetables if the gnocchi don't fill the entire dish.

Drizzle with béchamel or fonduta if desired and shower with shredded cheese. Cover loosely with aluminum foil and bake in the preheated oven for 20 to 30 minutes, or until the center is hot and the sauce is beginning to bubble. Remove the foil and broil 4 inches from heat until lightly browned.

Serve immediately.

GOAT & RICOTTA CHEESE GNOCCHI ON SPICY SPINACH SALAD

/ serves 6

Using gnocchi to top a salad may seem odd. However, it's not only delicious, it also makes a healthy one-dish meal, and is a quick way to use leftover gnocchi, be it already cooked or frozen. Change the salad ingredients, add cheese, switch out the sausage for chicken; use whatever inspires you or whatever you may have on hand in the refrigerator. In winter, consider wilting a hardy green such as kale for a warm main salad. Be creative — salads can be much more than lettuce and tomato.

/ FOR THE GNOCCHI

11 ounces fresh, soft goat cheese, at room temperature

4 ounces whole milk ricotta cheese, placed in a
    cheesecloth-lined colander set in a bowl and
    drained at least 30 minutes before using

2 large eggs

1 teaspoon salt

Freshly ground white pepper to taste

Pinch freshly grated nutmeg

¾-1 cup all-purpose flour + more for dusting

2 tablespoons extra-virgin olive oil

/ FOR THE SALAD

½ pound bulk or hot Italian sausage links,
    casings removed

½ medium red onion, thinly sliced

1 large shallot, minced

2 large garlic cloves, minced

3 tablespoons balsamic vinegar

⅓ cup currants

6 large handfuls baby spinach, washed and dried

About ½ cup extra-virgin olive oil

Salt and freshly ground black pepper to taste

½ cup sliced almonds, toasted, for garnish

In a bowl, whisk the goat cheese, ricotta, eggs, salt, and nutmeg until smooth. Gently fold in ¾ cup of flour until the dough begins to form a ball. Add more flour, 1 tablespoon at a time. Do not overwork the dough. Cover the bowl with plastic wrap and refrigerate 30 to 45 minutes.

Remove the dough from the refrigerator and turn it out onto a lightly floured board. Knead a few times to smooth out the dough. Take a walnut-size portion of dough, roll it into a 2-inch log, and cut into thirds. Test cook the three gnocchi until they rise to the surface. Check the texture and add more flour if necessary — ⅛ cup at a time. The gnocchi should hold together without being gummy.

Divide the remaining dough into 4 to 6 pieces and roll each piece into a finger-thick rope on a lightly floured board. Cut each rope into ¾-inch pieces and shape with a gnocchi paddle or the reversed tines of a fork to create small pockets and ridges. Place the finished gnocchi close together on a lightly floured tray. Refrigerate until ready to cook.

Place a sauté pan over medium heat, add the sausage and cook until the sausage begins to brown. Add the red onion

and sauté until it begins to caramelize. Stir in the minced shallot and garlic and continue to cook about 2 minutes. Remove from heat, add the balsamic vinegar and currants and set aside.

Cook the gnocchi in a pot of lightly salted simmering water and remove as soon as they float to the top. Drain and place in a large warmed bowl and toss to coat with olive oil. In another large bowl, toss the spinach with extra-virgin olive oil to lightly coat the leaves. Add the sausage-vinegar mixture and toss. Divide the salad between 6 serving plates. Arrange the gnocchi equally on each salad and garnish with toasted sliced almonds.

Alternatively, you can lightly brown the cooked, drained gnocchi over medium-high heat in a large sauté pan lightly coated with olive oil. Toss gently while cooking to brown all sides. Top the salads with the warm gnocchi and garnish with the almonds.

These gnocchi can be frozen after forming for up to two weeks. See Freezer Notes, page 250.

POTATO GNOCCHI WITH GORGONZOLA & SAUTÉED GREENS

/ serves 6

Kale, spinach, dandelion, chard, beet, and mustard greens, to name a few, are a historical staple of the Italian diet. Once foraged wild in the fields, they are now available year round in markets in all regions of Italy and are the basis for many a healthy main or side dish. Already cooked greens of various kinds, premeasured into kilo-sized balls, are also readily available at many grocery counters. Fresh gnocchi are also sold, usually on Thursdays, at fresh pasta shops.

Hungry for gnocchi years before I learned how to make it, I was inspired by ingredients I found in the Florence markets while renting an apartment there — fresh gnocchi, cooked greens, and Gorgonzola Dolce. I put them all together to make a quick meal that's still one of my favorite vegetarian combinations — and is particularly quick to prepare when you have frozen potato gnocchi on hand.

1 recipe Potato Gnocchi, with or without egg,
   page 20 or 23

1 recipe Gorgonzola Cream Sauce page 180

1 recipe sautéed greens page 227

Lemon slices for garnish

½ cup lightly toasted pine nuts

Prepare the potato gnocchi through the testing and shaping stage, but do not cook.

Prepare the Gorgonzola sauce and set aside, covered.

Sauté the greens and keep them warm, or reheat just before serving.

Cook the gnocchi according to directions.

To serve the gnocchi, put a portion of the warm sautéed greens in a heated, shallow pasta bowl, drizzle a portion of the sauce over the greens, then place a portion of the cooked gnocchi on top. Garnish with lemon slices, sprinkle with toasted pine nuts, and serve immediately.

GREEN POTATO GNOCCHI WITH TOMATO, FLAT BEAN & ARUGULA SAUCE

/ serves 6

Here is a recipe shared by my friend Lorenza Santo from San Quirico d'Orcia, in Tuscany. She and her family are proprietors of Il Rigo, a beautiful farmhouse B&B where guests are fortunate to enjoy her marvelous cooking when staying with her. I first met her in Santa Fe when she came to teach some cooking classes and we immediately bonded, sharing the language and passion for food.

I've taken the liberty of adding some details for American cooks, but otherwise the recipe written here is as she gave it to me. It's one of her favorite gnocchi recipes: "Perfect in April or May when the flat beans are available. They are sometimes called piattoni *here. It's almost a meal!"*

I prefer to use Yukon Gold potatoes and bake or microwave them when making gnocchi in the U.S. Beans in particular are always cooked very soft in Italy and should be cooked at length for this recipe in order to marry well with the soft texture of the gnocchi. You may cut them into pieces or leave them whole.

2½ pounds potatoes

Fresh spinach, boiled and carefully squeezed

   (about 1 pound)

1 egg

1 tablespoon salt

1½ cups flour, + extra for shaping

1 onion

Extra-virgin olive oil

About ¾ pound flat Italian Romano beans,

   cut at an angle into ½-inch pieces

1-pound can of chopped tomatoes

2 generous handfuls of clean, chopped arugula

Place potatoes in a large pot over high heat and cover with cold water. When they reach a boil, add salt. Cook potatoes, skins on, for about 20 minutes, or until tender when pierced with a knife. While potatoes are still hot, peel and press them through a ricer onto a clean, flat wooden work surface. Allow to cool.

Purée the spinach and distribute it over the potatoes. Sprinkle with the flour. Using your hand and a dough scraper, combine potatoes, spinach and flour until a dough forms. Divide the dough into pieces and roll into long, regular snakes. Cut the dough snakes into ¾-inch lengths and roll each piece off the tines of a fork or a gnocchi paddle to create a grooved texture.

Cook the gnocchi in boiling water just until they float, about 2 or 3 minutes. Remove with a slotted spoon and serve immediately, with the following sauce or other sauce of your choice. The gnocchi must be prepared immediately. The dough cannot be left to stand. If you want to prepare the gnocchi in advance, they can be frozen after boiling until they float.

Plunge the gnocchi in cold water, then place on a tray with a drizzle of olive oil. The gnocchi are now ready to be frozen or they can be left on a tray for up to 2 hours until it's time to serve them. To reheat, plunge into boiling water and retrieve with a slotted spoon once they return to the surface. Toss hot, cooked gnocchi with the sauce and serve immediately.

/ FOR THE SAUCE

Chop the onion and sauté in extra-virgin olive oil over medium heat until softened. Add a pinch of salt and the green beans. When the beans have softened, add the chopped tomatoes. Simmer on low heat for about 20 minutes. Before you switch off the heat, stir in some fresh arugula.

NEW YEAR'S EVE POLENTA GNOCCHI WITH LENTILS

/ serves 6 to 8

Lentils — which represent coins and good luck — are ritually served at the Italian midnight New Year's Eve meal. Included here in a warm and satisfying recipe with polenta gnocchi, the lentils can be made ahead of time and reheated hours later. The gnocchi can also be prepared in advance.

If you can find lentils from Castelluccio, Umbria, where they have been grown for centuries and are cultivated mostly by hand, by all means use them. They require a short cooking time and have a wonderful creamy texture while maintaining their shape. Look for them in gourmet shops or the specialty section of larger grocery stores. If they are not available, substitute French lentils. Stores that slice prosciutto often sell ends and pieces that are much cheaper than slices. If available, substitute an end piece for the sliced prosciutto and chop it finely.

1 recipe Polenta Gnocchi (page 87)

4-5 cups homemade broth OR a high-quality,
   low-sodium store-bought version

1½ cups dried lentils from Castelluccio
   OR French green lentils, cleaned of
   debris and rinsed

1 small onion, finely chopped to make ½ cup

1 small carrot, finely chopped

2 cloves garlic, minced

2 tablespoons extra-virgin olive oil

¼ pound prosciutto, thinly sliced and finely chopped

¼ cup simple tomato sauce
   OR 2 tablespoons tomato paste

Salt and freshly ground black pepper to taste

¼ cup finely grated fresh semi-aged pecorino
   OR other semi-hard grating cheese of choice

A few handfuls arugula, washed and dried

Extra-virgin olive oil for drizzling

Prepare the Polenta Gnocchi. Shape into 1-inch balls and place them close together, but not touching, on a baking sheet lined with parchment paper. Refrigerate, covered, while preparing the lentils.

In a saucepan pan over medium heat, warm the olive oil with the prosciutto and cook until the fat has rendered. Add the onion, carrot, and garlic and cook until the vegetables are softened, about 5 minutes. Add the tomato sauce or paste and stir to evenly coat the vegetables. Add 4 cups of the broth and the lentils.

Bring the pot to a boil and simmer over low heat, stirring occasionally, for 25 minutes. Check for doneness and continue simmering until the lentils are tender, adding more liquid as necessary, for a total cooking time of about 40 to 45 minutes. The lentils should be creamy but still hold their shape. Season to taste with salt and freshly ground black pepper. Set aside and keep warm while finishing the gnocchi.

When ready to cook the gnocchi, heat the remaining butter in a large nonstick skillet over medium-high heat. Cook gnocchi in two batches, turning and shaking the pan gently until browned on all sides, 6 to 8 minutes per batch. Keep warm while finishing the second batch, adding more butter to the pan if necessary.

Divide the lentils among 6 to 8 warmed, shallow serving bowls. Top with the polenta gnocchi, drizzle with extra-virgin olive oil and garnish with the arugula and grated cheese.

Serve immediately.

The gnocchi can be prepared and shaped, covered loosely and refrigerated, up to 2 days in advance. The lentils can be prepared in advance and refrigerated or frozen.

/ SAVORY STUFFED GNOCCHI

Gnocchi that have been stuffed, then cooked and sauced, are a very special variation of gnocchi not often available to tourists except in the finest high-priced restaurants. Even today's home cooks will avoid the extra time it takes to stuff each little gnocco with a filling as it's being prepped for cooking. In the Italian tradition, it's not uncommon to find this type of gnocchi served for special occasions, prepared with the help of a group of friends who gather to enjoy the process and gossip, or *chiacchierare*, as their nimble fingers quickly stuff and shape.

I consider stuffing gnocchi meditative, much like other repetitive cooking processes, and the results are definitely worth the bit of extra effort. Recipes included here are for traditional round or oval gnocchi. Sometimes the dough is rolled out no less than ¼-inch thick, cut into small circles, stuffed, and reformed into half-moons, much like one would stuff ravioli. You can use this method with any of the recipes in this section.

Potato-based dough is most commonly used for stuffing, but I prefer the basic ricotta recipe on page 90 because it will hold up to the extra manipulation that stuffing requires without becoming tough or gummy. That said, any of the gnocchi doughs, including bread-based canederli, will produce a satisfying result. Check the index for other specific stuffed recipes.

If you wish to experiment with different fillings, I've made a few suggestions. It's imperative that the filling ingredients are finely chopped and relatively dry; a wet filling will cause the dough to break down. For the best results, keep your flavor combinations simple — and don't be tempted to use more than a rounded ½ teaspoon of stuffing or the gnocchi will break open when cooked.

/ SUGGESTED VARIATIONS

* Soft or fresh cheese that will hold its shape when stuffed into gnocchi: Gorgonzola, fontina, Taleggio, or goat cheese are good choices

* Salamis, cooked sausage, prosciutto, or speck, finely chopped

* All firm ravioli fillings

* Cooked, minced vegetables bonded with cheese

FIG-STUFFED RICOTTA GNOCCHI WITH SAGE BUTTER & ORANGE ZEST

/ serves 6 to 8

This is my signature gnocchi recipe, one I've served at many a dinner party over the years and promised to publish in my cookbook. It's somewhat time consuming, but worth every bit of extra effort to make an outstanding gnocchi dish for any special occasion. Prepared in advance, you can direct your attention to other meal details and finish the gnocchi at the last minute. The slightly sweet fig filling is the perfect foil for the buttery sage sauce, and the smoked ricotta adds a surprising finish, typical of northern Italian cuisine where smoky cheeses are common.

See page 236 for more information on smoked ricotta. If you have a smoker, you can make your own, or substitute a mild, crumbly goat cheese from a local producer if smoked ricotta is not available in your area.

1 recipe ricotta gnocchi made with ricotta salata
(page 90)

1 recipe Sage-Butter Sauce (page 185)

1 recipe Fig Filling (page 163)

Sage leaves, grated smoked ricotta, and finely grated orange zest for garnish

Prepare the Fig Filling and set aside.

Prepare the Sage-Butter Sauce and set aside.

Prepare 1 recipe Ricotta Gnocchi through the testing stage.

Shape, stuff, and finish the gnocchi as follows:

With floured hands, break off a 1-inch size piece of dough and roll into a ball. Place it in the palm of one hand, flatten slightly, and make an indentation in the middle with the forefinger of your other hand. Fill with a small amount of the fig filling, about rounded ½ teaspoon. Close the dough around the filling and shape into balls or ovals. Place the finished gnocchi close together, but not touching, on a lightly floured tray. They should measure about 1¼ inches in diameter.

Bring a very large, deep pot of water — no less than 1 gallon — to a simmer. Add 1 to 2 tablespoons salt and drop in the gnocchi, cooking no more than half the batch at a time. Stir a couple of times with a wooden spoon so the gnocchi move gently. The water should remain at a simmer rather than a rolling boil. As the gnocchi rise to the surface, remove with a slotted spoon, draining well of all excess water.

Alternatively, you can cook all the gnocchi at the same time in two separate pots.

To serve the gnocchi, place a portion in each warmed serving dish, drizzle with sage butter, and garnish with grated smoked ricotta or dollop of a mild, soft goat cheese. Sprinkle with orange zest and sage leaves as desired.

These gnocchi can be frozen after forming for up to two weeks. See Freezer Notes, page 250.

PRUNE-STUFFED RICOTTA GNOCCHI WITH MADEIRA & FRIED SAGE

/ serves 6 to 8

A traditional stuffing, soft cooked prunes are often used whole. The gnocchi are then lightly sauced with sage butter when served as a first course. In the following recipe, the filling and sauce are enriched with Madeira and the results are both more elegant and richer in flavor. You can make this a dessert course by serving the stuffed gnocchi in a pool of macerated strawberries with a mint sprig garnish, a dollop of Vanilla & Orange Scented Mascarpone (page 206), or dribbled with Saba (page 205).

1 recipe Basic Ricotta Gnocchi (page 90)

/ FOR THE FILLING

20 whole pitted prunes

1 cup Madeira

2 tablespoons finely chopped fresh sage

½ cup finely chopped pancetta, sautéed over medium
   heat until barely crisp (optional)

/ FOR THE SAUCE

¼ pound unsalted butter

2 shallots, minced

10 whole black peppercorns

1½ cups Madeira

/ FOR THE GARNISH

½ cup extra virgin olive oil

Small bunch fresh sage leaves

MAKE THE FILLING

Put the prunes, Madeira and sage in a saucepan and bring to a boil. Turn heat down and simmer over medium heat until almost all the liquid has cooked away. Allow to cool. Chop very fine. Add the optional cooked pancetta and set aside.

MAKE THE SAUCE

Put the shallots, Madeira and peppercorns in a medium saucepan and cook until reduced and slightly thickened. Strain into a bowl to remove the solids. Return strained sauce to the saucepan. Over low heat, whisk in the butter, a tablespoon at a time, just until it's melted. Keep warm over a bowl of hot water.

PREPARE THE GARNISH

Line a plate with paper towels. In a saucepan, heat the olive oil to a simmer. Add the sage leaves and fry until they begin to change color to a deep green. Remove with a slotted spoon to drain and crisp. Set aside.

SHAPE, STUFF, AND FINISH THE GNOCCHI

With floured hands, break off a 1-inch size piece of dough and roll into a ball. Place it in the palm of one hand, flatten slightly, and make an indentation in the middle with the forefinger of your other hand. Fill with the prune filling. Close the dough around the filling and shape into balls or ovals. Place the finished gnocchi close together on a lightly floured tray. They should be measure about 1½ inches in diameter.

Bring a very large, deep pot of water — no less than 1 gallon — to a simmer. Add 1 to 2 tablespoons salt and drop in the gnocchi, cooking no more than half the batch at a time. Stir a couple of times with a wooden spoon so the gnocchi move gently. The water should remain at a simmer rather than a rolling boil.

Have ready warmed serving bowls and a large mixing bowl with half the sauce portioned into it. As the gnocchi rise to the surface, remove with a slotted spoon, toss with the sauce, garnish with the reserved fried sage, and serve immediately. Repeat with the remaining gnocchi and sauce. Alternatively, you can cook all the gnocchi at the same time in two separate pots and toss them all together in one large bowl of sauce.

These gnocchi can be frozen after forming for up to two weeks. See Freezer Notes, page 250.

APRICOT or PRUNE STUFFED GNOCCHI IN CINNAMON-SUGAR CRUMBS

/ serves 6

Fruit-stuffed potato gnocchi are often served as a savory first course rather than a dessert course in many parts of Italy. Here, in a recipe from Umbria, the filling and crumbs have a touch of sweetness that can lean either way, depending on how you choose to serve them. If you prefer to make them a dessert, you can pool a sweet sauce or rich cream next to them as you divide them among serving bowls.

1 recipe potato gnocchi with egg (page 20)

1 generous cup dried, very soft apricots, pitted prunes, or a combination

4 tablespoons granulated sugar, divided

¾ cup unsalted butter

1½ cups coarse, plain, dried breadcrumbs, preferably homemade

½ teaspoon ground cinnamon

½ cup finely grated fresh Parmigiano-Reggiano

Prepare the potato gnocchi dough through the testing stage. Set aside, covered, while preparing the filling.

Chop the apricots and/or prunes into pea-sized pieces. If serving as a dessert, mix with 2 tablespoons sugar.

With floured hands, break off a 1-inch size piece of dough and roll into a ball. Place it in the palm of one hand, flatten slightly, and make an indentation in the middle with the forefinger of your other hand. Fill with a small amount of the stuffing, about a rounded ½ teaspoon. Close the dough around the filling and shape into balls or ovals. Place the finished gnocchi close together, but not touching, on a lightly floured tray. They should measure about 1½ inches in diameter.

Melt the butter in a small saucepan. Transfer 4 tablespoons of the melted butter to a large skillet. Add the breadcrumbs and cook, stirring frequently, until golden — about 5 minutes. Add the cinnamon and 2 tablespoons sugar. Transfer to a pie plate to cool. Lightly mix in the Parmigiano-Reggiano and set aside.

Bring a very large, deep pot of water — no less than 1 gallon — to simmer. Add 1 to 2 tablespoons salt and drop in the gnocchi, cooking no more than half the batch at a time. Stir a couple of times with a wooden spoon so the gnocchi move gently. The water should remain at a simmer rather than a rolling boil. As the gnocchi rise to the surface, remove with a slotted spoon, draining well of all excess water.

Alternatively, you can cook all the gnocchi at the same time in two separate pots.

Toss with the breadcrumbs to evenly coat, divide among warmed serving bowls, and serve immediately, drizzling with the reserved butter from the saucepan and sprinkling with any extra breadcrumb mixture.

These gnocchi can be frozen after forming for up to two weeks. See Freezer Notes, page 250.

SAUSAGE-STUFFED POLENTA GNOCCHI IN TOMATO SAUCE

/ serves 6 to 8

This is a good gnocchi dish to take to a potluck where you have access to an oven. It can be easily prepared in advance and baked off at the party just before serving. Be sure to use fine polenta for this recipe; medium and coarse polenta will not hold together well enough to form balls.

1½ cups fine white or yellow polenta

½ cup whole milk

3½ cups water

3 tablespoons unsalted butter, divided

10 ounces bulk Italian sausage, mild or hot

1 tablespoon extra-virgin olive oil

2 cloves garlic, finely chopped

1 tablespoon each (or to taste) rosemary and sage, finely chopped

1 recipe Basic Tomato Sauce (page 208)

Kosher salt and freshly ground black pepper

2 tablespoons unsalted butter, cubed

¾ cup finely grated fresh Parmigiano-Reggiano

Bring the water and the milk to a simmer in a large, deep pan. Add salt to taste. Keep the liquid simmering over medium-low heat and add the cornmeal in a very thin stream, showering it over the water while stirring vigorously with a whisk.

Reduce heat to low and cook, stirring frequently with a wooden spoon, until it pulls away from the sides of the pan and forms a mass, 35 to 40 minutes. Do not be tempted to shorten the cooking time. Remove from heat, add 1 tablespoon of the butter and set aside to cool. It will be soft but still hold its shape.

Meanwhile make the tomato sauce and let it cook while finishing the gnocchi.

In a skillet, brown the sausage with the olive oil, chopped garlic, and herbs. Set aside.

Preheat the oven to 350°F. and spread the tomato sauce in the bottom of an 8-inch-x-12-inch ovenproof baking dish, or any size large enough to hold the gnocchi in a single layer.

Using a 1½-inch scoop, remove some of the polenta, and use your finger make a deep indentation in the dough. Insert a bit of sausage and close the opening. As they are stuffed, place the gnocchi in a single layer, barely touching each other, on top of the tomato sauce in the prepared dish. (Alternatively, you can use a spoon and wet hands to shape the balls, but I've found the scoop much easier as the dough is a bit sticky.)

Dot with butter and shower with Parmigiano-Reggiano. Bake in the preheated oven until the cheese melts and the gnocchi are bubbly and heated through, 20 to 30 minutes. Put under the broiler for a minute or two to brown the top if desired. Serve immediately.

Vegetarian variation: Substitute pieces of *mozzarella di bufala* for the sausage and garlic, and add the sage and rosemary to the polenta after it has cooled.

Do not freeze.

MUSHROOM FILLING

/ enough for 6 servings

The following recipe is one of my favorite gnocchi fillings. It can be tweaked to your liking by changing the kind of mushrooms used or by adding a small amount of your favorite herb. Experiment with it as you wish.

1½ pounds firm, fresh, white button mushrooms

3 cloves garlic, finely minced

¼ cup extra-virgin olive oil

¼ cup fresh parsley, finely chopped

Zest of 1 lemon, finely minced

Salt and freshly ground black pepper to taste

Brush any loose dirt from the mushrooms and finely chop by hand or in a food processer. You should have about 5 cups prepared mushrooms.

Heat the oil and minced garlic together in a large sauté pan over medium-high heat until fragrant. Do not brown. Add the chopped mushrooms and sauté, stirring frequently, until all the liquid has evaporated. They should be quite dry.

Remove from the heat and stir in the chopped parsley and lemon rind. Season with salt and pepper to taste. Set aside to cool to room temperature.

This filling will keep, refrigerated, for 3 days.

FIG FILLING

/ makes about 2 cups

This is a versatile filling that can also be used to stuff dessert gnocchi. If you plan to use it in a sweet rather than savory presentation, I suggest you add some mild honey to taste after the filling has cooled. Leftovers are perfect as an appetizer served with Italian cheeses.

Refer to the Sweet Sauces section (pages 205–207) for additional dessert presentation ideas.

2 cups finely chopped Black Mission figs

¼ cup brandy

½ cup orange juice

Grated rind of 1 orange

¼ cup water

Place the figs, brandy, orange juice, grated orange rind, and water in a medium saucepan. Bring to a simmer over medium-high heat. Reduce the heat to low, cover, and cook, stirring frequently, until the figs are soft and thickened — about 15 minutes. Add more water if necessary to keep from sticking.

Cool to room temperature before using.

This filling will keep for up to two weeks, refrigerated, in an airtight container. Bring to room temperature before using.

FARE LA SPESA

/ Food Shopping in Italy

No other culture celebrates food with such fervor as Italy.

I'm forever impressed with the interest Italians take in the food they eat. The knowledge of chefs and others involved in the food industry is one thing; to have a 30-minute conversation with my hairdresser over the nuances of great pizza is another — a perfect example of the everyday Italian's interest in how *si mangia bene*, how one eats well.

Most Italians, however, are not equally interested in eating the foods of other countries. As one Italian told me, they "eat how they speak." Since Italian food is the best, why would they bother eating anything else?

This attitude carries over from region to region within the country, as Italians will argue heatedly over who makes the best *salsa di pomodoro*, or tomato sauce, for instance, or what ingredients a given dish should include. I've even been told, "I only eat what my mother cooks" — which leaves me wondering what chance a new bride has to impress her husband.

Friends renting an apartment in Bologna once attempted to buy fresh tagliatelle to serve with pesto for their evening meal. They were firmly informed that tagliatelle and pesto are NOT eaten together, and that ragù Bolognese was the only sauce they should use. Needless to say, they bought the ragù and enjoyed a wonderful meal.

Although transportation of food around the country is much more common than it once was, most Italians continue to eat locally and seasonally — with regional customs and traditional recipes still dictating the availability of some items. Smoked ricotta cheese, for example, is difficult to find outside of the mountainous regions of northern Italy, while salted ricotta is nearly impossible to purchase in the north. Italians have a profound knowledge of their own cuisine and I respect their desire to maintain its traditions — even though at times it can seem overly strict.

Until I had access to my own kitchen, with the ability to prepare meals from the superior Italian ingredients I found locally, my experience of Italian food was limited to restaurants, which offer only a small glimpse of the country's diverse cuisine. When I began spending longer periods of time in Italy and rented apartments where I could cook, I began shopping Italian style — searching for the best of everything in small, specialized shops — *panifici* (bakeries) *macellerie* (butchers), *mercati ortofrutticoli* (fruit and vegetable markets), *latterie* (cheese and milk vendors), and *alimentari* (general household and a bit of everything). I still prefer this kind of shopping, and have formed relationships with a number of merchants over the 20 years I've lived in Perugia.

Farmers, butchers, bakers, and fishmongers are respected artisans, practicing a craft that is most often passed down from one generation to the next. My butcher has worked in his profession for almost 50 years and his son is now taking over the business. The same is true for my favorite fishmonger, although he's a bit younger. Italians believe the ability to be the best in any craft is passed down in the genes and finely tuned with practice. My experience suggests that to be true.

These relationships centering on food have also given me a closer connection to the Italian culture than I would otherwise have experienced. The best way to intimately know a culture is through sharing its food, which also involves shopping for it. I learned very quickly not to touch the fruits and vegetables with bare hands. Break that golden rule and even a foreigner who doesn't know better will be severely chastised. I once overheard an Italian woman *di una certa età* (of a certain age) being scolded for searching through a local vendor's peaches. After 30 years, she was told, she should know better.

Unlike larger supermarkets where so many products are prepackaged, in small shops one can order only what one actually wants. A slice of bread, a morsel of cheese or 10 olives? No problem. The norm in Italy is to purchase what one needs for a short period of time and eat it right away. This habit requires some daily shopping, but it's healthy and less wasteful.

I also appreciate that the origins of food products are always noted in great detail, including the area of the sea in which a particular fish was caught; where the fruits and vegetables were harvested; the locale of the milk used to make a container of yogurt; and the date it was laid stamped on each and every egg. All meat and poultry is registered as well and small local slaughterhouses are the norm. I was confused once when my butcher said I would need to wait a few days to purchase a pork tenderloin because *"e ancora calda"* — "it's still hot." The pig had just been slaughtered a few kilometers from Perugia and the flesh needed to cool down before it was dressed.

Markets have changed over the 30 years I've been spending extended time in Italy. There are now supermarkets, or "Iper-stores," on the edges of all the towns — just as in the U.S. — and many Italians, with their busy and changing lifestyles, prefer to shop there. I've learned to save stops at these stores for things I buy in large quantities, and heavy items, like wine and laundry detergent.

On a daily basis, I'm still old school. I love the smell of prosciutto when I enter a *salumeria* (delicatessen) or butcher shop. I enjoy having the fishmonger clean and trim fish if I request it. The vegetable vendor puts aside mature fava beans for me, and the butcher will grant some of my more unusual requests, like grinding part of a lamb leg for a special non-Italian recipe. And watching him hand-cut prosciutto with a precision learned only after years of practice is a marvel. My favorite cheesemonger once relabeled and vacuum-packed a small wheel of aged pecorino that had been given to me as a gift so I could bring it back to the U.S. without having problems in customs.

Various vendors have also taught me how to prepare local recipes not found in any cookbooks. Italians rarely toss anything edible and I've learned how to use every part of every vegetable. I now know that raw, shredded beets are fantastic in salads or simply seasoned and served on their own. And that beet stems added to risotto give the dish a beautiful pink hue (as well as make it more nutritious). I've been introduced to new vegetables that I crave in the off-season, such as fava beans, fresh borlotti beans, and *agretti*, a Mediterranean vegetable also known as *Barba di frate* in other parts of Italy. I make special trips to buy absolutely fresh *mozzarella di bufala* from a van that arrives daily from Naples. And olive oil? It's not just for cooking! It will silence a squeaky door as well as preserve its finish and add luster to your hair and complexion.

Community gardens are still prevalent and *prodotti nostrali*, or local products, are always available. Parallel to the spread of large supermarkets, there is a growing trend to double back to previous methods of smaller, less industrialized food production. I find it encouraging to know that the younger generation has a renewed interest in becoming farmers, vintners, and olive oil producers.

When buying fruits and vegetables from a local farmer, it's considered a matter of trust and respect to let him or her choose the produce for you. They may ask, for example, when you want to consume a melon. *"Oggi o entro un paio di giorni?"* Today or in a couple of days? For hygienic reasons, in larger markets, plastic gloves are provided to wear when selecting produce. After you've made your selection, you weigh it yourself on a scale that pops out the price. It certainly saves time at the checkout.

Sometimes the daily food shopping can be frustrating for a foreigner who isn't used to the cultural differences — like older women cutting ahead in line while they pretend innocence. I'm constantly amazed at this behavior, but I've realized that to some Italians it's an accepted practice, so I take a deep breath and even chuckle at the many sly techniques women have practiced and undoubtedly passed on to their daughters over the years. *Pazienza* (patience) is definitely a virtue to be cultivated. In recent years, the practice of issuing numbers at some shops has helped a great deal, but at others one still needs to jockey for position. Having your groceries carefully bagged for you, as in the U.S., does not happen in Italy, not even in the larger markets. It takes some quick thinking and agility to pack, pay, and get moving as quickly as possible to allow the next person to be served. But it's worth the effort.

My second home is in Umbria — the Green Heart of Italy — which is one of the country's most fertile and nurturing regions, with sheep and pig farms, lush green hills, rolling mountains, rich fertile valleys, vineyards, olive groves, and, of course, wonderful fresh fruits and vegetables within easy reach. At the very center of the Italian peninsula, it is the only landlocked region of Italy, with no coastline or border with other countries. Even with a profusion of hilltop towns, villages, and old castles, as well as visible remains of Etruscan and Roman communities, it has remained untouched by heavy tourism.

For all these reasons, and more, I've always felt grounded and centered in Umbria, or *piantata* — planted like a sunflower — in one of its many rich fields.

— CHRISTINE HICKMAN

Exceptional gnocchi require an exceptional sauce — and a strong repertoire of sauces to draw on means you have abundant choices to present a particular dish. I've made sauce suggestions at the end of each gnocchi recipe that follow certain guidelines, and you may find your own favorite combinations as well. Some recipes are traditional, while others reflect more "modern" movements as restaurants begin more and more to feature gnocchi on their menus.

The serving sizes, (how many gnocchi servings per sauce) are only a guide. When saucing gnocchi or pasta, Italians will use less sauce, while Americans tend to use more. As I often suggest in my classes, "Americans eat gnocchi with their sauce, while Italians eat sauce with their gnocchi." My personal preference is for the Italian way …

In general, the richer the sauce, the less you need. With pesto, for example, only a heaping tablespoon is required per serving. Too much of any pesto is overwhelming. And if you're a gnocchi novice, and not sure how much sauce you'll want, make more and save it for another dish. Almost all of the sauces will keep at least a few days refrigerated. Some sauces work equally well for meats, fish, or chicken, bruschette, vegetables, or pasta — so purposely making extra or using up leftovers can give you a head-start on another meal in the future.

My hope is that the large range of sauces included here will expand your ideas about what to serve for dinner, and serve as a go-to reference guide for more than just how to make the best gnocchi you've ever eaten.

SAUCES

/ CREAM, CHEESE & BUTTER SAUCES

Cream, cheese, and butter sauces are one of the most popular and traditional sauces to combine with nearly any style of gnocchi. From the familiar Gorgonzola Cream or Brown Butter & Sage to a Savory Zabaglione with Horseradish Cream, there are a wide range of choices — all of which are best when freshly made and used quickly. These sauces will not freeze well; when the milk proteins break down, the sauce loses much of its flavor. But a few days in the refrigerator, if absolutely necessary, will not severely harm any of them, except where noted in the recipes.

/ PESTOS & PESTO-STYLE SAUCES

Pesto — made from a combination of Genovese basil, pine nuts, garlic, olive oil, and Parmigiano-Reggiano — originated in Liguria, Italy. In today's kitchen, it encompasses a range of sauces based on the process of pounding, from the verb *pestare*, meaning "to pound, beat up, crush, or bruise." The pounding can be done the old-fashioned way, by hand, or mechanically, with a small food processor.

Basil pesto has long been a favored sauce for potato gnocchi, and is often served in restaurants across Italy, but I've included many other variations in this chapter because of their versatility, ease and speed of preparation, and the fact that they can be made days in advance. I always have at least one pesto on hand in my refrigerator to use as a sauce for pasta, a spread for bruschette, or to dollop on fish, chicken, meat, or vegetables.

/ SAUCES WITH MEAT

Prosciutto, pancetta, sausage, and other inexpensive meats are often used in gnocchi sauces, along with a variety of vegetables that can take either a primary or secondary role in the final recipe. These are a few examples of the huge range of possibilities.

Although any of the following meat sauces can be frozen up to two weeks, it's not recommended as texture and flavor can be adversely affected. For advance preparation, you can store them, tightly covered, in the refrigerator for a few days.

/ RAGÙS

Ragù, a quintessential sauce for pasta and potato gnocchi, varies with every region of Italy and with every family and cook that prepares it. By definition, ragù is a meat-based sauce that may or may not include tomatoes, depending on the region of origin.

Southern Italians call it Sunday Gravy, and it has plenty of tomatoes. Italian immigrants from southern Italy introduced this version of ragù to America, and it's the style Americans think of first when ragù is mentioned. Traditionally, in southern family homes the tender meat is removed from the sauce and served as the main course for the Sunday family meal, while the remaining red "gravy" is used to sauce the pasta for the first course. As noted in the Basic Southern Ragù recipe, any bone-in, fatty meat can be used to vary the sauce, but the cooking process is always the same.

In northern Italy, ragù usually refers to the Bolognese style — a finely chopped meat sauce that has very little tomato and is traditionally served with tagliatelle. Why so few tomatoes in the Bolognese versus the southern-style ragùs? Because, historically, tomatoes were not an abundant crop in northern Italy. Again, the meats used can vary but the preparation is always the same.

In other regions of Italy, white ragùs are more popular. All but the White Chicken Ragù require a long simmer. Don't get discouraged about the time required, as the recipes can be easily doubled and made days in advance or frozen for up to a month. I highly recommend you make enough to tuck away some for a future meal of pasta or polenta.

Critically important in making a successful ragù is browning the meat until "brown bits" form on the bottom of the pan. It is an essential part of the process as it caramelizes the meat and adds depth of flavor to the ragù. The sauce will suffer if you shortcut that step. And don't be tempted to shorten the long cooking time once all the ingredients have been added; this is what tenderizes both the meat and vegetables. Keep an eye on the pot and keep the temperature low, stirring occasionally to keep the sauce from burning on the bottom.

/ SWEET SAUCES

These are just a few of my favorite Italian sweet sauces to compliment the dessert gnocchi recipes in this book — but don't feel limited to what's presented here. Any favorite jams, marmalades, chocolate or fruit sauces, purées, or syrups will do the job.

/ TOMATO SAUCES

No collection of gnocchi recipes would be complete without a variety of tomato sauces to compliment them. Over the years, I've experimented with different preparations, some with meat and some without — but all with tomato as the core ingredient. I've separated tomato sauces from ragùs by this simple definition: ragù sauces may or may not contain tomatoes, and tomato sauces may or may not contain meat.

From green to red, large to small, fresh, canned, cooked, and raw, these are some of my favorite ways to "tomato" a sauce.

/ VEGETABLE-BASED & MISCELLANEOUS SAUCES

Historically, Italians followed a diet that was naturally vegetarian because they could not afford meat — and their traditional sauces do not suffer for it.

Today there are many variations of vegetarian diets that not only eliminate meat, but also some of the ingredients in these recipes. Hopefully, everyone will be able to find at least a few sauces that will fit their lifestyle.

Many sauce recipes in this book, mostly in the cheese and/ or pesto sections, also fall into the vegetarian — but not the vegan — category.

BASIC FONTINA SAUCE

/ enough for 6 servings

Fontina is one of the more famous (and popular) cow's-milk cheeses of northern Italy. Recipes for Fontina Sauce are abundant, but this is one of the easiest and most flavorful I've come across. It's easily modified by changing the combination of herbs, or by substituting other semi-soft or melting cheeses such as Asiago, Taleggio, Emmental, Gruyère, or provolone.

5 tablespoons unsalted butter

1 tablespoon finely minced shallot

2 tablespoons minced fresh parsley

2 tablespoons snipped chives

1 tablespoon minced fresh thyme

1 tablespoon minced fresh marjoram or oregano

1 tablespoon minced fresh sage

6 ounces fontina, cut into ¼-inch cubes (about 1½ cups)

In a large skillet, melt the butter and shallot together over medium heat until fragrant, about 2 to 3 minutes. Add the herbs and heat just until they begin to sizzle. Set aside while finishing the gnocchi.

When ready to serve, add the cubed fontina, then the cooked gnocchi, to the warm butter and herb mixture. Toss lightly just until the fontina begins to melt — a few chunks will remain in the sauce. Serve immediately.

BLACK TRUFFLE SAUCE

/ enough for 2 to 4 servings

Bottled black truffles are a viable substitute for fresh black truffles, even though they don't have as strong a flavor. Look for black truffles from Umbria, the biggest black truffle-producing region in all of Italy. Don't substitute white truffles in this sauce as they lose flavor when heated.

2 fresh or bottled black truffles

¼ cup fresh unsalted butter, softened

¼ cup extra-virgin olive oil

1 large clove garlic, minced

1 tablespoon Armagnac or brandy (optional)

Salt and freshly ground black pepper to taste

Mince one truffle, place in a mortar and pestle, and pound to a fine paste. Add the garlic and a little salt and pound again to integrate the ingredients. Add a few grindings of black pepper, mix in the softened butter, and set aside.

Cut the remaining truffle into paper-thin rounds using a truffle slicer or mandoline. In a small saucepan, warm the olive oil over low heat, add the truffle slices and set aside to steep for about 10 minutes. Add the optional Armagnac or brandy if using.

Cook the gnocchi until they rise to the surface. With a large, wide slotted spoon, remove the gnocchi and place in a wide sauté pan. Add the truffle-butter mixture to the pan and toss lightly to heat.

Serve at once, topping each portion with some of the reserved truffle slices.

You may also drizzle each serving with a few drops of natural commercial white or black truffle oil to enhance the flavor. (See notes on page 243) Don't heat the truffle oil.

Do not refrigerate.

BROWNED BUTTER & PRESERVED LEMON SAUCE
WITH RICOTTA

/ enough for 4 servings

Browned butter, creamy cheese, basil, and small bits of salty lemon rind make a simple gnocchi sauce. Finely chopped lemon zest would be a more traditional substitute for the preserved lemon, although it doesn't have the surprising zing of the preserved lemon. Common in Indian and North African cuisine, preserved lemons are available online, at specialty food stores, and sometimes at the deli counter of larger markets. Refrigerated in a tightly closed jar, they keep practically forever. If you can't buy them, preserved lemons are easy to make — but they can take at least two weeks to ferment properly, so plan ahead. There are recipes available on the internet, including some for "quick" preserved lemons that can make an acceptable substitute in a pinch.

1 large, whole preserved lemon, rind only, finely chopped

6 tablespoons unsalted butter

Freshly ground black pepper

1 cup whole-milk ricotta cheese, whipped until
    smooth OR 1 cup mascarpone

½ cup fresh basil, shredded

In a skillet, heat the butter over medium-low heat, swirling occasionally, for about 5 minutes or until it is a golden brown. Be careful not to burn it. Add the chopped preserved lemon and a generous grinding of black pepper and set aside. Remove half of sauce to a small bowl, leaving the remaining sauce in the skillet.

Cook half the gnocchi until they rise to the surface and transfer with a slotted spoon to the skillet as they are done. Heat quickly on medium-high, swirling the pan, until the gnocchi are just heated through. Divide the gnocchi into bowls and top with a dollop of the ricotta and some shredded basil. Serve immediately. Repeat with the remaining gnocchi and sauce. Do not refrigerate.

CABBAGE & CHEESE SAUCE

/ enough for 6 servings

This is a richly flavored sauce that combines ingredients from the northern regions of Italy. It's perfect for both canederli and the more robust varieties of gnocchi, such as those made with buckwheat and potato.

½ pound Savoy cabbage, finely shredded

3 tablespoons unsalted butter, divided

2 cloves garlic, minced

½ small white onion, finely chopped

2 cups whole milk

Salt and freshly ground black pepper to taste

¾ cup grated Italian fontina cheese

¾ cup grated Gruyère or Emmental cheese

In a deep, heavy skillet over medium heat, melt half the butter. Add the cabbage and sauté until soft and golden, about 6 minutes. Transfer to a bowl and set aside.

In the same skillet, melt the remaining butter and sauté the garlic and onion together until onion is soft, about 3 minutes. Add the milk, bring to a simmer, and allow to cook and thicken slightly, about 5 minutes. Add the cheese a small handful at a time and heat gently, stirring, until melted. Stir in the cooked cabbage, season to taste with salt and pepper, and set aside while cooking the gnocchi.

CARBONARA SAUCE

/ enough for 6 to 8 generous servings

*A well-known pasta sauce, rich and creamy carbonara gets
its name from the abundance of black pepper added just
before serving. This is not a traditional sauce for gnocchi,
but for those who love spaghetti carbonara, the gnocchi
offer a delicious alternative to the usual pasta. I've
suggested a simple potato-based gnocchi here, but other
varieties that do not contain cheese could also work.*

*Be sure to use genuine Parmigiano-Reggiano purchased
in a wedge, and grate it just before using. The cheese takes
center stage in this recipe and the quality of the star
ingredient makes a noticeable difference in the flavor.*

1 recipe potato gnocchi, ready to cook

6 ounces pancetta cut in a single thick slice

   OR 6 ounces thick-sliced, smoky slab bacon

2 tablespoons olive oil

1 tablespoon unsalted butter

4 garlic cloves, peeled and lightly crushed

¼ cup dry white wine

Salt to taste

3 large egg yolks*

¾ cup finely grated fresh Parmigiano-Reggiano

¼ cup heavy cream

Fresh, coarsely ground black pepper to taste

1 cup baby arugula leaves

Cut the pancetta into strips and chop into small dice, about
¼-inch.

Put the oil, butter, and crushed garlic into a small sauté pan
set over medium-high heat. When the garlic turns a light
gold, remove and discard it. Add the diced pancetta to the
pan, and sauté until it begins to crisp on the edges. Add
the wine, bring to a boil, and reduce for 2 minutes. Remove
from the heat and set aside.

In a large bowl, beat the egg yolks with the heavy cream.
Add the freshly grated Parmigiano-Reggiano and lots of
fresh, coarsely ground black pepper. Put half of the mixture
into a second large bowl.

Cook the gnocchi in two batches. As they rise to the
surface, add them to one of the bowls of sauce. Add a bit of
cooking water if the sauce is too thick, and toss thoroughly,
making sure the gnocchi is well coated. Reheat the pancetta
quickly over high heat, then pour half the contents of the
pan over half the gnocchi. Toss thoroughly again and serve
immediately, garnished with the baby arugula. Repeat with
the remaining gnocchi.

Alternatively, you can cook all the gnocchi at the same time
in two separate pots and toss them all together in a large
skillet with all the sauce.

Do not refrigerate.

**If your immune system is compromised or you are concerned
about Salmonella, you may want to avoid this recipe.*

CREAMY LEEK SAUCE

/ enough for 6 to 8 servings

Simple and rich, this sauce compliments some of the more earthy gnocchi of northern Italy — like Potato-Buckwheat or Meat and Potato Affogati. Leeks are more commonly used in European cuisine than onions. Milder and more delicately flavored than other alliums, they can assume a principal role without being overwhelming. A bonus: this sauce can be made in advance and refrigerated up to two days.

5-6 large leeks

2 tablespoons extra-virgin olive oil

2 tablespoons butter

3 garlic cloves, minced

1 cup half-and-half

Salt and freshly ground black pepper

About ½ cup finely grated fresh Parmigiano-Reggiano
    + more for serving

Finely chopped parsley for garnish

Cut the leeks an inch or two above the white part of the stalk and discard the dark green leaves. Slice the leeks in half lengthwise, then slice thinly into half-moons, about ⅛-inch thick, working your way down to the root end. Discard the end and put all the slices in a colander. Run cold water over them, shaking off the excess. Set aside.

Put the oil, butter, and minced garlic into a large skillet. Cook the garlic over medium heat until it begins to sizzle. Add the sliced leeks to the pan and cook, stirring frequently, until they become very soft, almost creamy, about 10 minutes. You may need to add up to ¼-cup water if they begin to dry out.

When the leeks are completely soft, raise the heat to high and continue cooking, turning them over a few times, until they turn a pale golden color. Add the half-and-half and reduce the sauce over high heat until it is moderately thick. Add salt and freshly ground black pepper to taste. Pour half the sauce into another skillet and set aside.

Cook half the gnocchi as directed. Using a slotted spoon, transfer it to one of the skillets with half the warm sauce. If the sauce is too thick, thin it with some of the gnocchi cooking water. Add half the freshly grated Parmigiano-Reggiano to the skillet and toss thoroughly five or six times. Portion the gnocchi into shallow serving bowls, garnish with the parsley, and serve at once. Repeat with the remaining gnocchi and sauce.

Alternatively, you can cook all the gnocchi at the same time in two separate pots and toss them all together in a large serving bowl with the appropriate amount of sauce.

Pass the additional finely grated fresh Parmigiano-Reggiano at the table.

CREAMY LEMON, PEAS & PROSCIUTTO SAUCE

/ enough for 6 servings

Perfect for a one-dish meal, I enjoy this sauce when fresh peas are available in the springtime markets of Italy. For a vegetarian alternative, omit the prosciutto garnish. It's equally good without the meat.

Note that you can substitute cooked fresh fava beans for the peas. Two pounds fresh favas in the pod will yield the 2 cups shucked fava beans for the recipe. Don't forget to immerse the shucked beans in boiling water for 2 to 3 minutes in order to slip off the outer skins.

2 tablespoons unsalted butter

3 large shallots, minced

1 cup homemade or low-sodium canned chicken broth

¾ cup heavy cream

3 teaspoons finely grated lemon peel

1 teaspoon finely grated orange peel

Pinch hot pepper flakes

2 cups frozen OR fresh green peas (about 1½
    pounds in the pod)

3 tablespoons minced fresh mint leaves

1 tablespoon fresh lemon juice

1 tablespoon extra-virgin olive oil

6 thin slices prosciutto, shredded

Freshly grated Parmigiano-Reggiano for serving

If using fresh peas, shuck the peas and immerse them in lightly salted, boiling water for 2 to 3 minutes. Drain well and set aside. Frozen peas can be used without thawing.

Melt the butter in a large nonstick skillet over medium heat. Add shallots and sauté until translucent, about 2 minutes. Add the broth and simmer over medium-high heat until liquid is reduced to ½ cup, about 3 minutes.

Add cream, lemon and orange peels, and pepper flakes. Simmer until sauce thickens slightly, about 3 minutes. Add the peas and simmer until heated through, about 2 minutes. Stir in mint and lemon juice. Season to taste with salt and pepper. Set aside.

In a medium sauté pan, heat the prosciutto shreds with the olive oil until slightly browned.

Toss the sauce with the cooked gnocchi. Divide the gnocchi among six warmed serving bowls and garnish with the prosciutto. Pass the freshly grated Parmigiano-Reggiano at the table.

CREAMY ROASTED GARLIC & PARMIGIANO-REGGIANO SAUCE

/ enough for 6 servings

This basic sauce is easily varied. If you are not serving it with the porcini gnocchi, you can substitute ½ cup dry white wine and ½ cup chicken broth for the porcini liquid. You could also try adding 2–3 tablespoons freshly grated horseradish to serve it with beet or squash gnocchi. Garnish the sauce with other herbs, diced pancetta, or crumbled and cooked sausage — or use other hard cheeses, such as aged pecorino.

You may want to roast a few extra heads of garlic for making bruschette (Italian toasts), to add to sauces or salad dressings, or to use wherever you want the mild flavor of roasted garlic. Squeeze the cloves into a small container, cover with olive oil, and refrigerate for up to two weeks — or tightly wrap and freeze for longer storage.

1 small head garlic

1 tablespoon extra-virgin olive oil

1 tablespoon unsalted butter

1 small shallot, minced

1 cup reserved porcini liquid (or other broth)

1½ cups heavy cream

¼ cup finely grated fresh Parmigiano-Reggiano
    + more for passing at the table

2 tablespoons finely chopped parsley for garnish

½ cup finely chopped and lightly sautéed prosciutto
    for garnish (optional)

Preheat the oven to 400°F.

Trim about ¼ inch off the top of the head of garlic to expose the cloves. Place the head on a sheet of foil, drizzle with the olive oil so it sinks into the cloves, sprinkle with bit of kosher salt, and pinch the top of the foil closed. Roast the garlic for about 20 to 30 minutes, or until it's completely soft. (Check by inserting the tip of a paring knife into the center of the head.)

Let the garlic cool slightly, then squeeze the cloves into a small bowl. Add salt and freshly ground black pepper to taste, and mash to combine. Set aside.

Heat the butter and minced shallot in a small saucepan over medium-low heat. Sauté until barely softened, about 3 minutes. Add the reserved porcini (or other) liquid, bring to a boil, and reduce it to ½ cup.

Add the heavy cream and roasted and mashed garlic to the mixture, stirring to combine. Return the pan to medium-low heat and reduce the sauce to about 1½ cups or less.

Remove from heat and stir in ¼ cup of the freshly grated Parmigiano. Add salt and freshly ground black pepper to taste. Set aside and keep warm while you finish the gnocchi.

FONDUTA

/ enough for 6 to 8 servings

Fonduta is the Italian version of fondue — a specialty of the Piedmont and Valle d'Aosta regions. It is made with fontina, a young cow's-milk cheese that melts much like mozzarella and tastes like other Alpine cheeses, such as Gruyère and Emmental. You can replace some of the fontina with Taleggio or fresh mozzarella if desired. String mozzarella prepackaged in plastic, often used in making American pizza, will not melt. Although the cheese used is similar, Italian fonduta is made with milk, cream, butter, and egg yolks rather than the cornstarch, wine, and garlic found in American fondue. Fonduta is wonderful with any gnocchi that calls for a rich, creamy cheese sauce. Often eaten with chunks of crusty bread, like fondue, it's also a favored sauce for canederli of all kinds. Garnish with truffle shavings if desired.

½ cup heavy cream

¾ cup whole milk

4 large egg yolks

4 tablespoons unsalted butter

2 cups coarsely grated Italian fontina cheese

Freshly ground white pepper

½ teaspoon kosher salt

Truffle shavings for serving (optional)

Beat the eggs with the milk and cream until well combined. Add the salt and pepper and set aside.

In the bowl of a double boiler, or in a medium bowl set over simmering water, melt the butter. Add a small handful of cheese and about 2 tablespoons of the milk mixture to the butter and stir until the cheese has melted and combined with the milk. Continue adding cheese and milk, a bit at a time, until everything has melted and the smooth sauce coats the back of a spoon. Keep warm until ready to use. Do not refrigerate.

GORGONZOLA CREAM SAUCE

/ enough for 6 servings

I've been using this recipe for one of the more traditional rich and creamy sauces for potato gnocchi in my classes for years. It's quick and yummy, and the flavor is "sweet" enough for this recipe. You can use more Gorgonzola Dolce if you like, but older, aged Gorgonzola is strong and can overwhelm this sauce — so be aware of the flavor of the cheese you purchase. (For more information on Gorgonzola Dolce, a creamy, soft cheese sometimes labeled cremificato, *see page 232)*

4 ounces Gorgonzola Dolce

½ cup milk

3 tablespoons unsalted butter

Pinch of salt

½ cup heavy cream

Put the Gorgonzola, milk, butter, and salt into a heavy saucepan over low heat. Stir with a wooden spoon, mashing the cheese with the back of the spoon. Continue to heat for a couple of minutes until the sauce is smooth, dense, and creamy. Set aside until you're ready to serve.

Shortly before the gnocchi is cooked, add the heavy cream to the sauce and stir it over medium-low heat until it is slightly reduced. It should be thin enough to lightly coat the back of a wooden spoon. Add more milk if necessary.

Do not refrigerate.

GREEN OLIVE-CREAM SAUCE

/ enough for 6 servings

The Castelvetrano olives called for in this recipe are such a brilliantly bright green, one would think they've been dyed — but the color comes from the fact that they are harvested young and cured in mildly salty brine, which also produces a more delicate, slightly sweet flavor. Named after a town in northern Sicily where they're primarily grown, they're readily available jarred or at some olive bars. You can substitute any green or black olive, or an assortment of your choice, for the Castelvetranos. Experiment until you find your favorite combination.

1½ cups homemade or canned low-sodium broth

½ cup heavy cream

1 tablespoon extra-virgin olive oil

1 tablespoon unsalted butter

1 large onion, finely chopped

3 garlic cloves, minced

⅔ cup Castelvetrano olives, pitted and coarsely chopped

Salt and freshly ground black pepper to taste

¼ cup finely chopped Italian parsley or basil

¼ cup finely grated fresh Parmigiano-Reggiano

+ more for serving

6 tablespoons toasted, finely chopped walnuts (optional)

In a saucepan, boil the broth until reduced by half. Transfer to a bowl and stir in the cream. Wipe out the saucepan.

Heat the olive oil and butter in the same pan. Add the onion and garlic, and cook over moderately low heat, stirring occasionally, until softened, about 5 minutes. Add the cream mixture and boil until slightly thickened, about 5 minutes. Add the olives and 2 tablespoons of the chopped herbs and season with salt and pepper to taste. Set aside, covered, while cooking gnocchi. Rewarm if necessary before serving.

Toss the cooked gnocchi with the green olive sauce and ¼ cup of the Parmigiano-Reggiano. Transfer to serving dishes and sprinkle with parsley or basil and optional walnuts. Pass extra finely grated fresh Parmigiano-Reggiano at the table.

LEMON & GARLIC SAUCE

/ enough for 4 to 6 servings

If you want an intensely flavored lemon sauce, this is the one for you. It's my favorite sauce for fish gnocchi or canederli, substituting fish broth for the chicken broth called for in the recipe. For a less astringent sauce, substitute Meyer lemon for the regular lemon in equal amounts. You can also tone it down by adding the optional cream.

3 tablespoons extra-virgin olive oil

3 cloves garlic, finely minced

1 cup chicken broth, homemade or canned low-sodium

OR ¾ cup chicken broth and ¼ cup heavy cream

1 lemon, finely zested

¼ cup lemon juice

Kosher salt and freshly ground black pepper to taste

¾ cup very finely chopped fresh flat parsley leaves

Finely grated fresh Parmigiano-Reggiano, ricotta salata or aged pecorino for serving (optional)

In a small, deep skillet, heat the olive oil with the minced garlic over low heat. Sauté, stirring frequently, for about 10 minutes. Increase the heat to medium, add the broth, and simmer until the liquid has reduced by half.

Add the lemon juice and zest and cook another 2 minutes. Add the cream if using and simmer another minute or two to reheat the sauce. Add the finely chopped parsley, stir to blend, and use immediately.

LEMON, THYME & SCAMORZA SAUCE

/ enough for 6 servings

This is a versatile, rich, and creamy sauce with the distinct flavor of lemon and smoky cheese that can be used with both gnocchi and canederli. When serving with canederli, I prefer to pool the sauce in the serving dish and place the canederli on top. It makes a more pleasing presentation.

1 lemon

3 sprigs thyme

2 tablespoons unsalted butter

1 cup heavy cream

Freshly ground pepper

3 ounces Scamorza (or smoked mozzarella),
   finely grated

Strip the leaves from the thyme and set aside. Finely grate the zest from the lemon and set aside.

In a large skillet over medium heat, melt the butter. Add half the chopped thyme and half the grated lemon zest, and sauté until fragrant, a minute or two. Add the heavy cream, season with salt and pepper, and stir. Bring to a simmer, reduce heat to low, and cook until thickened.

To serve, toss gnocchi with the sauce or pool the sauce in the bottom of warmed serving bowls and top with canederli. Sprinkle with the scamorza, and garnish with the reserved lemon zest and remaining thyme leaves.

If you prefer, you can melt the cheese into the sauce after adding the cream. Chopped rosemary or even sage can replace the thyme.

MASCARPONE CREAM SAUCE

/ enough for 6 servings

Widely known as the Italian cheese used in tiramisu, there is no substitute for the slight tang of mascarpone. It is widely available in the U.S., although the product is often a bit grainy as a result of rapid production techniques. If you want to be assured of the best mascarpone, which is silky smooth, thick, and rich with a slight tang, it's easy enough to make at home. You'll find easy-to-follow recipes on the internet.

3 small shallots, minced

2 tablespoons unsalted butter

1 cup mascarpone cheese

⅓ cup finely grated fresh Parmigiano-Reggiano

Salt and freshly ground black pepper to taste

2 tablespoons minced flat-leaf parsley

In a heavy saucepan, sauté the shallots in the butter over medium heat for 5 minutes, or until translucent. Fold in the mascarpone, and salt and pepper to taste. Keep warm until ready to serve.

Stir the Parmigiano-Reggiano into the warm sauce just before serving.

Do not refrigerate.

MEYER LEMON-BUTTER SAUCE

/ enough for 6 servings

This is one of my favorite lemon sauces for gnocchi or pasta. It's even more tasty with the optional grated bottarga garish.

1 cup homemade or low-sodium chicken broth

¼ pound chilled unsalted butter, cut into pieces

Freshly grated Meyer lemon zest to taste

Shredded fresh basil to taste

Grated bottarga (optional; see page 244 for
   more information)

In a small saucepan, reduce the chicken broth over high heat to a ½ cup. Remove from heat and quickly whisk in the butter, one piece at a time, until the sauce is thick and creamy. Stir in the Meyer lemon zest and set aside while cooking the gnocchi.

Reheat over very low heat before serving (higher heat will separate the butter). Serve garnished with shredded basil and optional grated bottarga.

PARMIGIANO-REGGIANO CREAM SAUCE

/ enough for 6 servings

This sauce also makes a very rich and creamy soup — just increase the liquid to 1 quart, and substitute low-sodium chicken broth for half the cream. Add the broth once the cheese has dissolved into the cream.

1 tablespoon unsalted butter

1 tablespoon unbleached all-purpose flour

2 cups heavy cream or half-and-half, warmed

1½-2 cups finely grated fresh Parmigiano-Reggiano

Salt and freshly ground pepper

In a heavy saucepan, melt the butter over medium heat. Add the flour and stir with a wooden spoon to mix well. Cook 2 to 3 minutes. Slowly add the warmed cream, stirring constantly with a wire whisk, until the mixture is thick and smooth.

Add the grated Parmigiano-Reggiano to taste. Heat, stirring constantly, just long enough for the sauce to reach a creamy consistency. Adjust the seasoning with salt and freshly ground pepper. Do not allow the sauce to boil. If reheating, do so over low heat.

PINE NUT-BUTTER SAUCE

/   enough for 4 to 6 servings

Thick like a pesto, this is a tasty gnocchi sauce that is also delicious on grilled or roasted vegetables, pasta, bruschette, fish, or chicken. A mortar and pestle produces a superior product both in taste and texture, but if you don't have that old-fashioned tool, you can use a small food processor. Whichever way you go, be sure to process the ingredients to a smooth paste.

½ cup pine nuts, divided

2 cloves garlic, minced

1 teaspoon minced fresh marjoram or thyme

Salt and freshly ground black pepper to taste

½ cup unsalted butter, softened

Using a mortar and pestle, pound 6 tablespoons of the pine nuts to a fine paste. Add the minced garlic, marjoram or thyme, and pound until ingredients are smooth and well combined. Gently fold in the butter and remaining 2 tablespoons of pine nuts until the pesto is creamy. Add salt and freshly ground black pepper to taste.

Use immediately or refrigerate for no more than 24 hours. Bring to room temperature before using.

POPPY SEED-MINT BUTTER SAUCE

/   enough for 4 to 6 servings

I love the combination of popping seeds and fresh mint when I bite into gnocchi served with this sauce. It's my favorite with ricotta and beet gnocchi, but it goes equally well with any delicate variety, such as winter squash, carrot, or fish.

½ cup unsalted butter

1 shallot, minced

2 tablespoons poppy seeds, or to taste

2 teaspoons finely grated lemon zest

Salt and freshly ground black pepper to taste

¼ cup fresh mint leaves, shredded

Freshly grated Parmigiano-Reggiano for the table

Melt butter in large skillet over medium heat and add minced shallot. Cook, stirring, until soft, about 2 minutes. Add poppy seeds and cook, stirring constantly, until fragrant, about 2 minutes. Remove from the heat; stir in the lemon zest and season with salt and freshly ground black pepper to taste.

Add cooked gnocchi and shredded mint to the sauce. Toss to coat.

SAGE-BUTTER SAUCE

/ enough for 4 to 6 servings

Sage butter is the quintessential sauce for many popular gnocchi, especially the potato-squash gnocchi from the northern regions of Italy. Experiment by varying the basic recipe with some of the suggested garnishes. My favorite variation is to add smoked ricotta and cinnamon to the sauce, with or without the hazelnuts. The sauce is equally good dribbled over roasted vegetables, such as slightly sweet kabocha or butternut squash.

4 small shallots

½ cup unsalted butter

Salt and freshly ground black pepper to taste

16 fresh sage leaves, finely slivered (or to taste)

Fried whole sage leaves for garnish (recipe below)

Peel and thinly slice the shallots. Put the butter and shallots in a small, light-colored saucepan over medium heat. Cook 5 to 10 minutes, or until shallots and butter are golden brown. Watch carefully so the butter doesn't burn. (Using a light-colored saucepan will allow you to see the true color of the butter.)

Add the slivered sage leaves, freshly ground black pepper, and salt to taste. Set aside and keep warm. When ready to serve, toss the sauce with the cooked gnocchi and garnish with the fried sage leaves (page 222).

Variations: Eliminate shallots and brown the butter; add ½ cup toasted and chopped hazelnuts; garnish with smoked ricotta, cinnamon, and a dash of sugar.

SAGRANTINO CREAM SAUCE

/ enough for 6 to 8 servings

Because Perugia is my second home, I'm partial to the fact that Sagrantino, the grape varietal that makes this recipe so special, grows only in the hilltops surrounding Montefalco, Umbria, and nowhere else in the world. The grape's origins are unknown, and whether or not it's indigenous to the area is debatable. Indisputable, however, is that the wine produced is Umbrian at its soul. It's a gutsy, powerful, and tannic wine with deep purple and ruby colors, usually taking at least 10 years of aging to be appreciated. The sauce will be pink — a bit shocking to some — but the subtle, deep wine flavor and creamy texture is sublime.

You can substitute a naturally cured, unsmoked bacon for the guanciale with good results, as long as it's sliced paper thin and minced. If you want a creamier sauce, you can purée it in a blender before reheating and serving.

1 tablespoon extra-virgin olive oil

1 tablespoon unsalted butter

2 ounces guanciale or pancetta, minced

1 small yellow onion, grated, about ½ cup

1½ cups robust red wine, such as Sagrantino

1¼ cups heavy cream

Freshly ground black pepper to taste

¼ cup finely grated fresh Parmigiano-Reggiano
    + more for garnish

Fresh parsley, finely chopped, for garnish

Melt oil and butter in a 12-inch skillet over medium-low heat. Add guanciale and cook slowly until the guanciale renders its fat, about 5 minutes. Add the onion and cook until soft. Add the wine and cook until the liquid is reduced by half, about 10 minutes. Add the cream, salt, and pepper. Bring to a simmer to blend flavors and remove from heat.

When ready to serve, add the freshly grated Parmigiano-Reggiano to the sauce and reheat over low heat, stirring well to combine. Garnish with the additional finely grated fresh Parmigiano and finely chopped parsley.

THYME-GARLIC BUTTER SAUCE

/   enough for 4 to 6 servings

A simple sauce that's easy to make and divine with any
savory gnocchi that screams for butter.

1 medium shallot

1 large clove garlic

½ cup unsalted butter

1 tablespoon chopped fresh thyme

2 teaspoons finely grated fresh lemon zest

Salt and freshly ground black pepper to taste

Crispy sautéed strips of thinly sliced prosciutto or
    speck (optional)

Finely grated fresh Parmigiano-Reggiano (optional)

Finely mince the shallot and garlic. In a small saucepan, heat the butter, garlic, and shallot over medium
heat just until the garlic and shallot begin to sizzle.
Be careful not to brown them. Remove from the heat
and add the chopped thyme and lemon zest. Season
to taste with salt and freshly ground black pepper. Set
aside until ready to use. Toss with cooked gnocchi and
garnish if you choose.

SAVORY ZABAGLIONE WITH HORSERADISH CREAM

/   enough for 6 to 8 servings

This is a savory version of the traditional sweet zabaglione.
It's rich and creamy, and balances beautifully with the slight
sweetness of beet gnocchi or canederli. It's also wonderful with
cabbage- or carrot-based gnocchi. You can adjust the thickness
of the sauce with light or heavy cream, or extra white wine.
You can also use Champagne instead of white wine — but
don't substitute prepared horseradish for the fresh; it contains
chemicals and additives that will adversely affect the flavor
of the sauce.

¼ cup dry white wine

8 large egg yolks

⅔ cup finely grated fresh horseradish, or to taste

1½ teaspoons salt

Fresh coarsely ground black pepper to taste

4-6 tablespoons heavy cream

In a medium saucepan, bring 2 to 3 cups of water to boil.
Place the wine and egg yolks in a copper or stainless
mixing bowl that can sit over the water without touching
it. Whisk vigorously until smooth, then place the bowl over
the simmering water. Cook the eggs and wine, whisking
constantly, until the sauce becomes frothy and thick, 5 to
10 minutes.

Remove from the heat and whisk in the horseradish, salt,
and generous grindings of black pepper to taste. Thin the
sauce with heavy cream until it resembles thick buttermilk.

Cover and keep warm while finishing the gnocchi. Make
and serve the sauce immediately. Do not refrigerate.

WHITE TRUFFLE & CREAM SAUCE

/ enough for 4 to 6 servings

White truffles have a following — and those who love them are willing to pay a high price for the privilege of eating them. They are more intensely aromatic than black truffles and do not stand up to heat, thus are not interchangeable in recipes where heat is applied. The aromatics that give the white truffle its distinctive flavor are not sensed by the tongue, but by the nose. The aromatics evaporate when heated, so they are always added to a dish just before serving. All you need to showcase a white truffle is a very simple sauce of butter, cream, high-quality Parmigiano-Reggiano — and a simple potato or ricotta cheese gnocchi to compliment it.

Plan on 5 to 6 grams of truffle per person, or about 5 servings per ounce. Fresh white truffles have a short season, from September through December, and can be purchased through a variety of sources in the U.S. It's possible to purchase canned white truffles, but they are inferior to fresh ones. White truffle oil lightly splashed over the finished dish is another viable way to extend the truffle flavor, but be sure to purchase natural rather than synthetic oil. (See page 243 for more information.) This is a dish I save for very special occasions; once enjoyed, it is never forgotten.

½ cup unsalted butter at room temperature

1 cup heavy cream

¾ cup finely grated fresh Parmigiano-Reggiano

About 1 ounce fresh white truffle, for garnish

White truffle oil, for garnish

In a saucepan large enough to hold the gnocchi once it's cooked, heat the cream and butter over low heat. Add the grated cheese and continue to heat, stirring, until the cheese has melted. Keep warm while cooking the gnocchi.

As the gnocchi rise to the top, remove with a slotted spoon, drain well, and toss them with the sauce. Portion into warmed serving bowls and garnish with very thin shavings of truffle and a splash of white truffle oil, if using. Serve immediately.

ARUGULA PESTO

/ enough for 10 servings

Be sure to use baby arugula; older arugula can be too sharp and bitter for this pesto. Plan on 2 to 3 tablespoons per serving. If you're an arugula fan, this mild pesto may become a favorite of yours so be sure to make some extra to top your favorite pasta, sautéed chicken, grilled fish, or bruschette.

⅓ cup shelled pine nuts

1 clove garlic, chopped

2 cups packed, chopped baby arugula

1 tablespoon finely grated lemon zest

½-1 cup extra-virgin olive oil

¼ cup finely grated semi-aged pecorino
    (not Pecorino Romano)

¼ cup finely grated fresh Parmigiano-Reggiano

Salt and finely ground black pepper to taste

BY HAND

Using a large mortar and pestle, crush the garlic and pine nuts with ½ teaspoon salt, then add the arugula leaves. Grind them until you have a fine paste. Add the lemon zest and drizzle in the olive oil, beating the mixture all the while with a wooden spoon. Stir in the cheeses. Add more olive oil if necessary to make a sauce-like consistency. It should be thinner than a pesto. Add salt and freshly ground black pepper to taste.

IN A FOOD PROCESSOR

Use the same ingredients in the following order: Process the garlic, salt, and pine nuts until finely chopped, then add the arugula, lemon zest, and olive oil. When smooth, add the cheese and process just to combine. It should be thinner than a regular pesto. Add salt and freshly ground black pepper to taste.

Toss the pesto with hot gnocchi in a bowl. Never heat the sauce in the pan or it will cook the cheese. It will keep in refrigerator for two weeks with a thin layer of olive oil covering it. A loss of color does not affect the flavor.

Variation: Top each serving with a small handful of halved cherry tomatoes that have been tossed with a bit of extra-virgin olive oil and salted to taste.

BASIL PESTO GENOVESE

/ enough for 10 to 12 servings

Although the modern food processor makes it easy to make pesto, it's well worth making it by hand. The process of hand grinding the ingredients produces a pesto that tastes remarkably better. Use Genovese basil for best results. Even better, grow your own year round on a sunny windowsill. Plan on 1 heaping tablespoon per serving, always starting with less rather than more.

2 large garlic cloves

3 tablespoons pine nuts

3 cups loosely packed basil leaves, stems removed, leaves washed and dried, torn into small pieces

½ cup finely grated fresh Parmigiano-Reggiano

½ cup extra-virgin olive oil

Salt to taste

BY HAND

Using a large mortar and pestle, crush the garlic with ½ teaspoon salt and the pine nuts to break them up, then add the basil leaves a handful at a time. Grind them, using a circular motion, until you have a fairly fine paste. Drizzle in the olive oil, beating the mixture all the while with a wooden spoon. Stir in the Parmigiano-Reggiano. Taste for salt and adjust the seasoning.

IN A FOOD PROCESSOR

Use the same ingredients but in the following order: Process the garlic, salt, and pine nuts until fairly finely chopped, then add the basil and olive oil. When smooth, add the cheese and process just to combine. Taste for salt and adjust the seasoning.

If using the pesto to sauce gnocchi or pasta, toss it in a bowl while they are hot. Never heat the sauce in the pan or it will cook the cheese.

The pesto will keep in the refrigerator for two weeks with a thin layer of olive oil covering it. A loss of color does not affect the flavor.

SAGE PESTO

/ enough for 8 to 10 servings

This pesto is made the same way as a traditional basil pesto, substituting sage and mint for the basil. It compliments any of the gnocchi that are traditionally sauced with browned butter and sage, and makes an interesting replacement for basil pesto. I love it with a simply prepared chicken, fish, lamb, or pork, slathered on bruschette, dolloped on bean soup, and as a pasta sauce. Plan on 2 tablespoons per serving, always starting with less rather than more.

1 cup packed fresh young sage leaves

⅛ cup packed fresh mint leaves

2 garlic cloves, sliced

1 teaspoon grated lemon zest

½ cup chopped walnuts

½ cup finely grated fresh Parmigiano-Reggiano

About ½ cup extra virgin olive oil

Finely chop the sage and mint leaves and place in a food processor. Add the walnuts, lemon zest, and garlic. Pulse a few times until mixture is coarsely ground. Add about ¼ cup olive oil and pulse until well combined. Add the cheese and pulse again. Add the remaining oil and process until the mixture is thick, but still chunky. Do not overmix. Place in a bowl and add salt and freshly ground pepper to taste.

If serving this pesto with gnocchi, thin the sauce with about ¼ cup of the hot cooking water before tossing with the cooked gnocchi.

Toss the pesto with hot gnocchi in a bowl. Never heat the sauce in the pan or it will cook the cheese.

This pesto will keep in the refrigerator for two weeks with a thin layer of olive oil covering it. A loss of color does not affect the flavor.

SUN-DRIED TOMATO & OLIVE PESTO

/ enough for 8 servings

This is another one of my favorite pestos to keep on hand for a variety of uses. I particularly love it with sautéed shrimp for a quick dinner. Or try it with grilled chicken, fish, or your favorite pasta. It's extremely quick and easy to prepare, especially if you start with already pitted olives. Plan on 2 tablespoons per serving, always starting with less rather than more.

20 sun-dried tomatoes in oil, without herbs or
    added flavorings

2 large garlic cloves, minced

1 teaspoon hot red pepper flakes (or to taste)

¾ cup extra-virgin olive oil

40 salt-cured black olives, such as Gaeta, pitted

1 tablespoon minced fresh thyme leaves

2 tablespoons minced fresh rosemary

In the bowl of a food processor, combine all the ingredients and process until the sauce is lightly emulsified but still coarse and a bit chunky. Do not overprocess.

Toss the pesto with hot gnocchi in a bowl. It will keep in the refrigerator for two weeks with a thin layer of olive oil covering it. This pesto can also be frozen.

PISTACHIO-ALMOND PESTO

/ enough for 8 to 10 servings

The combination of pistachio, almond, and orange make this a Sicilian classic. Semi-aged pecorino is the more traditional cheese in this pesto, but Parmigiano-Reggiano can be used with equally good results.

½ cup shelled unsalted pistachios, toasted

½ cup whole almonds, toasted

Pinch hot red pepper flakes

1 clove garlic, peeled and roughly chopped

⅓ cup packed fresh mint leaves, finely chopped

1 teaspoon finely grated lemon zest

1 teaspoon orange flower water (optional)

½ cup extra-virgin olive oil

¼ cup finely grated fresh Parmigiano-Reggiano or
    semi-aged pecorino

Salt and freshly ground black pepper

WITH A MORTAR AND PESTLE

Crush the garlic with a pinch of salt and the pepper flakes until it forms a rough paste. Add the pistachios and almonds. Continue pounding until the mixture forms a coarse meal. Add the mint, lemon zest, and optional orange flower water to the nuts, and pound until combined. Drizzle in the olive oil, beating the mixture all the while with a wooden spoon. Stir in the pecorino or Parmigiano-Reggiano. Add salt and pepper to taste.

IN A FOOD PROCESSOR

Process the garlic, salt, pepper flakes, and nuts until fairly finely chopped, then add the mint, optional orange flower water, lemon zest, and olive oil. The mixture should resemble a coarse meal, not a smooth paste. Empty the pesto into a bowl and stir in the cheese. Add salt and pepper to taste. Be careful not to over-process. Toss the pesto with the hot gnocchi in a bowl. Never heat the sauce in the pan or it will cook the cheese. This pesto will keep in the refrigerator for two weeks with a thin layer of olive oil covering it.

RADISH & TURNIP PESTO

/ enough for 12 servings

This unique, and very welcome addition to the pesto collection was created by my friend and dedicated recipe tester, Anne Ritchings. Feta cheese and bitter greens create a spin-off from the usual basil pesto. Plan on 3 generous tablespoons per serving.

"Whenever I buy vegetables with their tops attached, such as radishes, beets, or turnips," Anne said, "I am a bit mystified by what to do with those leafy greens. Sometimes I sauté them and serve them with whatever else is on the menu, but that doesn't seem quite the right solution in spring. With this batch of beautiful, leafy tops I decided that I would make pesto. I adapted Martha Phelps Stamps' recipe for Spring Pesto from Martha's at the Plantation as the basis for this, and I have to say that the result is extremely tasty."

3-4 cups, packed, soft leafy greens from vegetables, such as radish, Daikon radish, and Japanese turnip greens, thoroughly washed, tough stems removed, and coarsely chopped

¾ cup finely grated fresh Parmigiano-Reggiano

3 cloves garlic, roughly chopped

2 tablespoons capers

Juice and zest of 1 lemon

Salt and red pepper flakes to taste

1 cup of olive oil

Place the mixed greens in the bowl of a food processor. Pulse to coarsely chop. Add the remaining ingredients and process to a roughly textured paste. Toss the pesto with hot gnocchi in a bowl. Never heat the sauce in the pan or it will cook the cheese. This pesto will keep in the refrigerator for two weeks with a thin layer of olive oil covering it. A loss of color does not affect the flavor. This pesto can also be frozen for up to 1 month.

Recipe contributed by Anne Ritchings

UMBRIAN HERBED PESTO

/ enough for 4 to 6 servings

Years ago I started making this pesto in Italy, where I have an herb garden on the balcony. The combination of basil, mint, and chives is an aromatic marriage like no other. And, because it all is chopped together rather than ground in a mortar and pestle, the texture is not like that of a more traditional pesto. Plan on 2 tablespoons per serving, always starting with less rather than more. One of my favorites!

⅛ teaspoon salt, or more to taste

2 large cloves garlic

1 cup tightly packed, coarsely chopped fresh chives

3 tablespoons tightly packed fresh basil leaves

1 tablespoon tightly packed fresh mint leaves

½ medium red onion, halved

⅓ cup pine nuts

2 tablespoons + 2 teaspoons extra-virgin olive oil

Freshly ground black pepper

Finely grated fresh Parmigiano-Reggiano for the table

Make a small pile of the salt on a chopping board. Crush the garlic into it with the side of a large knife and finely chop. Add the herbs and half the onion and chop until finely minced. Add the pine nuts and coarsely chop. Blend in 2 tablespoons of the oil right on the board and season to taste with the pepper.

Finely chop the remaining onion. In a small skillet, heat the remaining 2 teaspoons of the oil, add the onion, and sauté until it softens. Remove from heat. Add the herb mixture from the chopping board to the skillet, stir to mix well, and taste for seasoning.

Toss the pesto with hot gnocchi in a bowl. It will keep in the refrigerator for two weeks with a thin layer of olive oil covering it. A loss of color does not affect the flavor.

ZUCCHINI PESTO

/ enough for 6 to 8 servings

A variation of the traditional Genovese-style pesto, the addition of zucchini makes a lighter tasting sauce. It's good with any gnocchi where a strong basil flavor is desired. Plan on 3 tablespoons per serving, always starting with less rather than more.

4 tablespoons extra-virgin olive oil

1 medium zucchini (about 2 cups sliced)

¼ cup pine nuts

12 large fresh basil leaves

1 clove garlic, minced

Pinch red pepper flakes

Warm 2 tablespoons of olive oil in a skillet over medium heat and add the zucchini. Sauté 5 minutes, until soft, and most of the liquid is evaporated. Transfer to a food processor along with the pine nuts, basil, garlic, and red pepper flakes. Pulse, adding the remaining 2 tablespoons olive oil in slowly.

Toss the pesto with hot gnocchi in a bowl. It will keep in the refrigerator for two weeks with a thin layer of olive oil covering it. A loss of color does not affect the flavor.

CAVOLO NERO & HORSERADISH PESTO

/ enough for 6 to 8 servings

An odd combination? Perhaps — but it's a delicious and versatile one. Known as rafano *or* barbaforte *in Italian, horseradish grows in the colder regions of Italy, including Friuli Venezia Giulia, Veneto, Lombardia, Emilia-Romagna, and Piedmonte, where it's a commonly used ingredient in sauces and a favored accompaniment to Bollito Misto, or mixed boiled meats, a classic northern Italian stew often served on festive occasions.*

Plan on 2 to 3 tablespoons per serving. You can also try this pesto on your favorite pasta or grilled meat.

¼ pound Italian cavolo nero or other kale leaves, stems removed

2 cups fresh basil leaves

⅓ cup pine nuts, toasted

2 cloves garlic, minced

2 tablespoons finely grated fresh horseradish

½ cup extra-virgin olive oil

⅓ cup finely grated fresh Parmigiano-Reggiano

Kosher salt and freshly ground black pepper to taste

Lightly blanch the kale leaves in boiling water for about 1 minute. Remove and drain until cool enough to handle. Using a dishtowel or paper towels, squeeze all the water from the kale and coarsely chop.

In a food processor, process the garlic, pine nuts, and horseradish until fairly finely chopped, then add the basil, kale, and olive oil. When the pesto is smooth, add the cheese and process just to combine. Taste for salt and adjust seasoning. Toss the pesto with hot gnocchi in a bowl. Never heat the sauce in the pan or it will cook the cheese.

This pesto will keep in the refrigerator two weeks with a thin layer of olive oil covering it. A loss of color does not affect the flavor.

GARLIC SCAPE PESTO

/ enough for 8 servings

Garlic scapes, commonly found in Italian markets in late spring, are becoming a popular item in farmer's markets in the U.S. as well. Scapes are the soft stems and unopened flower buds of the garlic. Removed to encourage the plant to increase the size of the bulb, they can be used to replace garlic in any recipe. Scapes have a slight sweetness and a milder flavor than mature garlic, which makes them a perfect candidate for pesto. If you grow your own garlic, trim off the scapes before the flowers open. Plan on 2 to 3 tablespoons per serving, always starting with less rather than more.

10-12 garlic scapes sliced into ½-inch pieces to
    make 1 cup

½ cup pine nuts, unsalted pistachios, or sunflower seeds

1 tablespoon freshly squeezed lemon juice

⅓ cup extra-virgin olive oil

¼ cup finely grated fresh Parmigiano-Reggiano

Kosher salt and freshly ground black pepper to taste

Pulse the garlic scapes in a food processor for about 30 seconds, or until they are broken down. Add the nuts and pulse until well combined. Add the lemon juice and olive oil and process until smooth. Add the cheese and mix just to combine. Season with salt and pepper to taste.

Toss the pesto with hot gnocchi in a bowl. Never heat the sauce in the pan or it will cook the cheese.

This pesto will keep in the refrigerator for two weeks with a thin layer of olive oil covering it. A loss of color does not affect the flavor.

OLIVE-MINT PESTO

/ enough for 8 to 10 servings

I try to keep this pesto on hand because of its versatility. It's wonderful with lamb, chicken, and pork as well as with cheeses, bruschette, and many of the gnocchi in this collection. You can easily vary the flavor of the pesto by changing the combination of olives you choose, or by eliminating the anchovies. Plan on 2 to 3 tablespoons per serving, always starting with less rather than more.

¼ cup chopped flat-leaf parsley

½ cup chopped mint leaves

1 cup cured mixed green and black olives, such as
    Sicilian, Kalamata, and oil-cured, pitted and chopped

1 lemon, finely zested

2 anchovy fillets, rinsed and minced (optional)

1 garlic clove, minced

⅓ cup extra-virgin olive oil

Salt and freshly ground black pepper to taste

On a chopping surface, combine the parsley, mint, olives, lemon zest, optional anchovies, and garlic. Finely chop all the ingredients together until mixed well. Scrape into a small bowl, add the olive oil, and mix well. Season with salt and pepper and set aside.

Toss the pesto with hot gnocchi in a bowl. It will keep in the refrigerator for two weeks with a thin layer of olive oil covering it.

ARTICHOKE & SAUSAGE SAUCE

/ enough for 6 servings

This is a wonderful sauce to celebrate the spring or fall artichoke harvest. It will complement any basic gnocchi such as potato, ricotta, semolina, or canederli. Use only fresh artichokes for this sauce, stem included.

4 medium artichokes

1 lemon

2 tablespoons extra-virgin olive oil

2 cloves garlic, minced

8 ounces sausage, casings removed, crumbled

¼ cup pine nuts, lightly toasted

Freshly ground black pepper

¾ cup low-sodium chicken broth, preferably homemade

¾ cup warm water

2 tablespoons butter

½ cup finely grated fresh Parmigiano-Reggiano

2 tablespoons finely chopped parsley

Squeeze a lemon into a large bowl of water and drop the lemon into the water. Snap off the dark green outer leaves of the artichoke. Slice off all but 1 inch of the remaining leaves. Peel and trim the bottom stem of the artichoke. Halve the artichokes and scoop out the furry choke. Cut the artichoke halves in half again and add to the lemon water, stem and all. Remove the artichokes from the water and finely chop the stems and hearts into small pieces, no larger than ⅛ inch.

Put the olive oil, garlic, and the crumbled sausage in a skillet over medium heat and sauté until the sausage is browned. Add the artichoke pieces, season with salt and pepper, and cook until the artichoke pieces are lightly browned and begin to soften. Add the chicken broth and water and simmer over low heat for about 10 minutes. Add more water if needed to keep the artichokes from drying out. Add the butter, other ingredients, or herbs, and stir to mix well. Toss with the cooked gnocchi. Garnish with Parmigiano and parsley.

CHESTNUT, PANCETTA & SAGE SAUCE

/ enough for 6 to 8 servings

This is a wonderful sauce to celebrate fall and winter. Even though fresh chestnuts may be available, the texture and flavor of the bottled ones work best because of their added sweetness and softer texture. A fine complement to squash or sweet potato gnocchi, this is an equally good sauce with simple potato or ricotta gnocchi. If I'm not in the mood for gnocchi, I also use this sauce to dress various hefty pasta shapes, such as penne, strozzapreti (another name for priest strangler), or the Sicilian whole-grain pasta called busiate.

¼ pound thinly sliced pancetta, shredded

1 tablespoon extra-virgin olive oil

1 small onion, halved and very thinly sliced

4 garlic cloves, minced

2 tablespoons finely shredded fresh sage

10 ounces bottled roasted whole chestnuts, coarsely crumbled (2 cups)

1 cup low-sodium chicken broth, preferably homemade

½ cup heavy cream (optional)

Finely grated fresh Parmigiano-Reggiano, OR Grana Padano for garnish

In a heavy sauté pan, cook the pancetta in olive oil over medium heat, stirring frequently, until it begins to render its fat, about 2 to 3 minutes. Add the onion and continue to sauté, stirring frequently until onion is translucent, about 2 minutes more. Add the garlic, stir for 1 minute, and add the shredded sage. Add chestnuts and chicken broth. Bring to a boil and reduce the sauce for 1 minute, or just until it begins to thicken.

For a creamier and richer sauce, add the heavy cream. Reheat until bubbles form, then set aside and keep warm.

CHICKEN SAUSAGE & FENNEL SAUCE

/ enough for 6 to 8 servings

Cooked fennel has a unique flavor that marries well with mildly flavored chicken sausage. It's critical to slice the fennel very thin, or it will not melt into the sauce. It should be limp when cooked, not chunky.

1 pound chicken sausage, casings removed
   OR ground chicken

3 tablespoons extra-virgin olive oil

1 clove garlic, minced

One pinch of peperoncini flakes

1 teaspoon fennel seeds, ground fine in a spice
   grinder or mortar and pestle
   OR ½ teaspoon fennel pollen (page 245)

1 small fennel bulb, very finely sliced, to make 2 cups

½ cup dry white wine

1 cup low-sodium chicken broth, preferably homemade

½ cup heavy cream

Shaved ricotta salata for serving

Finely chopped fresh parsley leaves

In a sauté pan over medium heat, warm 2 tablespoons olive oil and add the sausage or ground chicken. Cook until it begins to brown. Put aside on a plate.

Add the remaining olive oil to the sauté pan and add the garlic, peperoncini, and ground fennel or fennel pollen. Stir and add the sliced fennel. Turn the heat to medium-low and cook, stirring, until the fennel is very soft and caramelized. Add the white wine and chicken broth, scraping up the browned bits from the bottom of the pan. Reduce the sauce over medium-high heat to 1 cup. Add the cooked sausage and the heavy cream, and simmer over low heat until the sauce reaches a medium-thick consistency. Toss with cooked gnocchi. Serve immediately garnished with shaved ricotta salata and chopped parsley.

MIXED MUSHROOM & SAUSAGE SAUCE

/ enough for 4 to 6 servings

This sauce includes a variety of mushrooms as well as meaty sausage. You can choose any available mushrooms, and even eliminate the porcini if you prefer a lighter flavored sauce. The sauce is relatively thin; if you want it thicker, add some heavy cream to taste. For a meatless mushroom sauce, see page 216.

½ cup dried porcini mushrooms

2 tablespoons extra-virgin olive oil

½ pound bulk sweet Italian sausage,
   OR links with casings removed

2 thinly sliced shallots

¼ pound shitake mushrooms, cleaned and
   coarsely chopped

¼ pound cremini or white mushrooms, cleaned and
   coarsely chopped

Salt and freshly ground pepper to taste

3 sun-dried tomatoes packed in oil, drained and
   coarsely chopped

2 tablespoons unsalted butter

Soak the porcini in boiling water until softened, about 15 minutes. Drain and reserve the soaking liquid. Strain through a very fine sieve if necessary to remove any dirt. Coarsely chop the porcini and set aside. In a skillet, heat 1 tablespoon of the oil over medium-high. Add the sausage and shallots and cook, stirring, until sausage is no longer pink. Remove to a bowl and set aside. Add the remaining oil to the skillet over medium-high heat. Add all the fresh mushrooms and cook until they are tender and release their moisture. Pour in the porcini, the soaking liquid, and the sun-dried tomatoes, and stir with a wooden spoon to release the browned bits from the bottom of the pan. Add the reserved sausage mixture. Cover and cook over medium heat for 4 minutes, adding more liquid if necessary to keep the sauce from drying out. Season with salt and freshly ground black pepper to taste. Take the pan off the heat, swirl in the butter, and sprinkle with parsley. The sauce will be thin.

FRESH FAVA BEAN & PANCETTA SAUCE

/ enough for 6 to 8 servings

Fresh fava or broad beans, a Mediterranean staple, arrive around the first of May in Umbria, and the season is short, lasting only into the first part of June. The first fava beans are usually sold when still small, and are traditionally eaten raw with salt, olive oil, good bread, and a hunk of fresh pecorino cheese. When larger and more mature, they make a wonderful simple soup, something I look forward to every year. I always freeze some of the older ones for using later in a variety of ways, such as a traditional purée for bruschette.

Look for fresh fava beans in your local markets. They're definitely worth the preparation time. One pound in the pod will equal about 1 cup shelled. For this recipe, I recommend medium-size favas for their creamier texture. You can substitute frozen lima beans for this sauce if fava beans are not available.

2 pounds fresh fava beans in the pod, to make 2 cups
   when blanched and peeled

4 ounces thick-cut pancetta or naturally smoked
   bacon, diced into ⅛-inch pieces

1 shallot, minced

1 clove garlic, minced
   OR 2 spring garlic shoots, chopped

2 teaspoons finely minced fresh thyme or rosemary

¾ cup dry white wine

½ cup heavy cream

Vegetable or chicken broth to thin the sauce (as needed)

Finely grated rind of 1 lemon

Salt and freshly ground black pepper to taste

Freshly grated ricotta salata or aged pecorino
   (not Romano) shavings

Slivered chives or finely chopped parsley

Shell the fava beans. Cook shelled fava beans in boiling salted water for 2 minutes. Transfer with a slotted spoon to ice water; cool and drain. Gently peel if skins are tough and set aside. You should have 2 cups.

In a large, deep sauté pan over medium heat, cook the pancetta until very crisp. Drain all but 1 tablespoon of fat, add the shallot, garlic, and rosemary to the pan and cook until the shallot just begins to soften, about 1 minute. Add the wine, deglazing the pan and scraping the bits from the bottom. When the liquid has reduced by half, add the heavy cream and lemon rind. Reduce slightly to make a creamy sauce. If desired, you may add some broth to thin it. Stir in the favas and keep warm while cooking the gnocchi.

To serve, toss the cooked gnocchi with the sauce, divide among warmed shallow serving bowls, and garnish with cheese and herbs.

Variations: Substitute ½ pound bulk Italian sausage for the pancetta and cook until it is no longer pink. Eliminate the pancetta and garnish with shavings of bottarga (See page 244 for more information.)

PANCETTA-ORANGE SAUCE

/   enough for 6 servings

This is a rich and deeply flavored sauce that should barely coat the gnocchi and leave a shallow pool in the bottom of the bowl so you can swirl each gnocco in the sauce before eating it. I particularly love this one with beet gnocchi showered with smoked ricotta.

4-6 ounces medium-thick sliced pancetta or natural
    bacon, finely chopped
2 cloves garlic, minced
½ cup dry white wine
¾ cup low-sodium chicken broth, preferably homemade
½ cup freshly squeezed orange juice
2 tablespoons unsalted butter, melted
1 tablespoon fresh rosemary, minced
Salt and freshly ground black pepper to taste
Heavy cream (optional)
Toasted walnuts, coarsely chopped
Finely grated orange rind
Freshly grated Parmigiano-Reggiano or other hard
    grating cheese for serving

In a medium sauté pan over medium-high heat, fry the pancetta until crisp and all the fat is rendered. Pour off all but 1 tablespoon of the fat. Add the minced garlic and heat until it begins to sizzle. Add the wine, broth, and orange juice. Turn the heat down to a simmer and reduce the liquid by half. Remove from the heat and quickly stir in the melted butter and minced rosemary. Add salt and freshly ground black pepper to taste.

This is a fairly thin sauce. If you prefer a thicker sauce, add a few tablespoons of heavy cream.

Toss immediately with cooked gnocchi, and garnish with toasted walnuts and orange rind. Pass the finely grated fresh Parmigiano-Reggiano at the table.

Variations: You may substitute red wine for the white, beef broth for the chicken, and sage or mint for the rosemary.

LAMB & ROASTED SWEET PEPPER RAGÙ

/   enough for 6 servings

One of my favorite ragùs typical of the Abruzzo region features lamb and peppers. Many regional recipes use ground lamb, but I prefer small chunks that cook down to make a tender, meaty sauce, along with roasted rather than raw peppers. The slightly smoky roasted flavor adds depth to the finished sauce. For maximum quality and flavor, roast your own peppers and buy the lamb from a local source when available; this will duplicate the Italian ingredients as closely as possible.

1 pound boneless lamb, trimmed of extra fat,
    coarsely chopped into ⅛-inch pieces
¼ cup extra-virgin olive oil
5 garlic cloves, thinly sliced
4 bay leaves
1 cup dry white wine
4 plum tomatoes, peeled, seeded, and diced into
    ¼-inch pieces
4 sweet bell peppers, red, orange, yellow, or mixed,
    roasted, peeled, seeded and cut into long thin strips
4-6 large fresh basil leaves, slivered
Salt and freshly ground black pepper to taste

Heat the olive oil, garlic, and bay leaves in a deep pot over medium heat. Cook about 1 minute, until the garlic begins to sizzle. Add the lamb, turn the heat to medium high, and cook, stirring frequently, until deeply browned, about 10 minutes. Add the wine and cook, stirring to deglaze the bottom of the pan. When the wine has evaporated, about 10 minutes, add the tomatoes and pepper strips. Cover and simmer about 2 hours, stirring occasionally, until the flavors have developed and the lamb is tender. You may need to add a bit of water to keep the sauce from sticking or burning. The sauce should as thick as a stew when done. Add fresh basil and salt and pepper to taste and remove bay leaves before serving.

The ragù can be made three days ahead. Cover and refrigerate it until ready to use. It also freezes well for up to 1 month.

BASIC SOUTHERN ITALIAN RAGÙ

/ enough for 6 to 8 servings

This is my go-to basic southern-style ragù with lots of tomato and chunks of meat. It can be easily varied by using a different braising meat, such as beef short ribs, chuck, round, brisket, pork shoulder, or Boston butt. Lamb shoulder and shanks, chicken thighs, venison, boar, pigeon, and rabbit are also often used in Italy. The key to a deeply flavorful ragù is to use bone-in, fatty cuts of meat — and not skimp on the browning process.

2 pounds braising meat

2 tablespoons extra-virgin olive oil

1 tablespoon each fresh rosemary and fresh thyme, finely chopped

1 medium onion, peeled and finely chopped

4-6 garlic cloves, peeled and finely chopped

1 carrot, peeled and finely chopped

1 stalk celery, finely chopped

2 tablespoons red wine vinegar

3 crushed dried red chile peppers, or to taste

Ground cloves and cinnamon, to taste (optional)

3 sun-dried tomatoes, chopped

1 cup dry red wine

1 28-ounce can plum tomatoes or equivalent fresh tomatoes, peeled and coarsely chopped

Salt and freshly ground black pepper to taste

Season the meat with salt and pepper. If the cut is large, cut into pieces that will fit into a heavy 4-5 quart saucepan.

Heat the saucepan and olive oil over medium-high until the oil begins to shimmer. Add the meat and sauté, turning occasionally, until the meat is deep brown on all sides. Turn the heat down to medium to protect the glaze that forms on the bottom of the pan, and cook about 10 minutes more, or until the meats are a deep brown. Add the herbs, onions, garlic, carrot, and celery. Turn the heat down again and continue to cook for another 5 minutes, or until the vegetables have softened. Add the vinegar, red wine, peppers, sun-dried tomatoes, and optional spices, raise the heat to medium-high, and continue to simmer until the liquid has almost cooked away.

Add the plum tomatoes and just enough water to cover the meat by a half inch. Cover and cook over low heat for about 2 to 3 hours, or until the meat is completely tender. Add more water if necessary to keep it from burning. The total cooking time will vary by the type of meat used.

Allow the ragù to cool slightly before removing the meat from the pan. Pull apart or chop the meat, discarding any bones. Skim the fat from the surface of the braising liquid and put the meat back in the pan. Cook, uncovered, at a slow simmer, until the sauce is thick. Season to taste with salt and pepper.

Set aside or keep warm until ready to use.

The ragù can be made three days ahead. Cover and refrigerate it until ready to use. It also freezes well for up to 1 month.

OXTAIL RAGÙ

/ enough for 12 to 16 servings

During a cooking/teaching trip to Ramekins Cooking School in Sonoma, California, my friend Lisa Lavagetto made this sauce for me — and it's undoubtedly one of the most deeply flavorful and satisfying ragùs I've ever tasted. A southern Italian-style ragù, the meat is cooked on the bone and the sauce includes a goodly amount of tomato. A large amount of chopped aromatic vegetables known as soffritto or battuto, form the flavor base of the sauce.

Oxtails can be difficult to find. As my butcher in Italy reminded me, c'e solo una coda per vacca — there's only one tail per cow — and the availability of oxtail will depend on the demand for this cut in your area. Ask before assuming it's not available: it's worth the search. In the U.S., you may find it in the frozen section of the market by the pet bones. The oxtail may be precut into pieces, or it may be one whole piece. If it's whole, ask your butcher to cut it between the joints.

2½ pounds oxtails, cut between the joints

Salt and freshly ground black pepper to taste

⅓ pound finely diced pancetta

   OR naturally cured bacon

2 medium yellow onions, chopped (about 2 cups)

2 medium carrots, peeled and shredded (about 1 cup)

1 cup chopped celery, with leaves

⅓ cup chopped fresh Italian parsley

3 garlic cloves, peeled and chopped

2 cups dry white wine

One 35-ounce can Italian plum tomatoes
   (preferably San Marzano) with their liquid, crushed

3 to 4 cups low-sodium chicken stock or broth,
   preferably homemade

Freshly grated Grana Padano or Parmigiano-
   Reggiano for serving

Soak the oxtails in cold water to cover for 30 minutes. Drain thoroughly and pat them dry. Season both sides of the oxtail pieces with salt and pepper.

Sauté the pancetta in a heavy pan or Dutch oven over medium heat. Add as many oxtail pieces as will fit without crowding into the pan. Cook, turning, until golden brown on all sides, about 10 minutes. If necessary, remove the pieces as they brown to make room in the pan for remaining pieces. Remove all the oxtail pieces from the pan.

Stir in the onion, carrot, celery, parsley, and garlic. Season lightly with salt and pepper and cook, stirring, until the vegetables are wilted, about 4 minutes. Pour in the wine, bring to a vigorous boil, and cook until the wine has evaporated, about 10 minutes. Pour in the tomatoes and their liquid. Bring to a boil, lower the heat so the sauce is at a lively simmer, and season lightly with salt and pepper. Tuck the oxtails into the sauce and simmer very slowly until the meat is falling off the bone and the vegetables have disintegrated into the sauce, about 3 to 5 hours.

As the oxtails cook, add the chicken stock, about ½ cup at a time, to keep the level of the liquid more or less steady during cooking. Cool the oxtails in the cooking liquid to room temperature, then refrigerate overnight. Leave the bones in the sauce as they continue to add flavor.

The next day, skim the excess fat from the sauce and remove the meat from the bones. Shred the meat coarsely or chop it finely, and return it to the sauce. Serve with gnocchi or pasta. You may serve the oxtails whole as a second course, if you prefer, reserving the extra sauce for gnocchi or pasta. That's the way it's done in southern Italy.

The oxtail ragù can be prepared and refrigerated for up to three days in advance. The recipe can be halved or the extra frozen up to one month.

Adapted from a recipe by Lisa Lavagetto, Ramekins Cooking School, Sonoma, California

RAGÙ BOLOGNESE

/ enough for 6 to 8 servings

On October 17, 1982, an "official" recipe for Ragù Bolognese was deposited by the Accademia Italiana in the Palazzo della Mercanzia, the Chamber of Commerce in the City of Bologna. It's not unlike Italians to establish official recipes in order to protect their heritage.

Still, Italians also are known to disagree over who makes the best of anything when it comes to food, and Ragù Bolognese is known for its numerous variations. There are some consistent factors that mark a Bolognese, however. Meats are ground or finely chopped, milk is added, very little tomato is used, and there's always a bit of wine. I often chop the meats by hand instead of purchasing them already ground. It's a bit time consuming, but I prefer the slightly chunky texture.

This recipe is one I've used for years to sauce lasagne Bolognese, pastas, and gnocchi. I credit the original recipe to my favorite Italian cookbook, Lynne Rosetto Kasper's The Splendid Table. *I've changed the recipe over time to suit my personal taste, but I still follow the basic Bolognese rules.*

2 tablespoons extra-virgin olive oil

2 ounces pancetta,

    OR uncured natural bacon, finely chopped

1 medium onion, minced

½ small fennel bulb with fronds, minced

1 medium carrot, minced

¼ pound ground veal

¼ pound ground pork

¼ pound mild or hot Italian sausage, casings removed

8 ounces lean ground beef

2 ounces sliced Prosciutto di Parma

    OR a 2-ounce end, finely chopped

⅔ cup dry red wine

1½ cups low-sodium chicken or beef broth,

    preferably homemade

2 cups whole milk

3 fresh plum tomatoes, peeled and seeded

    OR 3 canned pear tomatoes, coarsely chopped

Salt and freshly ground black pepper to taste

Put the olive oil, pancetta, and minced vegetables in a 4- to 5-quart saucepan over medium-high heat. Sauté, stirring frequently with a wooden spoon, for 8 to 10 minutes, or until the onions soften and begin to turn golden. Add all of the meat to the pan and continue to cook and stir over medium-high heat. Cook off any liquid that the meat gives off so that browning can begin. Stir often, and, as browning begins, turn the heat down to medium to protect the glaze that forms on the bottom of the pan. Cook about 15 minutes more, or until the meats are a deep brown. This is a critical step to create ragù with depth of flavor.

Add the wine to the saucepan, lower the heat to medium, and stir continuously until the wine has reduced to half, about 3 to 5 minutes. Scrape up the brown glaze from the bottom as the sauce simmers. Stir ½ cup of the stock into the saucepan and simmer slowly, about 10 minutes, or until completely evaporated. Repeat with another ½ cup of stock. Add the milk along with the remaining stock and bring to a slow simmer. Partially cover the pot and cook for 1 hour, stirring frequently to prevent sticking. Add the tomatoes. Cook, uncovered, at a slow simmer for another 45 minutes, or until the sauce is thick and meaty. Season to taste with salt and pepper.

The ragù can be made three days ahead. Cover and refrigerate it until ready to use. It also freezes well for up to 1 month.

SARDINIAN PORK & LAMB RAGÙ

/ enough for 6 servings

For me, Sardinia has the most beautiful seacoast of all the Italian islands, from swimmable beaches with mesmerizing blue pools of water to intimidating rocky cliffs beaten by high waves. Although the northern coast is more tourist-oriented, much of the remaining island is still untouched. Because Sardinia was prone to frequent invasions from the sea, it is historically pastoral and agricultural, with the population concentrated upland rather than near the shores. Fishing was not pursued, and only recently has seafood been embraced by the locals. The land is particularly well suited to pasturing both sheep and pigs. This recipe for a simple pork- and lamb-based ragù reflects the traditional Sardinian diet. Be sure to thoroughly brown the meat to add richness and depth of flavor to the ragù.

2 tablespoons extra-virgin olive oil

3 ounces pancetta

   OR smoked natural bacon, thinly sliced and

   finely chopped

1 medium onion, finely chopped

4 ounces ground pork

12 ounces ground lamb

½ cup dry red wine

1¼ pounds fresh pear-shaped tomatoes, skinned and

   coarsely chopped OR 28-ounce can Italian

   pear-shaped tomatoes, chopped, juice reserved

¼ cup finely chopped Italian parsley

1 tablespoon chopped fresh sage

¼ cup shredded fresh basil leaves, optional

Salt and freshly ground black pepper to taste

Place the olive oil, pancetta, and onion in a large skillet and sauté over medium heat until the onion is translucent and the pancetta is beginning to brown, about 8 minutes. Add the pork and lamb and continue cooking, stirring frequently, until a deep brown glaze has formed on the bottom of the pan, about 10 minutes. Be careful not to burn the meat.

Add the wine to the saucepan, reduce the heat to medium-low, and cook, stirring and scraping the brown glaze from the bottom of the pan, until the wine has reduced by half. Add the tomatoes and their juice to the saucepan, along with the parsley and sage, and bring to a boil. Reduce the heat and simmer about 1 hour, or until the sauce is thickened. Add water if necessary if it becomes too dry.

Remove the sauce from the heat, add the basil if using, and season with salt and freshly ground black pepper.

The ragù can be made three days ahead. Cover and refrigerate until ready to use. It also freezes well for up to one month.

SCIABBO (SICILIAN CHRISTMAS RAGÙ)

/ enough for 4 to 6 servings

This version of a Sicilian ragù uses ground pork instead of chunks of pork shoulder. It's a quick ragù, requiring less cooking time and fewer ingredients, resulting in less flavor development compared to ragùs that call for a 3-hour simmer. However, it's a very flavorful replacement for the long version and can be simmering away while you make the gnocchi.

1 medium onion, finely chopped

2 tablespoons olive oil

1 pound lean ground pork

½ cup red wine

3 tablespoons tomato paste

2 cups plain tomato sauce, homemade
    OR good quality canned

2 cups water

Salt and freshly ground black pepper to taste

½ teaspoon ground cinnamon

1½ tablespoons unsweetened cocoa powder

Coat the bottom of a heavy, medium saucepan with the olive oil, add the onion, and sauté over medium heat until the onion is soft, about 5 minutes. Add the pork and cook, stirring, until well browned and a glaze forms on the bottom of the pan, being careful not to burn the meat. Add the wine and the tomato paste, stirring with a wooden spoon to deglaze the pan. Add the tomato sauce and the water. Bring to a boil, reduce the heat, and simmer for about 40 minutes, or until the meat is tender and the sauce is thick. Add salt and freshly ground black pepper to taste. Stir in the cinnamon and cocoa.

The ragù can be made three days ahead. Cover and refrigerate until ready to use. It also freezes well for up to one month.

Adapted from Pomp and Sustenance *by Mary Taylor Simeti*

WHITE RAGÙ: PORK

/ enough for 6 to 8 servings

There are no tomatoes in this ragù, and, as is sometimes typical of northern Italian sauces, it contains unusual spices and combinations of herbs because of the ancient spice route through the region. Mint, rosemary, and coriander seeds, combined with lemon and olives, are not typically found in southern Italian ragù recipes, which makes this a uniquely flavored sauce. Look for green Taggiasca olives from Liguria, although any olive with a big flavor punch can be substituted.

2½ pounds pork loin, cut into 1-inch pieces

Kosher salt and freshly ground black pepper

2 teaspoons whole fennel seeds

2 teaspoons coriander seeds

1 teaspoon whole black peppercorns

4 tablespoons extra-virgin olive oil

2 medium onions, diced medium

3 carrots, diced medium

1 medium fennel bulb, cored and diced medium

1½ cups dry white wine

4 cups low-sodium chicken broth, preferably homemade

1 6-inch sprig fresh rosemary

1 cup pitted Taggiasca olives, coarsely chopped

2 tablespoons fresh lemon juice

1 tablespoon finely zested lemon rind

⅓ cup mint leaves, shredded

Kosher salt and crushed, dried red pepper to taste

Knead a teaspoon of kosher salt and some grindings of black pepper into the pork and set aside.

Heat a large enameled casserole or sauté pan over medium heat, toss in the fennel, coriander, and whole peppercorns and toast until fragrant. Remove to a bowl and set aside to cool, then coarsely crush.

Add 2 tablespoons of oil to the pan and and brown the pork over medium-high heat to a rich dark color. There should be a deep brown glaze on the bottom of the pan. Remove the meat to a dish and set aside.

Add the remaining olive oil to the pan. Add the onions, carrots, and fennel, and cook over medium heat, stirring frequently, until the vegetables are soft, about 10 minutes. Add the wine and bring to a boil, scraping up any brown bits from the bottom of the pan. Reduce by half. Add the chicken stock and the browned pork, along with the rosemary sprig, ½ cup olives and the crushed spices. Cover and simmer over low heat until the pork is very tender and falling apart, about 2 hours. Discard the rosemary sprig and continue to cook, uncovered, until the sauce is thick. Add the remaining olives, lemon juice, lemon zest, and mint leaves. Season to taste with crushed red pepper and salt.

The ragù can be made three days ahead. Cover and refrigerate until ready to use. It also freezes well for up to one month.

SICILIAN PORK SHOULDER & COCOA RAGÙ

/ enough for 6 to 8 servings

Cocoa is often added to Sicilian ragùs to deepen the rich, meaty flavor of the sauce. The addition of mint and other herbs commonly used in Sicily sets this ragù apart from Napolitano "Sunday Gravy" recipes. As with all good ragùs, the secret is in the browning of the meat and the long simmering process once the ingredients have been combined — so don't be tempted to take shortcuts. And be sure to make plenty of sauce for the freezer. You'll be thankful for that quick meal sometime in the future.

About ¼ cup extra-virgin olive oil

2-pound piece boneless pork shoulder, trimmed
    and cut into 2-inch chunks

Kosher salt and freshly ground black pepper

1 large yellow onion, finely chopped

4 medium carrots, finely chopped

1 small fennel bulb, finely chopped

4 garlic cloves, finely chopped

2 tablespoons minced rosemary, or to taste

2 tablespoons minced sage, or to taste

3 tablespoons unsweetened cocoa powder

2 tablespoons tomato paste

1 cup dry white wine

3 cups low-sodium chicken broth, preferably homemade

3 tablespoons chopped mint

2 tablespoons chopped fresh parsley

Pinch crushed red pepper flakes

1 tablespoon unsalted butter

Freshly grated Parmigiano-Reggiano or semi-aged
    pecorino for serving

Season the pork with salt and pepper, evenly coating all the pieces. In a large cast-iron casserole, heat the oil and brown the pork over moderately high heat, turning occasionally, about 10 minutes. You should have a nice brown glaze on the bottom of the pan. Transfer the pork to a plate.

Reduce the heat to medium. Add the onion, carrots, fennel, garlic, rosemary, and sage to the casserole and cook 4 to 5 minutes. Stir in the cocoa powder and cook over moderate heat until the vegetables are softened, about 5 minutes more. Add the tomato paste and cook, stirring, for 2 minutes. Add the wine and cook, scraping up any browned bits from the bottom of the pot, until the wine has almost completely evaporated, 5 to 10 minutes. Return the pork to the pot, add the stock and bring to a boil.

Cover and cook the sauce at a low simmer for 3 to 4 hours, or until the pork is extremely tender. Remove the meat from the pot and break it apart into large shreds, discarding any fat. Crush the vegetables to thicken the sauce, return the meat to the pot and stir in the mint, parsley, crushed red pepper, and butter. Simmer until the sauce resembles a thick, meaty stew.

The ragù can be made three days ahead. Cover and refrigerate until ready to use. It also freezes well for up to one month.

WHITE RAGÙ: CHICKEN

/ enough for 6 to 8 servings

White ragù is a meat-based sauce that uses only white meat and no tomatoes. I'm particularly fond of this recipe because it also includes a few of my favorite spring vegetables — artichokes, fava beans, and peas — which, with the addition of asparagus, is a celebrated combination for a Roman spring vegetable stew called vignarola. *Often served with pasta, it also makes a wonderful sauce for gnocchi — and is the perfect way to celebrate the change of seasons.*

Although I prefer the texture and deep flavor of chicken thighs, you can substitute chicken breasts or turkey if you wish. Any meat you choose should be finely chopped, not ground. Any fresh fava beans will work, although I search for more mature beans for this ragù because they have a wonderful meaty texture that complements the chicken. Frozen lima beans can be substituted if fava beans aren't available.

½ lemon

2 medium artichokes

1½ pounds fresh fava beans, shelled to make
    1½-2 cups

2 tablespoons extra-virgin olive oil

½ cup finely chopped fennel

2 large shallots, finely chopped

1 clove garlic, minced

1½ pounds boneless, skinless, chicken thighs,
    finely chopped

½ cup dry white wine

1 cup low-sodium chicken broth, preferably homemade

½-1 cup fresh or frozen peas

¼ cup finely chopped herbs (such as chives,
    marjoram, and thyme)

Salt and freshly ground black pepper to taste

Freshly grated Parmigiano-Reggiano or semi-aged
    pecorino for serving

Squeeze the lemon into a bowl of cold water, dropping in the lemon half. Starting at the base of each artichoke, remove as many rows of the outer leaves as necessary by pulling them downward and snapping them, breaking off the tough part and leaving the tender part of the bottom of the leaf attached to the stem. Do this until you reach the pale green leaves and can clearly see a separation between the green at the top of the leaves and the light yellow at the bottom. Cut off green tops with a serrated knife. Trim off stems and peel. Trim any dark green fibrous parts from base and sides of artichoke with a small sharp knife. Cut the artichoke in half lengthwise, and, with a melon baller or small spoon, remove the hairy chokes. Cut into medium dice and immediately drop into acidulated water. Repeat with remaining artichoke. Set aside.

Boil the shelled fava beans for 3 to 4 minutes, or until tender. Transfer the cooked beans to a colander and run under cold water to stop cooking. Peel and set aside.

In a large sauté pan, heat the olive oil, fennel, shallots, and garlic over medium-high heat until the vegetables soften, about 5 to 8 minutes. Add the chicken and cook, stirring frequently, until chicken is cooked through, about 5 minutes. Lower the heat to medium and add the wine, scraping the bottom of the pan until the liquid is reduced by half.

Drain the artichokes. Add artichokes, peas, and broth to the pan and bring to a simmer. Reduce heat to low and cook, covered, stirring occasionally, for about 15 minutes, or until the artichokes are tender. Stir in the fava beans and herbs, and season with salt and freshly ground black pepper to taste. Add more broth or reduce the sauce if necessary to make a thin gravy. Remove from the heat and cover to keep warm.

Toss the cooked gnocchi with the ragù. Serve immediately in warmed, shallow bowls and garnish with the freshly grated cheese. The ragù can be made three days ahead. Cover and refrigerate until ready to use. It also freezes well for up to one month.

SABA (FRESH GRAPE SYRUP)

/ makes about 2½ cups for drizzling

Depending on where you are in Italy, this deeply flavored, naturally sweet syrup is also known as sapa, vincotto, *or* mosto cotto. *Made from grape must, the leftovers of wine-making, it's been a favored sweet treat in the Italian kitchen for centuries. Poured over a scoop of freshly fallen snow, it's the original snow cone. Although it's commercially available in many Italian grocery stores or online, I prefer to make my own Saba. It enhances any of the sweet gnocchi recipes, can be dribbled on other savory gnocchi such as sweet potato, or compliment other Italian desserts where a touch of syrupy sweetness is desired. No sugar or sweetener is added — and none is needed.*

Start making the syrup two days before you want to use it. The recipe doubles easily and keeps months in the refrigerator — even longer if it's canned using the water-bath method.

4½-5 pounds flavorful red grapes, with or without
    seeds, preferably organic

1 cup dry red wine

Wash and stem the grapes. Fit a food processor with the steel blade and process the grapes, in a couple of batches, until finely chopped. Turn the crushed grapes into a glass or stainless steel container, cover, and refrigerate 48 hours. Strain the grapes through a fine sieve set over a large bowl. Press as much liquid as possible out of the grapes, and allow some of the pulp to be blended into the liquid by scraping the underside of the strainer.

Gently boil the strained grape juice, uncovered, in a wide, heavy nonreactive pan over medium-high heat until thickened and reduced to about 2¼ to 2¾ cups. This can take 1 to 2 hours. The syrup will foam with large bubbles as it approaches the proper thickness. Stir occasionally and check for burning. Do not let it caramelize. Blend in the wine, boil 1 more minute, and allow to cool. Poured into sterilized containers or bottles. Covered tightly and refrigerated, it will keep for months.

Adapted from The Splendid Table *by Lynn Rosetto Kasper*

FRESH PLUM SAUCE

/ enough for 6 to 8 servings

Many varieties of plums grow in Italy — and make their appearance, fresh or dried, in a large range of recipes, sweet or savory. This very simple plum sauce is absolutely delicious with any of the sweet gnocchi recipes. It's also lovely with panna cotta, one of Italia's well-known creamy desserts, as well as other dishes that would benefit from a fruit garnish.

Although any type of plum can be used, I recommend the small, oval, purple ones known as Italian prune plums. They are freestone and very flavorful — and have a lower water and higher sugar content than other varieties. Be sure to choose plums that feel soft but not mushy when gently pressed with your finger.

3½ cups peeled, pitted, and sliced Italian prune plums

¼-½ cup mild honey, or to taste

1 tablespoon fresh lemon juice, or to taste

1 teaspoon vanilla extract

Pinch ground cloves

Pinch ground cinnamon

Place the plums and honey in a medium saucepan. Cook over medium heat, stirring constantly, until the mixture comes to a boil. Add lemon juice to taste and continue to cook, stirring, until the fruit is softened but still hold its shape, about 6 to 8 minutes.

Remove from the heat, add the vanilla and spices, and adjust for sweetness. Cover and allow the sauce to cool to room temperature.

Use immediately or pour into a jar with a tight fitting lid and refrigerate for up to a week.

ROSEMARY-ORANGE SYRUP

/ enough for 4 to 6 servings

Rosemary is often used to enhance sweet dishes in Italian cuisine. I first experienced it when I ate the famous Tuscan sweet buns called pan di ramerino *popular in bakeries in Florence. Slightly sweet, sugar-glazed, packed with raisins and a touch of rosemary (*rosmarino *or* ramerino*), I was hooked. Now that bakery is my first stop when I get off the train in Florence from Perugia — morning street food at its best!*

I appreciate the combination of flavors in the buns and love the addition of orange in this syrup. It's simple to prepare, can be done well in advance and stored, refrigerated, much like a good maple syrup. Use it on fruit, gelato, or pancakes — wherever a touch of sweet will enhance a dish. I dribble it on fried gnocchi, or any of the other sweet gnocchi in this collection.

Wide strips of zest from 1 orange

¾ cup fresh orange juice

½ cup sugar

¼ cup water

6-inch sprig fresh rosemary

In a heavy 1-quart saucepan, simmer all the ingredients together until the sauce has reduced to about ¾ cup — about 15 minutes. Watch carefully to prevent burning, as the syrup will thicken quickly once it's nearly finished. It should be like thick maple syrup when done. Cool to room temperature.

Use immediately or pour into a jar with a tight fitting lid and refrigerate. Strain before using.

SWEET MASCARPONE CREAM

/ enough for 6 to 8 servings

I put a dollop of this creamy whipped cheese next to almost every sweet I make. It's a great substitute for whipped cream. Covered and refrigerated, it keeps for hours — and can be easily varied to accent a variety of desserts. Sometimes I add a couple tablespoons of my favorite liqueur, some ground espresso, substitute other flavorings for the orange rind, or drizzle it with Saba (page 205) — and even sneak a spoonful when no one is looking.

1 cup mascarpone, at room temperature

¾ cup heavy cream

2 teaspoons finely grated orange zest, optional

2 tablespoons confectioners' sugar

Pinch salt

In a large bowl, using an electric mixer, beat the mascarpone with the cream, orange zest, confectioners' sugar, and salt until soft peaks form. Chill until ready to use.

SWEET MACERATED FRUIT SAUCE

/ enough for 8 servings

4 cups seasonal fresh fruit such as strawberries, figs, raspberries, cherries, blueberries, or peaches, whole or roughly chopped

¼ cup fresh lemon juice

½ teaspoon finely zested lemon rind

¼ cup honey or to taste

Grappa or liquor of choice to taste (optional)

Mix the prepared fruit, lemon juice, lemon rind, and honey in a medium bowl. Add optional liquor to taste.

Cover and refrigerate up to 2 days.

SWEET SEARED FRESH FIG SAUCE

/ enough for 4 to 6 servings

Naturally sweet fresh figs make a simple but rich sauce for sweet gnocchi. For a savory version to serve with the potato-squash gnocchi, eliminate the honey and mint and garnish with a dusting of freshly grated Parmigiano-Reggiano and fried sage leaves.

10 large, fresh Black Mission, Kadota, or
    Brown Turkey figs, halved

2 tablespoons extra-virgin olive oil

2 tablespoons fine lemon zest

1 tablespoon Saba OR pomegranate molasses

Mild-flavored honey, to taste

Finely chopped fresh mint, to taste

¼-½ cup heavy cream

Salt to taste

½ cup walnuts, toasted and coarsely chopped for garnish

Finely grated semi-aged pecorino cheese for garnish

In a medium sauté pan, heat the olive oil over medium-high heat. Add the halved figs, cut side down, and sear them until browned on the bottom. Use tongs to turn the figs over and lightly sear the other side.

Remove from heat, scatter with the lemon zest and stir, crushing the halved figs to a slightly chunky but sauce-like consistency. Add the Saba or pomegranate molasses along with mint and honey to taste, mixing well. Stir in as much of the cream as you like and season with salt. Reheat the sauce before serving. Toss the cooked gnocchi with the warm sauce and garnish each serving with toasted walnut pieces and grated cheese.

WHOLE CHERRY SYRUP

/ enough for 4 servings

I usually arrive in Perugia every year just before cherry season, when I can look forward to basketsful of different varieties at both the commercial markets and roadside stands. If I'm lucky, a friend or neighbor will gift some of their overly abundant crop to me.

Cherries are a favored fruit for jam, called marmellata, *in Italy; they also make a tasty syrup for sweet gnocchi. You can vary the sauce by making it with different kinds of cherries, or adding a pinch of anise or clove, a bit of minced rosemary, or a spoonful of amaretto. You may need to adjust the quantity of sugar and cooking time to achieve the best end result — a sauce the consistency of warm honey.*

½ pound dark sweet cherries, pitted

½ cup water

1 cup sugar, or to taste

1 tablespoon unsalted butter, at room temperature

½ teaspoon vanilla

In a medium saucepan over high heat, bring the pitted cherries, water, and sugar to a boil. Reduce the heat to a simmer and cook until the mixture has thickened to a syrup. Be sure to wash down the sides of the saucepan with water and a soft-bristle brush to prevent crystals from forming.

Once glassy bubbles begin to form over the surface, remove the pan from heat and test for thickness by fast-cooling a small spoonful in the freezer. If the spoonful jells, you're done. If it's too watery, return pan to heat, cook a bit longer, and retest.

Remove from heat, stir in the butter, vanilla, and any optional flavorings. Serve the sauce hot with your favorite sweet gnocchi.

Make extra sauce during cherry season and either refrigerate in tightly covered containers or freeze. Chilled or frozen it will keep up to 2 months.

BASIC TOMATO SAUCE

/ enough for 6 to 8 servings

This is my go-to tomato sauce; I use it on just about everything. It's simple, quick to prepare, and infinitely variable. If the sauce seems bland, add salt — rather than sugar — to bring up the flavor. Sugar will overwhelm rather than compliment the tomato flavor, and can make the sauce cloyingly sweet. If fresh tomatoes are not in their prime, it's far better to use a high quality, pear-shaped canned tomato — such as Muir Glen or San Marzano tomatoes imported from Italy.

6 cloves garlic, minced

2 tablespoons extra-virgin olive oil

2½ pounds fresh, ripe, pear tomatoes, peeled and
    coarsely chopped, OR 3 cups canned plum
    tomatoes, coarsely chopped, juices reserved

⅓ cup shredded or torn fresh basil leaves, or to taste

Salt and freshly ground black pepper to taste

In a large sauté pan, heat the oil and garlic together over medium heat until the garlic begins to sizzle. Add the tomatoes, along with their juices, and turn the heat to medium-high. Cook about 20 minutes, stirring occasionally, until the sauce thickens. Remove from the heat, season to taste with salt and pepper, and stir in the basil.

/ VARIATIONS

* Add 1 cup oven-roasted cherry tomatoes along with the basil for a more intense tomato flavor.

* Add chopped capers along with the seasonings and herbs.

* Add 1 teaspoon red pepper flakes for an *all'Arrabbiata* (spicy) sauce.

* Add heavy cream to taste along with the basil.

* Sauté ground meat (beef, veal, pork, chicken livers, or pancetta) along with the garlic before adding the tomatoes.

* Use oregano, marjoram, or savory instead of basil.

* This sauce can be frozen up to 2 months.

OVEN-ROASTED CHERRY TOMATOES

/ enough for 6 to 8 servings

Small cherry tomatoes have a unique sweetness that becomes concentrated when they are roasted. Any tiny tomato variety can be substituted for the cherry type with equal results. Leftovers are particularly good on bruschette or as a side dish, so I recommended making extra for another meal.

2 pounds ripe cherry tomatoes

¼ cup extra-virgin olive oil

Kosher salt and freshly ground black pepper to taste

Chopped fresh basil, parsley, thyme, or mint

Preheat the oven to 400° F.

In a large bowl, toss the tomatoes lightly with olive oil. Spread them on a parchment-lined baking sheet in one layer, and sprinkle generously with salt and pepper. Roast for 10 to 15 minutes. Remove from oven when the tomatoes are soft and slightly collapsed. Sprinkle with chopped basil leaves, parsley, thyme, or mint to taste, and cool to room temperature.

Toss with hot, cooked gnocchi.

The sauce will keep up to three days, refrigerated, in a tightly covered container.

GREEN TOMATO SAUCE

/ enough for 6 to 8 servings

I was first introduced to a particular bulbous green tomato that Italians use in salads many years ago when I worked in a restaurant near Perugia. Naively thinking they were used because we were out of red ones, I quickly learned, when sent to the fruttivendolo *to purchase salad tomatoes, that they are treasured in salads for their low–acid content and mild flavor.*

The following sauce recipe uses those same green Cuore di Bue *tomatoes. You may find them in your local farmers market as part of the heirloom tomato family. In a pinch, you can substitute green pear tomatoes. They are more acidic but equally as good.*

I prefer this sauce nice and meaty, sometimes replacing the pancetta with salami or sausage. For a vegetarian version, eliminate the pancetta, add extra salt to bring out the sweetness of the tomato, and experiment with other herbs. Thinned with broth, it also makes a wonderful soup garnished with a dollop of creamy ricotta.

2 tablespoons extra-virgin olive oil

1 small onion, finely chopped (about ¾ cup)

4 cloves garlic, minced

6 ounces coarsely chopped pancetta
   OR unsmoked bacon (about 1½ cups)

Hot red pepper flakes, to taste

2½ pounds green tomatoes, coarsely chopped
   (5-6 cups)

½-1 cup water

¼ cup coarsely chopped parsley

Finely chopped basil, mint, or marjoram to
   taste (optional)

Salt and freshly ground black pepper to taste

Freshly grated Parmigiano-Reggiano or semi-aged
   pecorino for garnish

In a large sauté pan, heat the oil, onion, garlic, pancetta, and red pepper over medium heat until the onions are softened and the pancetta has released its fat, about 5 minutes. Add the tomatoes and water. Cook over moderate heat until the tomatoes have broken down and the sauce has thickened slightly, about 20 minutes. You may need to add more water to maintain a saucy consistency. .

Season with salt and pepper, add the parsley and other optional herbs, and set aside.

Toss with hot, cooked gnocchi when ready to serve.

This sauce can be frozen in airtight containers up to 2 months.

SUN-DRIED TOMATO SAUCE

/ enough for 6 servings

This is an intensely flavored tomato sauce that comes together quickly and can easily be made in advance and refrigerated for a week or more. Use it sparingly, the way you would use a pesto. I love this sauce with pasta, grilled fish, or a simple roasted chicken as well as to dress gnocchi.

There are a number of producers of oil-cured, sun-dried tomatoes on the market and their quality will vary. To maintain the integrity and freshness of the flavors, look for a jar without herbs or other additions.

½ cup extra-virgin olive oil

2 cloves garlic, minced

4-6 olive oil-packed anchovies, chopped (or to taste)

1½ tablespoons capers in brine, drained

1½ cups oil-packed, sun-dried tomatoes,
  coarsely chopped

¼ cup dry red wine

Freshly ground black pepper

In a medium sauté pan, cook the garlic, anchovies, and olive oil over medium heat, stirring constantly, until the anchovies are nearly dissolved. Add the capers and tomatoes and cook another minute or two. Add the wine and bring to a boil.

Transfer the contents to a food processor and pulse until coarsely chopped, being careful not to overprocess to a paste. The sauce should be chunky. Season with freshly ground black pepper to taste. Toss with hot gnocchi just before serving. Do not freeze.

TOMATO & OLIVE SAUCE

/ enough for 6 servings

My favorite sauce to serve with Roasted Pepper and Potato Gnocchi, it also compliments sautéed chicken or fish.

2 tablespoons extra-virgin olive oil

2 garlic cloves, finely chopped

1 cup Gaeta or Kalamata olives, pitted and halved

2 pounds ripe plum tomatoes, skinned and cut into
  ½ inch dice OR a 28-ounce can plum tomatoes,
  drained and cut into ½-inch dice, juices reserved

1 tablespoon fresh marjoram leaves OR ¼ cup fresh basil
  leaves, shredded

Finely grated fresh Parmigiano-Reggiano for the table

Heat the oil and chopped garlic in a large sauté pan over medium heat until the garlic begins to sizzle. Add the olives, tomatoes, and reserved juice, and cook over medium-high heat until the sauce thickens, about 15 minutes. The time will vary depending on the water content of the tomatoes.

Keep warm until ready to toss with hot gnocchi.

The sauce will keep up to 1 week, refrigerated, in a tightly covered container.

TOMATO, SAUSAGE & LEEK SAUCE

/ enough for 6 to 8 servings

Not all Italian sausage is alike, and many Italians favor their local butcher's variety. Search for a special sausage that suits your own taste — and remember you can always add extra peperoncini if you prefer a hotter sauce.

28-ounce can whole peeled plum tomatoes
    OR 2 pounds fresh plum tomatoes, peeled

½ pound hot or sweet Italian bulk sausage

2 tablespoons extra-virgin olive oil

1 red bell pepper, cored and finely chopped

1 large leek, white and pale green parts only, trimmed, halved lengthwise, rinsed and thinly sliced to make about 1½ cups

2 medium garlic cloves, smashed, peeled, and finely chopped

2 tablespoons chopped fresh flat-leaf parsley

2 sprigs fresh thyme, leaves removed and chopped

2 sprigs fresh marjoram, leaves removed and chopped

Kosher salt and freshly ground black pepper to taste

Chop the tomatoes, retaining their juice. Set aside. Heat 1 tablespoon of the olive oil in a deep skillet over medium-high heat. Add the sausage, breaking it apart, and cook until it begins to brown. Add the remaining olive oil to the skillet, along with the red bell pepper, leek, garlic, and herbs. Cook over medium heat until the pepper and leek begin to soften. Add the reserved tomatoes and their juices, stirring and scraping up the browned bits from the bottom of the pan until the mixture comes to a simmer. Reduce the heat to medium-low and continue cooking slowly until reduced to a medium sauce consistency, about 15 to 30 minutes. If the sauce becomes too thick, add a bit of water.

Keep warm until ready to toss with hot, cooked gnocchi. The sauce will keep up to five days refrigerated in a tightly covered container, or up to one month frozen.

SAVORY FIG SAUCE

/ enough for 6 servings

Figs, dried and fresh, are a favorite Mediterranean fruit, used in both sweet and savory dishes. Here, dried figs are married with savory herbs and meaty pancetta to make a very rich, slightly sweet and savory sauce that is wonderful with any simple gnocchi.

10 dried figs, coarsely chopped

1 cup Marsala wine

3 ounces pancetta, coarsely chopped

2 large shallots, peeled and minced

1 tablespoon extra-virgin olive oil

1 clove garlic, peeled and minced

1 teaspoon finely chopped fresh rosemary or sage

1 cup chicken broth

¼ cup coarsely chopped Kalamata olives

2 tablespoons small capers packed in brine, drained

¼-½ cup heavy cream (optional)

Kosher salt and freshly ground black pepper to taste

Freshly grated Parmigiano-Reggiano for serving

Fresh figs or rosemary sprigs for garnish (optional)

Place the chopped figs and Marsala in a small bowl and set aside until figs begin to soften, at least 30 minutes. Put the pancetta in a medium skillet and cook over medium-low heat until the fat is rendered and the pancetta is crisp. Remove the pancetta to a paper towel.

Drain all but 1 tablespoon of the cooking fat from the skillet and return to the heat. Add the olive oil, shallots, and garlic to the skillet and cook until soft, about 2 to 3 minutes. Add rosemary and stir a minute or two. Add the figs and Marsala. Cook until the pan is almost dry, 5 to 10 minutes more. Add the broth, reserved pancetta, capers, and olives. Reduce over high heat until it reaches the desired consistency. Add optional heavy cream to taste and reheat. Season with salt and freshly ground black pepper to taste. Toss with hot gnocchi. Garnish with freshly grated Parmigiano-Reggiano, fresh figs and rosemary sprigs if desired. The sauce will keep up to five days refrigerated in a tightly covered container. Do not freeze.

UNCOOKED FRESH TOMATO SAUCE

/ enough for 6 servings

This is a wonderfully refreshing sauce for the summer, using the sweetest vine-ripened tomatoes from the garden or local market. If available, a mix of red, yellow, orange, or even ripened green cherry tomatoes makes the sauce even more colorful. The hot oil slightly heats the tomatoes and brings out their richness — so don't skip this step.

If using plum tomatoes, cut a thin slice from the top stem end and peel them with a vegetable peeler. Halve the tomatoes crosswise, then remove and discard the core and seeds. Chop the tomatoes into ¼-inch dice before proceeding with the recipe.

4 tablespoons extra-virgin olive oil

2 cloves garlic, finely chopped

3 cups sweet cherry tomatoes, quartered,
    OR 2 pounds ripe plum tomatoes

½ cup lightly packed fresh basil leaves, finely shredded
    (or more to taste)

Kosher salt and freshly ground black pepper to taste

Fresh basil leaves for garnish

In a large bowl, mix the tomatoes and garlic together and let sit up to 2 hours before you are ready to serve the gnocchi.

Just before serving, warm the olive oil over medium heat in a 1-quart saucepan until it begins to shimmer. Pour the warm oil over the tomato mixture and season to taste with salt and freshly ground black pepper. Add the shredded basil and mix gently.

Toss with gnocchi and serve, garnished with additional fresh basil leaves.

This sauce does not keep well.

AVOCADO-ARUGULA SAUCE

/ enough for 6 servings

Historically, avocados were difficult to find in Italian markets, so they do not make an appearance in traditional Italian recipes. Today they are imported from North Africa or grown in Sicily. In the following recipe, a bit of avocado adds a creamy texture and tempers the bite of the arugula. It's a wonderful flavor and texture combination that you can pull together at the last minute. Guacamole gnocchi? Not quite — but you could add a touch of chile for an added kick.

3 cups packed, chopped baby arugula

½ small, very ripe avocado, peeled

½ red bell pepper, roasted, peeled, seeded
    and finely chopped

1 small scallion, thinly sliced

½ cup finely grated fresh Parmigiano-Reggiano

¼ cup extra-virgin olive oil

Kosher salt and freshly ground black pepper to taste

Fresh arugula leaves for garnish

Place all the ingredients except the olive oil in a food processor and pulse until well combined. Add the olive oil in a steady stream and continue mixing until a smooth creamy sauce forms. Empty the mixture into a bowl and add salt and freshly ground black pepper to taste.

Toss with hot gnocchi and serve immediately, garnishing with arugula leaves.

The sauce can be made a few hours in advance, but does not keep well over a longer period. Do not freeze.

Variation: Add some *mozzarella ciliegine* (small mozzarella balls) to the gnocchi when tossing with the sauce.

GARDEN 'PATÉ' SAUCE

/ enough for 6 to 8 servings

From Italy's Ligurian region, known for its aromatic basil, this sauce varies by the ingredients available at the time it's being prepared — so feel free to experiment with other seasonal vegetables and herbs, such as charred peppers or mint.

¾ cup sun-dried tomatoes packed in olive oil, drained

¾ cup baby artichokes hearts, packed in olive oil, drained

½ cup fresh basil leaves, washed

¼ cup shelled walnuts

Dried peperoncini (chile peppers) to taste,
    finely chopped

1 cup pitted Taggiasca or Niçoise olives, pitted

Extra-virgin olive oil as needed

Coarsely chop the sun-dried tomatoes, artichokes, basil, walnuts, and pitted olives together. They should be in equal-sized pieces. Put them in the bowl of a food processor, along with the peperoncini, and pulse a few times to form a coarse paste. Empty the contents into a bowl and add extra-virgin olive oil as needed to make a sauce-like consistency.

Covered with a thin film of olive oil, this sauce may be refrigerated up to two weeks. Do not freeze.

CABBAGE & APPLE SAUCE

/ enough for 4 to 6 servings

The mountainous region of northern Italy is apple country. Married with onion and cabbage, this is one of my favorite sauces for Sausage Canederli (page 83). For a substantial main course pair it with Liver Canederli or Whole Grain Buckwheat Canederli. And be sure to save any leftovers to serve with grilled or roasted pork. Refrigerated, it will keep a week or two.

1 medium onion, thinly sliced

¼ pound unsalted butter

1½ pounds red cabbage, washed and thinly sliced

½ cup full-bodied red wine

½-¾ cup chicken or vegetable broth,
    preferably homemade

1 tablespoon chopped fresh herbs such as mint,
    thyme, or rosemary

2 tart, crisp apples, peeled, cored, and grated

Salt and freshly ground black pepper to taste

Freshly grated Parmigiano-Reggiano for serving

In a large sauté pan over medium heat, cook the butter and sliced onion together until lightly browned. Add the sliced cabbage and cook together over low heat about 5 minutes, stirring occasionally, until cabbage is wilted and somewhat tender. Add the wine, along with the herbs, cover and simmer over very low heat for another 20 minutes, stirring occasionally and adding broth as necessary to prevent burning. The sauce should be thick but not dry.

Add the grated apple, salt, and freshly ground black pepper to taste. Keep warm, covered, while preparing the canederli.

FENNEL POLLEN-CREAM SAUCE

/ enough for 6 servings

This is one of my favorite sauces for any savory gnocchi, especially potato- or cheese-based recipes. The fennel purée's intense flavor comes from the addition of fennel seed and fennel pollen, and the smooth texture is enhanced by the addition of heavy cream. If fennel pollen isn't available, you can substitute ground fennel seed. (See page 245 for more information about fennel pollen.)

The recipe tester said this sauce was so good she ate the leftovers with a spoon. If you can resist following her example, a dollop or two also goes well with roasted or sautéed chicken or fish. And it compliments pasta as nicely as it does gnocchi.

3 tablespoons extra-virgin olive oil

1½ pounds fennel

2 cloves garlic

¼ cup minced shallot

1 teaspoon fennel seeds

1 cup heavy cream, or to taste

1 teaspoon fennel pollen

Salt and freshly ground black pepper to taste

Freshly grated Parmigiano-Reggiano for serving

Fennel leaves for garnish

Cut the stalks and feathery leaves from the fennel bulb. Reserve the leaves for garnish and the stalks for another use. Cut the trimmed bulb in half lengthwise, remove the core, then chop into 1-inch pieces. You should have 3½ to 4 cups of fennel.

In a large saucepan, heat the fennel pieces with 2 tablespoons olive oil and sauté over medium heat until softened, about 5 minutes. Add ½ cup water, cover, and cook about 10 minutes more until the fennel is very soft. Uncover and set aside to cool.

Drain the fennel over a small bowl, reserving the liquid. Purée the drained fennel in a food processor, blender, or with a blending wand, adding reserved cooking liquid as needed to make a very smooth purée. Set aside.

In a saucepan, heat the remaining tablespoon of olive oil with the garlic, shallot, and fennel seeds over medium heat. Sauté until the shallots are very soft but not brown. Add the fennel purée and cook, stirring constantly with a wooden spoon, for about 3 minutes. Slowly add the heavy cream and fennel pollen, blending well.

Using the wand, blender, or food processor, process again until smooth. Reheat the sauce over low heat and add salt and freshly ground black pepper to taste.

The sauce will keep up to five days refrigerated in a tightly covered container. Do not freeze.

ROASTED RED PEPPER PURÉE

/ enough for 6 to 8 servings

Red, yellow, or orange bell peppers are some of the more common vegetables in the Italian cuisine. Although any fully mature — but not green — pepper can be substituted in the following recipe, the red peppers make the most beautifully colored sauce — and they're naturally sweet and rich in flavor. Don't be tempted to substitute jarred roasted red peppers in this purée; they lack depth of flavor and the sauce will suffer for it.

2 large red bell peppers, about 12 ounces total

1 tablespoon extra-virgin olive oil

1 tablespoon unsalted butter

2-3 cloves garlic, minced

½ cup heavy cream

Kosher salt and freshly ground black pepper to taste

Shredded basil, thyme, or mint to taste

Freshly grated fresh Parmigiano-Reggiano for serving

Prick the peppers with a fork and place on a foil-covered sheet pan. Broil the peppers, turning occasionally, until they are blackened all over — about 15 minutes. Place the hot peppers in a paper bag to steam and cool, about 10 minutes. You may also use the flame of a gas stove to char the peppers. Place them in a paper bag to steam and cool.

Core the peppers, remove the seeds, and peel. The charred skin will slip off easily. Do not be tempted to rinse the peppers; rinsing will remove much of the flavor. Coarsely chop the peppers. Using a blender or food processor, purée the peppers until smooth. Set aside. Put the oil, butter, and minced garlic into a large frying pan. Sauté over medium heat until the garlic begins to sizzle and soften. Add the pepper purée and mix well. Lower the heat and whisk in the heavy cream. Add the salt and freshly ground black pepper to taste and cook, stirring, until slightly thickened, about 5 minutes. Remove from heat and stir in the optional basil, thyme, or mint. Keep warm. Toss the hot, cooked gnocchi in the pan with the hot sauce. Serve in warmed shallow bowls, garnished with grated cheese. This sauce will keep up to three days refrigerated in a tightly covered container, or up to one month frozen.

PANCETTA, RADICCHIO, PINE NUT & ROSEMARY SAUCE

/ enough for 6 servings

This is one of my favorite sauces — not just for its intense flavor and unusual texture, but also for its colorful presentation. It marries well with potato gnocchi, but also complements the flavor of gnocchi made with ricotta cheese, winter squash, carrot, chestnut, hazelnut, or buckwheat flours.

8 ounces very thinly sliced pancetta OR natural
    smoked bacon, coarsely chopped (optional)

2 large shallots, thinly sliced

2 large garlic cloves, minced

1 tablespoon extra-virgin olive oil

1½ cups finely shredded radicchio

4 sprigs Italian parsley, leaves chopped

1 sprig rosemary, leaves minced

Kosher salt and freshly ground black pepper to taste

½ cup finely grated fresh Parmigiano-Reggiano
    or to taste

3 tablespoons pine nuts, lightly toasted

In a large deep skillet over medium heat, sauté the chopped pancetta or bacon until crisp and golden.

Add the shallots and garlic. Sauté, stirring constantly, until the shallots have wilted. Turn heat to medium-high and add the radicchio and herbs, reserving 1 tablespoon chopped parsley for garnish. Toss until the radicchio is barely wilted and cooked through, about 2 minutes. Add salt and pepper to taste. Set aside and keep warm, covered, while cooking the gnocchi.

If the sauce thickens too much before serving, thin it with a little of the gnocchi cooking water. Toss sauce with gnocchi and portion into warmed, shallow serving bowls. Garnish with the grated Parmigiano, toasted pine nuts and remaining chopped parsley.

The sauce can be made a few hours in advance, but does not keep well over a longer period. Do not freeze.

PORCINI MUSHROOM SAUCE

/ enough to generously sauce 6 servings

The woodsy aroma and flavor of porcini, particularly those from Italy, is unequaled by any other mushroom. If fresh porcini are available, substitute them for the white mushrooms called for in the recipe. Dried porcini are so intense that 1 ounce is more than enough to flavor the sauce. Adding cream makes this sauce particularly good with pasta and meat dishes — anywhere the distinctive flavor of porcini mushrooms is desired. Or, if you choose, you can go in the other direction and eliminate the porcini altogether to make a simple mushroom sauce.

½-1 ounce imported dried porcini mushrooms

1 pound fresh, firm, white mushrooms

4 tablespoons extra-virgin olive oil

2 large cloves garlic, minced

1 small shallot, minced

1-2 tablespoons fresh rosemary, mint, or sage leaves, minced (optional)

1 cup low sodium chicken or vegetable broth, homemade or high-quality canned

½ cup heavy cream, optional

Kosher salt and freshly ground black pepper to taste

Finely grated fresh Parmigiano-Reggiano for serving

Soak the dried porcini mushrooms in 1 cup lukewarm water for 20 to 30 minutes.

Gently remove the mushrooms without stirring up the water. Check for any remaining grit and remove it. Finely chop the mushrooms and set aside. Filter the water in which the mushrooms were soaked through a very fine sieve or cheesecloth and set aside.

Clean the fresh mushrooms with a brush if necessary and coarsely chop them. In a large skillet put the olive oil, garlic, shallot, and herbs, if using. Sauté over medium-high heat, stirring with a wooden spoon, until the garlic and shallot just begin to sizzle and release a delicate aroma. Add the fresh mushrooms and cook for 5 minutes, stirring frequently until they begin to release their liquid. Add the porcini and their soaking liquid, and cook until all the liquid boils away. Stir in the broth, salt, and pepper to taste. Add the heavy cream if you are using it. Lower the heat to a simmer and cook the sauce for 3 or 4 minutes, just until everything is hot and the sauce thickens a bit.

Keep warm while cooking gnocchi of choice. Toss with the hot gnocchi. Serve with freshly grated Parmigiano-Reggiano at the table.

This sauce will keep up to five days refrigerated in a tightly covered container. Do not freeze.

ROASTED EGGPLANT SAUCE

/ enough for 6 servings

Creamy and slightly sweet, this rich, flavorful sauce combines wonderfully with potato or cheese gnocchi. Choose firm, fresh eggplant for this recipe — older eggplant tends to be bitter. There's no need to salt and drain the eggplant before using it; the extra liquid is drained off once it's roasted and chopped.

2-2½ pounds large, deep purple eggplant

¼ cup extra-virgin olive oil

Kosher salt and freshly ground black pepper

Pinch red pepper flakes

¼ cup coarsely chopped flat-leaf parsley

4 tablespoons pine nuts, lightly toasted

3 garlic cloves, coarsely chopped

¼ cup lightly packed fresh mint

1 tablespoon small capers packed in vinegar, drained

¾ cup finely chopped cherry tomatoes

2 tablespoons extra-virgin olive oil

Kosher salt and freshly ground black pepper to taste

Freshly grated Parmigiano-Reggiano or semi-aged
    pecorino for serving

Preheat oven to 400° F. Place a rack in the middle. Line a baking sheet with parchment paper.

Cut eggplants in half lengthwise. Using a small, sharp knife, score interiors in a deep diagonal cross-hatch pattern. Brush with 4 tablespoons extra-virgin olive oil, sprinkle with salt and pepper, and place cut side down on the baking sheet. Bake until tender, about 30 to 45 minutes.

Transfer baking sheet to a wire rack. Turn the eggplant cut-side up and cool for 5 minutes. Scrape eggplant from the skins and place flesh in a fine-mesh sieve set over a bowl. Drain for 10 minutes. Discard the liquid. Coarsely chop the flesh and place it in a large bowl.

On a cutting board, mound the pepper flakes, parsley, pine nuts, garlic, mint, and capers. Finely chop, then mix with the chopped eggplant.

Mix the finely chopped cherry tomatoes with the 2 tablespoons of extra-virgin olive oil; add salt and pepper to taste. Set aside for garnish.

Reheat the sauce if necessary, then toss it with the hot, cooked gnocchi. Ladle into warmed, shallow serving bowls, garnish with chopped tomato, and serve immediately, passing grated Parmigiano-Reggiano at the table.

This sauce can be made a few hours in advance, but does not keep well over a longer period. Do not freeze.

SQUID & ROE SAUCE

/ enough for 4 to 6 servings

Gnocchi served with squid may sound odd, but I think of it as a twist on the very popular calamari salad with cannellini beans that is often found on restaurant menus. The cannellini beans are optional in this recipe, but they add an interesting dimension to the finished dish. The addition of bottarga (dried, preserved fish eggs — see page 244 for more information) elevates the dish to a more sophisticated level.

Previously frozen calamari, which are more tender than fresh, are recommended for this recipe. Be careful not to overcook the calamari; it can become rubbery.

2-3 tablespoons extra-virgin olive oil

2 medium shallots, finely chopped

2 garlic cloves, finely minced

1 cup finely chopped carrot

½ teaspoon fresh oregano, chopped

2 tablespoons finely chopped flat-leaf parsley

1 pound cleaned squid (bodies and tentacles)
    chopped into ½-inch pieces

1 cup dry white wine

1 tablespoon vinegar-packed capers, drained
    OR salt–packed capers, soaked in water for
    30 minutes (optional)

Pinch peperoncini flakes

1 tablespoon finely grated lemon zest

½ pound cherry tomatoes, halved

½ cup cooked cannellini beans (optional)

Kosher salt and freshly ground black pepper to taste

3-4 ounces bottarga, finely shaved, for garnish (optional)

In a medium skillet over medium heat, cook shallots and garlic together, stirring occasionally, about 2 minutes. Add carrots, reduce heat to low, and cook, stirring occasionally, until carrots begin to soften, 3 to 5 minutes.

Stir in oregano and parsley. Add squid and stir to coat with oil. Add white wine and increase heat to medium. Cook another 3 to 5 minutes, or until the squid are tender and the wine has reduced by half. If needed, add some water to the pan to maintain a saucy consistency. Don't let it dry out. Add peperoncini, lemon zest, halved cherry tomatoes, optional capers and/or cannellini beans. Cook another 2 minutes to soften the tomatoes. Season to taste with salt and freshly ground black pepper.

Reheat sauce and toss it with hot, cooked gnocchi. Divide among warmed, shallow serving bowls, garnish with bottarga, and serve immediately.

Do not freeze.

WILD MUSHROOM &
BLUEBERRY SAUCE

/ enough for 4 to 6 servings

*The original recipe for this sauce was given to me by
Cinzia Ubaldi, a chef/friend since I first arrived in
Perugia. Traditionally, the sauce is made with* mirtilli
rossi, *small red berries similar in taste to cranberries.*
Mirtilli rossi *are abundant in the Dolomite region of
northern Italy, where a wonderfully tart jam (*marmalata*)
is made from them and often used to fill thin egg crepes.*

*American cranberries overwhelm the delicate mushroom
flavors, but I found that blueberries add a surprising
sweetness that complements the wild mushrooms. I don't
recommend using porcini mushrooms in this recipe because
their strong woodsy flavor is too assertive. This sauce goes
best with potato or ricotta gnocchi.*

4 tablespoons extra-virgin olive oil

2 medium cloves garlic, minced

1 large shallot, minced to make ¼ cup

1 cup fresh blueberries, washed and well-drained,
   ½ cup reserved for garnish

2 teaspoons sugar

¾ cup dry, full-bodied red wine such as Cabernet,
   Merlot or Sagrantino from Umbria

¾ pound chanterelles or a mix of mild-flavored wild
   mushrooms, such as oyster, trumpet, or enokitake,
   combined with white or cremini mushrooms,
   cleaned and coarsely chopped

½ cup deep-flavored low-sodium beef stock,
   preferably homemade

Kosher salt and freshly ground black pepper

2 tablespoons unsalted butter, chilled and cut into
   small pieces

Fresh mint leaves and Parmigiano-Reggiano shavings
   for garnish

Put 2 tablespoons of the olive oil, the minced garlic, and
shallots in a large skillet. Sauté gently over medium heat
until the garlic and shallots just begin to sizzle. Add the
wine, blueberries, and sugar, and reduce sauce by half.

Heat the remaining oil in another skillet. Add the fresh
mushrooms and cook, stirring, over medium-high heat
until they release their moisture. Add the mushrooms to
the reduced wine sauce. Add the beef stock, salt, and
freshly ground black pepper to taste. Melt in the chilled
butter and toss immediately with warm cooked gnocchi.

Garnish with mint leaves, a few fresh blueberries, and
some Parmigiano-Reggiano shavings.

Do not freeze.

FUNDAMENTAL RECIPES

Included here are some basic recipes used in the gnocchi preparations in this book. From homemade ricotta (*Yummmm!*) to the best Italian-style chicken broth I've ever tasted, you will want to refer to these recipes for all your Italian cooking.

BASIC FIRM POLENTA

/ makes about 3 cups

4 cups water OR a combination of milk and water

1½ cups medium-grain polenta, preferably stoneground

1 teaspoon kosher salt

2-4 tablespoons unsalted butter, softened

Bring the water to a simmer in a deep, heavy saucepan. Add the salt.

Keeping the liquid simmering over medium-high heat, add the cornmeal to the pan in a very thin stream, showering it over the water while stirring vigorously with a whisk.

When you have added all the cornmeal, reduce heat to low and cook, stirring frequently with a wooden spoon, about 35 to 40 minutes, or until polenta is smooth and very stiff — the texture of cold mashed potatoes. Do not be tempted to shorten the cooking time or the polenta will have a "raw" taste.

Remove from heat and stir in the butter.

FRIED SAGE LEAVES

½ cup extra-virgin olive oil,
    OR enough to fill a small saucepan to ½ inch

Fresh whole sage leaves

Dash salt

Heat the oil in a small saucepan over medium-high heat until a wooden skewer inserted in the oil begins to sizzle. Adding 5 to 6 sage leaves at a time and fry for about 15 seconds, or just until the oil stops sizzling. Remove the leaves quickly, before the sage begins to brown, or the leaves will be bitter.

Transfer the leaves to a paper towel-lined plate. The leaves will become crisp as they cool. Sprinkle lightly with salt.

BESCIAMELLA
(BASIC ITALIAN BÉCHAMEL)

/ makes 3 cups

Besciamella, or béchamel, thought by some to be of French origin, appeared first in Italian cookbooks and is believed to have been introduced to French cuisine by the great chefs of Italian-born Catherine de Medici, who married Henry II of France. In Italian legend, all the best food that France has to offer is a product of her influence.

Traditional béchamel is created by whisking hot milk into a cooked flour and butter mixture called a roux, made of equal parts butter and flour. The creamy, rich white sauce is the basis for many Italian dishes and is not difficult to make, but requires a bit of patient stirring as it thickens. If a thinner sauce is desired, more hot milk can be added once the cooking process is completed.

4 tablespoons butter

4 tablespoons sifted flour

2 cups hot whole milk

Salt and freshly ground black pepper

Few fresh gratings of nutmeg (optional)

Melt the butter in a medium saucepan over medium-low heat until it begins to froth. Sprinkle in the flour and whisk for 2 minutes, or until the paste begins to bubble. Do not allow to brown. Remove pan from the heat, cool slightly, then add the hot milk all at once, whisking constantly to avoid lumps. Season to taste with salt and pepper, lower heat to very low and continue whisking until sauce is the consistency of thick cream. Do not boil. Increase heat slightly, bring it to a simmer and immediately remove from the heat.

To cool this sauce for later use, cover it with parchment paper to prevent a skin from forming. To store in the refrigerator: Cool sauce completely, pour into container, and place a piece of cling film directly in contact with the surface of the sauce. It will keep 4 to 5 days.

HOMEMADE CHICKEN BROTH

I suggest you always make your own chicken broth and be wary of those available in supermarkets: with few exceptions, they lack flavor and contain too much salt. I prefer a deeply flavored broth and always keep a few containers of homemade in the freezer.

Being a fan of roast chicken, I reserve the leftover bones and skin, toss it all in a pot, cover it with water, and simmer it slowly for 1½ hours. Once cooled to room temperature, I strain it and freeze it in usable quantities. I find that the bones from one chicken will make about 3 cups of light- to medium-flavored broth usable in most recipes that call for additional liquid, not just gnocchi or soup recipes.

Once thawed, I adjust the intensity of flavor of the broth by cooking it longer to make it stronger or adding water to make it lighter. I then add salt and freshly ground pepper to taste to complement the recipe I'm using.

Alternatively, you can follow your favorite recipe for homemade broth and stock it in your freezer, or make a batch of the Italian Brodo on page 224. If you don't have any homemade broth available, substitute a high-quality commercially-made one, but make sure it has a low-sodium content. You can always add salt to taste, but you can't save an overly salty dish.

You can also substitute a high-quality, low-sodium vegetable or beef broth in any of the recipes that call for chicken broth.

My favorite store-bought brands are Swanson's and Progresso. Be sure they're labeled low-sodium broth, not stock.

ITALIAN BRODO

/   makes about 2 quarts

Homemade broth, be it for a soup or used as the liquid in other recipes, makes a significant difference in the outcome of any dish. In the U.S., adequate packaged substitutes can be purchased (see page 223 for suggestions) and used when necessary. In Italy, where canned products are not the norm, it's just not available. I encourage any serious home cook to make a big batch of brodo *(broth) and keep it in the freezer in conveniently sized containers.*

This recipe for brodo has a base of beef, chicken, and pork, and is designed specifically to serve as a soup base where the flavor is of utmost importance. It's also a good choice for any sauce that calls for the addition of broth.

4 chicken legs, thighs attached

2 beef shanks, cut into 1-inch pieces by your butcher

1 ham hock, 2-3 pounds

1 medium yellow onion

4 stalks with leaves cut from a fennel bulb

1 large carrot

5 large cloves garlic

4 fresh plum tomatoes

20 stems fresh parsley

8 (4-inch) sprigs fresh thyme

2 large bay leaves

2 teaspoons crushed peppercorns

1 teaspoon kosher salt

Parmigiano rind (if available)

Place the chicken, beef, and ham hock in a deep stockpot, large enough to hold all the meat comfortably. Cover with cold water and bring slowly to a simmer over medium-high heat. As impurities rise to the surface, skim them off with a fine-meshed sieve.

Peel and cut the onion into large dice. Cut the fennel stalks and carrot into ½-inch pieces. Peel and coarsely chop the garlic cloves. Halve and core the tomatoes, then cut into quarters.

Once the impurities have all been skimmed from the surface of the broth, add the prepared vegetables along with the herbs, peppercorns, salt, and Parmigiano rind. Partially cover the pot and simmer lightly for an hour.

Remove the chicken legs. When cool enough to handle, remove the meat and set aside for another use. Return the chicken bones to the broth. Continue to simmer an hour or two more, until the ham hock and beef shank are tender. Remove the beef and ham hock from the broth and allow to cool. Remove the meat from the bones and set aside for another use. Discard all the bones.

With a slotted spoon, remove and discard the heavy solids from the broth. Let the broth cool a bit, then strain through a fine-mesh sieve lined with cheesecloth. Season to taste with additional salt.

Cool and refrigerate. Remove any hardened fat and discard. At this stage, you may cook the broth for an additional period of time to concentrate it before freezing in desired portions.

Adapted from a recipe by Tony Minichiello in Rouxbe recipes

HOMEMADE FRESH RICOTTA

This is my favorite basic recipe for fresh ricotta cheese. It requires just a few utensils and ingredients, and is simple to make. If you want a different flavor and a more moist cheese, you can substitute buttermilk for the white vinegar and mix both milks together at the start.

Do not use low-fat or part-skim milk to make ricotta; the flavor comes from the cream in the whole milk. Pasteurized rather than ultra-pasteurized milk produces bigger, creamier curds with a higher yield. For desserts, add 1 pint heavy whipping cream along with the milk for a richer and creamier result. If you're lucky enough to have goat or sheep milk available, by all means use it as a tasty alternative. You can also substitute equal amounts of lemon juice for the vinegar if you prefer a slightly citrusy flavor.

The recipe halves easily.

EQUIPMENT

A large heavy pot

Cheesecloth

A cooking thermometer

Colander

INGREDIENTS

1 gallon whole milk

⅓ cup distilled white vinegar or lemon juice

½ teaspoon kosher salt

   OR 1 gallon whole milk

1 quart buttermilk

½ teaspoon kosher salt

Place 1 gallon of milk in a large, heavy, nonreactive pot on medium heat. Include the buttermilk if using. Add salt and stir briefly to dissolve. Allow milk to heat up slowly, stirring occasionally to prevent sticking or burning. This could take up to 30 to 40 minutes. Watch carefully and check the temperature with a cooking thermometer. You want it to reach 180 to 185 degrees, near scalding.

When the milk reaches the correct temperature, take the pot off the burner, add the vinegar or lemon juice if using, and give it one brief stir, just enough to disperse the acid. Don't stir up the milk too much or you risk breaking up the big ricotta curds into tiny, grainy ones. Cover with a dry, clean dishtowel and allow the mixture to sit undisturbed on the counter for a couple of hours or more.

When the ricotta has rested, dampen the cheesecloth and place it inside the colander. With a finely slotted spoon, carefully ladle the ricotta into the prepared colander, keeping the curd chunks as large as you can. The more they are handled the tougher they will become. Place the colander filled with ricotta inside a larger pan or bowl so it can drain freely. Let it drain for at least 30 minutes or up to 2 hours, depending on how creamy or dry you want the cheese to be.

Lift the cheesecloth by the four corners and twist gently. If the liquid runs clear, squeeze a little more. If the liquid runs milky, there is no more need to squeeze. Placed the cheese in a tightly sealed container and refrigerate for up to 10 days. Do not freeze.

What to do with the liquid leftover from making ricotta? If you make your own bread you can use it in place of the water called for in the recipe.

SAUTÉED GREENS

/ makes 3 to 4 cups

*Many recipes in this book use a variety of fresh greens.
Dark leafy greens are a staple of the Italian diet. Wild
greens, or* verde di campagna, *are prized when in season.
Unless otherwise noted, any kind of greens suitable for
cooking can be substituted for those suggested in the
recipes. Choose your favorite.*

*When cooking greens, rinse under cool water, shake off the
excess, and strip the leaves from stems. Save the stems for
another use. In Italy, deeply colored beet and chard ribs
are used to make a beautiful risotto or are added to pasta
sauces. I've learned from my local Italian farmers how
to use almost every bit of every vegetable; very little is
wasted in the Italian kitchen.*

3 pounds greens, such as curly endive, spinach,
    escarole, kale, dandelion, chard, beet, or mustard

Extra-virgin olive oil

3-4 large cloves garlic, slivered

Salt and freshly ground black pepper

Wash the greens well, strip away any large ribs, and
chop the greens. The water clinging to the leaves will
help prevent them from scorching. Lightly coat the
bottom of a large sauté pan with olive oil and set it
over medium heat. Add the garlic and heat just to
warm it. Do not brown.

Add the chopped greens to the pan, sautéing until
wilted and heated through, adding only enough water
to prevent browning. Be aware that different greens will
require different cooking times. Check occasionally and
add a small amount of water if necessary. If using
tougher greens such as kale or mustard that take
longer to cook, cover them tightly, reduce the heat
to a simmer, and cook until tender.

When greens are tender, proceed with the desired
recipe. If adding to gnocchi dough, finely chop,
then squeeze all excess water from the greens before
continuing. Any extra liquid will require more flour
in the dough and the resulting gnocchi will be tough.
Season with salt and pepper to taste and cover and
keep warm until needed.

SWEET CHESTNUT PURÉE

/ enough to stuff 1 recipe gnocchi

14.8 ounces roasted, peeled vacuum-packed chestnuts

1 cup sugar

1½ cups water

1 tablespoon vanilla extract

Roughly chop the chestnuts and place in a saucepan
with the sugar and water. Bring to a boil, cover and
simmer them for 30 minutes, or until the chestnuts are
softened and the liquid is thick and syrupy. Remove
the cover, if needed, to reduce the liquid. Remove from
heat and strain the chestnuts, reserving the syrup.

Purée the chestnuts in a blender with the vanilla,
adding syrup as needed, until the texture is smooth
and thick enough to hold its shape.

This purée can be refrigerated, completely covered,
for up to two weeks.

ROASTING PEPPERS

Place whole peppers directly on a gas burner or gas or charcoal grill. Roast the peppers until the skin becomes charred, wrinkled, and loose, turning them frequently with a pair of tongs.

The peppers can also be broiled in an oven, about 5 to 6 inches from the broiling element, until the skins are wrinkled and charred.

Once roasted, place the peppers in a bowl, put a plate on top, and let them steam at least 15 minutes to loosen the skins. Reserve any juice that has collected from the steaming peppers in the bottom of the bowl, then rub the skins off the peppers with your hand or a paper towel. Don't worry about getting every bit of skin — and don't rinse the peppers, as this will wash away a lot of the flavor.

Open the peppers and scrape away the seeds and veins. Cut as desired and return to the bowl of reserved juice. The peppers will keep for couple of days well covered and refrigerated. Be sure to make extra to top off your next panino, add to a frittata, or spark up a green salad.

PEELING TOMATOES

The easiest way to peel tomatoes and retain their fresh flavor is by lightly scalding them. While it may seem time-consuming and messy, it's a necessary step to guarantee a smooth sauce.

Bring a large pot of water to a boil. Fill a large bowl with ice water and set it next to the stove.

Remove any stems and slice a small x in the bottom of the tomatoes. Working in small batches, drop the tomatoes into the boiling water for 30 to 45 seconds. As soon as the skins start to wither, remove them with a slotted spoon and transfer to the ice water. Be sure to remove the tomatoes from the boiling water before they begin to cook.

When cooled just enough to handle, transfer to a cutting board and either peel them with a pairing knife or slip the skins off with your fingers. Repeat until all the tomatoes have been poached and peeled.

Cut the tomatoes in half. Seed them if desired, then chop according to recipe directions.

TOASTING NUTS

In the past, when a recipe called for toasted nuts, I would think for a moment of avoiding that step, not wanting to turn on the oven, use the energy, and dirty yet another pan. But I knew that the time and energy spent on this task is of utmost importance to the final dish and not to be overlooked.

I don't remember how or why I began doing this, but I now roast all nuts using a microwave. It's quick, easy, uses little energy, and is far superior to the stovetop method as the nuts are cooked all the way through. I will often roast extra nuts to keep on hand for adding to salads.

There isn't a definitive recipe for roasting nuts in a microwave oven. The timing depends on how many nuts you are processing, the power of your oven, and the kind of nut you're toasting. Pine nuts, walnuts, and pecans are the most delicate, while almonds and hazelnuts take a bit longer.

Start with the quantity of nut you want to toast, place them on a paper towel or a microwavable dish, put the power on medium and set the timer for 1 minute. Test after 1 minute and continue to test at 30 second to 1 minute intervals until the nuts are toasted to your liking. Eventually, you'll find a time and setting that works best for you. Remember that the nuts will crisp up as they cool.

TOSSING A GREEN SALAD

Commercial salad dressings, which can be cloyingly heavy, aren't used in Italy. When you order a mixed green salad in an Italian restaurant, the oil and vinegar is usually brought to the table and you add it to taste yourself.

Try experimenting with the Italian way of dressing a salad the next time you serve your favorite greens:

* Wash and spin-dry all the greens and place them in a large, roomy salad bowl.

* Dribble with your best extra-virgin olive oil. Using your hands, lightly toss the greens, adding more olive oil as needed until the ingredients begin to glisten. Sprinkle with coarse salt and freshly ground black pepper to taste. Toss lightly with your hands again and check for salt, adding more if desired.

* Sprinkle the salad with the acid ingredient of your choice — fresh lemon juice or a favorite vinegar — and continue to lightly toss and taste until you reach the desired balance. If you like to add herbs, shallots, garlic, or mustard to your dressing, they can be premixed with the acid and added at the same time.

* Add finishing ingredients — such as grated cheese, chopped dried fruit, or prepared vegetables — last.

* Toss the salad again and serve immediately; if you allow the salad to rest, it will begin to wilt.

Tossing a salad in this way gives you more control over the balance of dressing, seasoning, greens, and other ingredients. Adding the oil first coats the delicate greens and prevents the loss of moisture caused by salt and acid attacking the unprotected leaves. Experiment with different acids and oils to find those that go best with the greens and other ingredients you choose for each salad.

THE FULL PANTRY

This chapter explains the most important Italian ingredients used in recipes in this book, as well as other useful information. Included is a discussion of cheeses, flours, fats, cured meats, tomatoes, potatoes, miscellaneous ingredients, tools, and storage tips that will guide you through the gnocchi-making process.

Gnocchi is part of the *cucina povera*, or common, simple cooking tradition — so all the ingredients and tools are easily available in Italy, and, with few exceptions, in the United States as well. If you live in a large city or small but sophisticated food town, most everything you will need to make gnocchi can probably be found at a local natural foods or specialty shop, or an Italian delicatessen. If your community cupboard is bare, there are many good mail-order sources available online or by phone. A few of my favorite sources include D'Artagnan, Gourmet and Dean & Deluca for ingredients, and Fante's Kitchen Shop for tools. You can also check online for purveyors of specific products.

CHEESES

The number of wonderful cheeses found in Italy can't be replicated in the U.S. Even though many varieties are imported, many are not allowed into the country due to U.S. regulations. The recipes is this book are based on cheeses readily available in the U.S., but I also suggest you try experimenting with what's available near you, especially if you're fortunate enough to live in an area with a good Italian market. Also keep in mind that replacing one cheese with another in any of the recipes requires that the consistency be equal.

/ ASIAGO

A popular unpasteurized cows' milk cheese from the northern Italian region of Veneto, this cheese is produced only on the Asiago plateau in the foothills of the Dolomites. It's available fresh, as Pressato, which has a smooth texture, or as Asiago d'allevo which is aged and crumbly. The mild-flavored Pressato is the Asiago used in the recipes in the book. It's also my favorite cheese for burgers and pianini.

/ FONTINA

Fontina Val d'Aosta is an unpasteurized cows' milk cheese from the Aosta Valley in the Italian Alps south of France and Switzerland. It has a mild, nutty flavor, melts evenly, and is extremely aromatic. It's typically used in northern Italian cheese sauces in combination with other melting cheeses such as Gruyère or Emmental, and is a favorite in Italian fondue. Fontina cheese from countries other than Italy is not as complex or flavorful.

/ GOAT CHEESE

Caprino refers to any of a variety of Italian cheeses made from goats' milk. For the few recipes here that call for it, you can substitute a soft chèvre. It's very similar and easy to find in American markets.

/ GORGONZOLA

Produced for centuries in northern Italy and named after the commune of Gorgonzola where it originated, Gorgonzola is one of the world's oldest blue-veined cheeses. Made from whole, pasteurized cows' milk, it is usually aged for two to three months before arriving in the markets as Gorgonzola Dolce. The rich and creamy texture and delicate flavor can become quite firm and strong as the cheese matures. Cheeses up to six months old are sold as Gorgonzola Piccante or Gorgonzola Montagne. For cooking purposes, I recommend Gorgonzola Dolce for its melting properties and savory richness. Look for it at your local cheese shop. There are no substitutions.

/ GRANA PADANO

Grana Padano is made over a much wider area of Italy with different regulations and controls. The name comes from *grana* or grain, which refers to its crystalline texture, and Padano, which refers to the Pianura Padano valley where it originated. Following the same basic cheese-making process as Parmigiano-Reggiano, the main difference between the two cheeses is that cows producing Grana Padano are allowed to ingest silage, preservatives, and antibiotics, while cows producing milk for Parmigiano-Reggiano eat only grass and grains. And while Parmigiano-Reggiano is made from whole and partially-skimmed milk, Grana Padano is made from 100 percent whole milk. For the recipes in this book, one can be substituted for the other with equal results.

/ GRUYÈRE & EMMANTAL

Similar and interchangeable in cooking, both Gruyère and Emmantal are cheeses from Switzerland that are often used in Italian recipes originating in the Piemonte, Val d'Aosti and Lombardia regions of Italy that border that country.

/ MASCARPONE

Technically not a cheese, mascarpone is simply cream coagulated with an acidic agent after which the whey is removed. What is left is a luxuriously smooth, thick and luscious product that can be used in both savory and sweet dishes. In the U.S. it's well known as the cheese used in tiramisu, while in Italy its use extends far beyond the dessert arena. It's readily available in the dairy section of your local grocery store.

/ MOZZARELLA

Originally made from buffalo milk near Naples, Italy, most mozzarella today is produced from cows' milk. *Mozzarella di bufala*, if you can find it, is creamier and contains more fat. Feel free to substitute it for the cows' milk variety called for in any of these recipes. All the recipes in this book call for fresh, whole cows' milk mozzarella packaged in whey or water rather than the low-fat, low-moisture factory "string cheese" mozzarella usually packaged in plastic logs. Fresh mozarella usually comes in two to three different sizes: *ovoline* (balls weighing 4 ounces each);

bocconcini (small bites about 1-inch round); and *ciliegine* (small balls about the size of cherries). The cheese should be mild and delicate, and taste of fresh milk. Ciliegine are an especially nice addition to tomato-based gnocchi sauces since they're about the same size as the gnocchi and marry well with tomato. Fresh mozzarella doesn't keep well, so use it as soon as possible after purchase.

/ PARMIGIANO-REGGIANO

Undoubtedly the "King of Cheeses," Parmigiano is the Italian word that refers to cheeses that have been produced on hundreds of artisanal dairies in the provinces of Parma, Reggio Emilia, Modena, and parts of Mantua and Bologna for over 900 years. What the cows eat, which farm the milk came from, the *casaro* (cheesemaker) responsible, and the date the cheese is made are all controlled and recorded so that each wheel can be traced to its origin.

It takes 600 liters of milk to produce one cheese wheel weighing about 40 kg or 85 pounds. Each wheel is assigned a unique number and allowed to mature a minimum of 12 months, after which it's examined by experts of the *Consorzio del Formaggio Parmigiano-Reggiano* and either rejected or fire-branded with the month and year of production and its cheese dairy registration number, after which it's either sent for sale or for further aging up to 30 months. After 18 months, the mark "Export" or "Extra" is added to the label. Any further maturation identity is noted with a colored seal of either Red (18 months), silver (22 months) or gold (30 months).

Other cheeses labeled "Parmesan" or "Parmigiano" manufactured outside of the European Union, such as in Australia and the U.S., for example, do not follow the same rules and regulations and are not of equal quality.

Should you have the interest or opportunity to view the Parmigiano cheese-making process — and you don't mind rising about 4 a.m. — you can make an appointment at a *caseificio* (cheese factory) to watch the production. It's an amazing experience that will no doubt convince you why Parmigiano-Reggiano is the "King of Cheeses."

/ PECORINO CHEESE

To an American, pecorino cheese usually means pecorino romano, the sheep's milk cheese most often associated with Italian cuisine and most often found in American markets. The cheese — whose name refers to Romans, not Rome — is produced principally on the island of Sardinia, the area of Tuscany known as Maremma, and Lazio, the region that includes Rome. One of the most ancient Italian cheeses, it was a staple part of Roman soldiers' diets when they were at war.

In Italy, pecorino (from *pecora*, the Italian word for sheep) refers to any cheese made from sheep's milk. It can be sold as *fresco* (fresh, mild, and young); *semi-stagionato* (semi-aged, from 40 days to 4 months, a firmer and slightly sharper variation); and *stagionato* (aged at least 4 months,

rich and crumbly). The flavor may vary subtly by the region in which it's produced, with some of the best coming from Sardinia or Tuscany.

Pecorino romano is very hard, very sharp and extremely salty. Because of its dry and granular texture, it is often used instead of Parmigiano-Reggiano for grating over pastas, but it can easily overwhelm rather than compliment the dish. However, a good semi-stagionato or stagionato pecorino can be used in place of Parmigiano-Reggiano to finish dishes, and is often the choice of most Italian regions from Umbria down to Sicily. In the U.S., one can find a good aged pecorino in specialty cheese shops, although it is not as readily available as Parmigiano-Reggiano or pecorino romano.

/ PIAVE

One of my all-time favorite Italian cheeses is Piave, a cows' milk cheese produced in the province of Belluno in the Dolomites region. Named after the Piave River, it has a DOP or Protected Designation of Origin. I first tasted it on a trip to the Dolomites, and later found it available in the U.S. at the semi-hard aged stage as Piave Vecchio (blue label) and the aged Vecchio Selezione Oro (red label). Readily available in specialty cheese shops, it has an intense, buttery, slightly sweet flavor similar to a young Parmigiano.

/ PROVOLONE & SCAMORZA

The major difference between these two cheeses is the region in which they are made and the names they are given. Otherwise, they are similar in both taste and style of production. They are formed the same way as mozzarella, using the stretched-dough method, then allowed to ripen for two or more weeks, reaching a semi-soft and elastic texture comparable to a firm, dry mozzarella. Both are available smoked and can be used interchangeably, so look for what's available in your area.

/ FRESH RICOTTA

Ricotta, which means recooked, refers to a fresh Italian cheese made from whey left over from the cow, sheep, goat, or Italian water buffalo cheese-making process, with some fresh whole milk added to the mix. Creamy white, slightly sweet, and perfectly smooth, a high-quality ricotta is unmatchable, and is used in every dish imaginable, from appetizer to dessert, in the Italian cuisine.

The cows' milk variety is readily available in the U.S., but you will need to read the label closely to make sure it doesn't contain any added ingredients, such as gums or carrageenan, which will cause it to retain moisture. These additives will adversely affect the texture and flavor of the ricotta and will ruin a recipe. Ricotta should contain only milk, an acid and salt. Only use ricotta made from whole milk. Should it weep liquid, drain it in a strainer lined with fine cheesecloth and placed over a bowl for 30 minutes or longer to remove any excess whey. If it's a bit grainy in texture, beat it until it's creamy. Ricotta is highly perishable. Refrigerated, it will keep no more than a week once opened or freshly made.

I've included a recipe in the Fundamental Recipes chapter for making it at home. It's very simple and produces a far superior product to what's available in U.S. markets. Should you be lucky enough to have access to sheep or goat milk, by all means use it.

Pressed for time? The best commercial substitute I've found is Trader Joe's brand whole milk variety.

/ RICOTTA SALATA

In central and southern Italy, ricotta is pressed, salted, dried, and aged as a means of preserving the cheese. This cheese is firm, with a salty tang, and is used for grating, crumbling, or shaving to complement other foods. Good quality ricotta salata is readily available in many U.S. markets.

Smoking ricotta is another method of preserving the cheese readily found in northern Italy, but rarely imported to the U.S. There are recipes on the internet for making it at home — all you need is a simple stove-top smoker. Ricotta affumicata plays an integral role in many of the northern Italian gnocchi recipes included here, and is worth searching out or making. Check the internet for mail-order sources. Ricotta affumicata has a slightly grey crust and a delicate charred wood aroma. In a pinch, smoked mozzarella or provolone can be substituted to provide the smoky flavor, but the texture is very different.

I first tasted ricotta affumicata during a trip to the Dolomites, where it was lightly grated over a simple bowl of buttered pumpkin gnocchi. When I searched for the cheese at my local *salumeria*, or cheesemonger/delicatessen, I quickly learned how many local Italian foods remain just that: local. Ricotta affumicata, common in northern Italian cuisine, is rarely available south of Bologna, and ricotta salata, common in southern Italy, is rarely available in the north.

It's easy enough to imagine that, with the readily available supply of wood used to heat homes in the north, smoking food to preserve it was a natural development in the mountain regions. In southern Italy, it's warm year-round and houses are not heated with wood; salt from the sea is more abundant and thus more commonly used to preserve food. So — I make sure to pick up some smoked ricotta during my yearly hiking excursion in the Dolomites, and save a space for it in my suitcase for the return trip to the U.S.

Produced in the Lombardia region and named after Val Taleggio, where it originated, Taleggio is one of the oldest soft cheeses produced. Because it's also one of Italy's most well-known and popular cheeses, it's generally available in the U.S. Taleggio has a thin, washed rind and a soft, sumptuous interior with a strong aroma that can be stinky and off-putting. The flavor, however, is relatively mild and slightly fruity. It melts well due to its high fat content and will nearly dissolve into a bowl of hot gnocchi when added at the last minute.

POTATOES

The potato appeared in Italy around 1562. First thought to be poisonous, potatoes were slowly accepted as they are easy to sow and harvest and are more productive than grains. Recipes for the first potato gnocchi appeared not long after the spuds gained a foothold in the country's cuisine.

Worldwide, there are over 4,000 varieties of potatoes that fall into three categories: starchy, all-purpose, and waxy, with the majority either starchy (farinose) or waxy (cerose). The starchy varieties are generally preferred for frying and baking as they break up easily when cooked; the waxy varieties, which maintain their structure when boiled, work well in salads and slicing. In between are the all-purpose potatoes, which are moderate in starch content and suitable for all preparations.

Potatoes found in Italian markets are historically more numerous and diverse than varieties available in the U.S. — although the starchy potato known as a russet is not found in Italy, nor is it equal to any of the starchy potatoes available in Italy. The russet baking potato that has over-whelmed markets in the U.S. was primarily developed to supply McDonald's with raw material for French fries.

I disagree with the many American chefs who recommend using russets for potato gnocchi. After years of experience preparing them, I've found that russets tend to produce an undesirably grainy texture. Waxy, or other non-starchy potatoes, don't work well either; potato gnocchi made with these varieties are often gummy and heavy.

Italian experts usually suggest using "yellow" or all-purpose potatoes for gnocchi — and those are the kind I used when first making gnocchi with my friend, Anna Maria Rodriguez d'Amato. Yukon Golds, now readily available in U.S. markets, are the best substitution for the all-purpose yellow potatoes used in Italy. They have a very thin skin, a superior potato flavor, a wonderfully smooth texture, and a beautiful golden color, and can be baked, microwaved, or boiled with equally good results. Gnocchi dough made with Yukon Golds is very easy to work with and freezes far better than dough made with russets.

Purple potatoes, a starchy potato sometimes used for gnocchi in Italy, make a violet gnocchi that have a very nice potato flavor and can be substituted in the basic potato recipe. The unusual color can make them a fun alternative, although the violet hue is unappealing and visually challenging to pair with many sauces.

TOMATOES

Today Italian food and tomatoes are almost synonymous, although that is a relatively recent phenomenon. Pomi d'oro, so called because of their golden or reddish color when mature, were first noted in Italy in 1548. Introduced by the Spaniards, tomatoes — along with potatoes and eggplants — were initially thought to be poisonous, and used more as ornaments than foodstuffs. The oldest known Italian recipe using tomatoes didn't appear until 1692 in Naples — more than 100 years later — where the overripe ones were turned into tomato sauce.

Over the next several hundred years, unique varieties have been developed for other uses, including dried tomatoes, sauce tomatoes, pizza tomatoes, and tomatoes meant for long-term storage. Local markets overflow with every shape and color from tiny green, yellow and red ciliegini (cherries) or datarini (little dates) to small red and green elongated Marinda, to pear-shaped Roma and San Marzano, to beautifully ridged Cuore di Bue (bull's heart) and bulbous green to deep red salad tomatoes — each favored for its particular properties.

Tomatoes grown in Italy are known to have a more intense flavor, partly because of the climate and also because of the soil. San Marzano tomatoes are a prime example of this. The name applies both to the specific geographic region in which they are grown as well as to the tomato variety. Although San Marzano tomatoes grown anywhere other than the San Marzano region around Naples can be perfectly fine, they're not as delicious. San Marzano tomatoes from San Marzano are what one wants.

In Italy, I use fresh tomatoes for sauce — San Marzano when available, or pear-shaped paste tomatoes that are part of the same variety. They are meatier, less acidic, and cook down to a wonderful, naturally rich sauce.

In the U.S., I usually use fresh, in season, pear tomatoes, or I look for one of three canned varieties: *Cento certified San Marzano* tomatoes (best for pizza sauce), Cento "San Marzano Style" tomatoes, or Muir Glen Organic pear tomatoes, for pasta or gnocchi sauce. These brands produce the most authentically flavored Italian tomato sauces; many U.S. brands add sugar in the canning process and the resulting sauce is cloying sweet.

FLOURS

/ BUCKWHEAT FLOUR

Grano saraceno, or buckwheat, has long been consumed in northern Italy, particularly in the Alpine valley of Valtelina in Lombardy, where it's used in crêpes, polenta *taragna* and pasta *pizzoccheri*. It can be used alone to make gnocchi, or as an addition to potato-based gnocchi. It has a unique, earthy flavor and is a gluten-free alternative to wheat flours.

/ CHESTNUT FLOUR

Farina di Castagne, or chestnut flour, is slightly sweet and widely used in cakes and desserts in the Liguria, Tuscany, and Emiglia-Romagna regions of Italy. It also makes a wonderful delicately flavored gnocchi. Made from ground chestnuts, it has less fat content and more carbohydrates than other nut flours, with many of the same properties of wheat flour. Readily available on line, it's highly perishable and is best stored frozen in a tightly sealed plastic bag for up to six months.

/ CORNMEAL

Cornmeal appears in many gnocchi recipes from the northern region of Italy. First introduced to the country in the second half of the 17th century in the region of Bergamo, it quickly joined chickpea flour, chestnut flour, millet, barley, and other grains as one of the peasant porridge staples still enjoyed today. Polenta, which historically refers to the popular dish and not the grain, has been complicated by U.S. manufacturers that have begun labeling their uncooked ground corn as polenta, corn flour, cornmeal, corn grits, etc.

When purchasing cornmeal for gnocchi-making in the U.S., I look for the grind (fine, medium, or coarse) rather than the description or name used on the label. I never choose grits (traditionally made from a softer corn variety), or instant or quick-cooking polenta, which lack flavor and texture. Worse yet is cooked polenta packaged in tube form, which contains preservatives and other ingredients that affect the flavor.

Use the specific grind and cooking time recommended for each recipe and be aware that cooking times vary according to grind. It's important to fully cook the cornmeal for easy digestion, so don't be tempted to shorten the process even though the porridge looks or tastes done.

Cornmeal is available prepackaged as well as in the bulk aisles of natural foods stores. For the best flavor, look for meal that is stoneground and preferably organic.

/ FARRO

Farro is an ancient grain — still widely cultivated in Italy, mostly in Abruzzo and Tuscany — that is gaining in popularity both as a wheat replacement and a whole-grain addition to salads and main dishes. Although it's not gluten-free, it has a considerably lower gluten content than commercial wheat. Usually made from spelt (or *farro grande*), it's available in most natural food stores.

/ GARBANZO/CHICKPEA FLOUR

Farina di ceci, better known in the Near East, has always played a visible roll in Italian cuisine, particularly in Liguria, where it's used to make a flatbread called *farinata* or *cecina*, and in Sicily, where it's used to make *panelle*, a kind of fritter. Garbanzo flour, which has a strong, slightly nutty flavor, is widely available, particularly in natural foods markets. It can be used to replace some, but not all, of the regular flour when making potato gnocchi.

/ NUT FLOURS

Hazelnuts from northern Italy and almonds from Sicily are widely available in Italy. Roasted and ground into flour, they make a wonderfully delicate gnocchi when used to replace some — but not all — of the flour in a recipe. If you make your own nut flour, lightly toast the nuts and grind in a food processor, being careful not to make nut butter. They will be coarser than commercial nut flours, so if you want a finer texture, pass them through a fine sieve. Walnuts and pine nuts are more often used in pesto or sauces than in gnocchi dough.

/ ROVEJA FLOUR

Made from a variety of pea cultivated during Neolithic times, roveja is staging a comeback in the central regions of Umbria and Le Marche, where many farmers want to re-establish heirloom crops. Traditionally used in soups, the peas have a strong, but pleasant, almost herby flavor. As a flour, roveja is gluten-free and is a great alternative to wheat flour in a few of the gnocchi recipes (like alla Romana) where gluten is not required to form the dough. Recipe headnotes will tell you where you can make successful substitutions.

I discovered roveja recently in my Italian hometown of Perugia and use it interchangeably with chickpea flour. It's not yet easy to find in the U.S., although you can mail order from Italy at the following site: www.saporidinorcia.com. Look for *farecchiata* when ordering. Production is presently low, but with more people searching for gluten-free products, it stands a chance of gaining in popularity. If you travel to central Italy, save room in your suitcase for a pound or two.

/ SEMOLINA FLOUR

Semolina, from the Italian word meaning bran, is the coarsely ground endosperm — the nutritive tissue within the seeds of flowering plants — of durum wheat. A beautiful golden color and very high in protein, it's used to make quality *pasta asciutta* (dried pasta), as well as some Italian breads. A sweet pudding made from semolina and milk has been eaten since Roman times; a savory version was used to make the first gnocchi — you'll find a recipe included in this collection.

/ WHEAT FLOUR

American and Italian wheat flours are not interchangeable, and the differences between them can be confusing. In the U.S., flours are categorized by their protein content; in Italy, they're categorized by how finely the wheat has been ground, using a scale of 2 (very coarse) to 000 (the finest). Each grind can then vary greatly in its protein content.

The protein content of flour impacts the elasticity of the dough. The higher the protein, the higher the gluten content, and the higher the gluten, the more elasticity in the dough. This factor is critical when making potato and other vegetable gnocchi, where the balance of water content and flour affects the tenderness of the gnocchi. The drier the ingredients, the less flour is required to make the dough — and more tender the cooked gnocchi.

Durum wheat, with a mid-range protein content of 11 to 12 percent, is the norm in the U.S. To complicate matters even more, the durum wheat grown in Europe produces a grain with a lower protein content. Most American all-purpose flour is in the 11 to 12 percent mid-range, with a grind comparable to an Italian 0 flour, while Italian wheat flour used in gnocchi-making is 00 (or very fine) and has a protein content around 9.5 percent.

While all-purpose unbleached flour can be used for any of the recipes in this book with very good results, you may choose to replace one-third of the flour in the potato and other vegetable gnocchi recipes with cake flour. I've found that the lower protein and more finely ground cake flour can produce a more tender and finely textured gnocchi, closer to gnocchi in Italy.

King Arthur Flour is producing an American "Italian-Style" 00 flour with a protein content of 8.5 percent, which can make a viable substitute for all-purpose flour — but I find substituting cake flour for one-third the amount of all-purpose flour called for will produce equally good results at a lower price.

/ WHITE-BEAN FLOUR

While testing recipes and playing with ingredients, I substituted white-bean flour for garbanzo-bean flour with equally good results. It's readily available in most natural food stores and can add variety to your gnocchi in recipes where gluten is not necessary.

OILS, BUTTER AND OTHER FATS

/ COOKING OIL

I've learned from Italians to use olive oil for almost everything, even to clean and revitalize my front door every spring, or to silence squeaky hinges. In the kitchen, the only time I substitute another oil is when I want a neutral flavor. Sunflower oil is the most widely used alternative cooking oil in Italy, and is considered one of the healthier neutral-flavored choices.

/ LARDO

Lardo — a unique type of *salumi*, or cured meat, served as an appetizer — is pork back fat that has been spiced and cured for six months. It is NOT Italian lard, which is a different fat used in cooking known as *strutto*.

Animal fat in general has a bad reputation, but sliced extremely thin and eaten in small amounts, one could easily argue that lardo should be forgiven for its possibly bad health effects. It's just that good! Rich and creamy, it's a unique product that deserves special attention and guilt-free consumption. It also adds a special richness when substituted for other cooking fat in a recipe.

The best lardo comes from Carrara, where quarries supplied marble for Michelangelo and where marble vats for making lardo are still used today.

/ OLIVE OIL

What's the best olive oil? There are so many on the market it's not possible to suggest one "best" — but I do recommend you consider the following before buying an oil:

Always purchase extra-virgin, first cold-pressed oil, preferably from one type of olive, from whatever origin or country you prefer. Olive oils produced this way are considered the highest quality, with the best flavor and the proper acid balance. Look for oil that is labeled with the date it was bottled — which is not the same as the "use before" date. Also important, if the information is available, is noting where the olives were grown, not where the oil was bottled. Many processors import olives from various sources or countries, then label it as "Italian," for instance, because it was processed in Italy.

For cooking, purchase an olive oil you like, remembering that the subtleties of the oil will be overpowered by other ingredients.

Reserve expensive olive oils and those with your favorite flavor nuances for dribbling on bruschette, soup, or anywhere the flavor will shine.

Neither the price nor the color of the oil is a guarantee of taste or quality. Unfiltered olive oils, called *grezzo*, or rough, in Italian, usually have a deeper, more pronounced olive flavor that will last up to six months. Oil from recent olive harvests will have a piquant bite that will slowly disperse as the oil ages. If you like that peppery aspect, purchase an oil within a month of harvest or bottling.

Store unopened olive oil in a cool dark place for up to two years. The oil will mellow like an aged wine, but remain edible. If, when opened, the oil smells even slightly rancid, it's spoiled. Once opened, store the oil in a dark, cool place and use it within two months. You may also keep it in the refrigerator for a longer period; it will become cloudy when cold, but once it returns to room temperature it will clear up and run freely.

/ UNSALTED BUTTER

Although salted butter is available in Europe, unsalted butter is always preferred because it's fresher, and you can control the salt content to suit your taste. Salt acts as a preservative and adding it to butter became common practice in the U.S. to increase shelf life. Unfortunately, it can also hide off-flavors. Always use unsalted butter.

European butter contains more fat than American butter, and if you care to use it in the sauce recipes, go ahead. It's readily available in U.S. markets. A bowl of gnocchi swimming in fresh, unsalted European butter is an eating experience that will likely convert you to the practice.

MEATS

/ GUANCIALE

As with many other Italian foods, guanciale is a regional delicacy, not commonly found outside the regions of Umbria and Lazio. The name comes from *guancia*, meaning cheek, and is the cured flesh from — you guessed it — pork cheeks. It's what gives the well-known *alla Matriciana* pasta sauce its authentic deep pork flavor. Pancetta can be substituted, although it doesn't deliver the smooth richness that guanciale imparts. It's available at Italian markets and via email order. Vacuum packed, it will keep frozen for a month or so.

/ PANCETTA

Although it is often referred to as Italian bacon, pancetta — unlike bacon — is not smoked. Both are made from pork belly sides, but that's where the resemblance ends. The Italian version is seasoned with salt and pepper, usually curled into a tight roll, wrapped to hold its shape, and cured. Bacon is brined flat and then smoked.

Pancetta may be difficult to find, but it's worth the hunt: its distinct flavor is more authentic to these recipes. Bacon can be substituted but the resulting dish will taste different. Both freeze equally well.

/ PROSCIUTTO

Although now available from U.S. producers, I prefer prosciutto made in Italy. As with other ingredients, similar production and processing techniques will differ according to their source; even within Italy, prosciutto varies from region to region. Prosciutto di Parma, the most popular kind found in the U.S., comes from specially bred and fed Italian pigs and is aged more than 14 months.

When recipes call for prosciutto that is chopped rather than thinly sliced, I always look for "ends" that are sold at a discounted price.

/ SPECK

Speck is cured and smoked pork from the northern Trentino-Alto Adige region of Italy. It has a more delicate flavor than bacon and is closer to prosciutto in consistency. If you can't find it, substitute prosciutto, not bacon. You will miss the subtle, smoky flavor of the speck, but retain the preferred texture.

MUSHROOMS & TRUFFLES

/ PORCINI MUSHROOMS

Boletus edulis, known as porcini in Italy, are a common mushroom in Europe and North America and are highly prized in the Italian cuisine. Available fresh in the fall and sometimes in the spring, they are used to flavor soups, risotto, and pasta, thinly shaved to be served raw in salads, or — my favorite — grilled and eaten as a main course with a hunk of fresh bread to soak up the juices.

Porcini retain their distinct, earthy flavor when dried, which makes them easy to reconstitute and add to sauces and ragùs. Only a small amount is needed as the flavor of dried porcini is intense. Porcini powder can be added sparingly for the same purpose.

/ TRUFFLE OIL

Most truffle oils are olive oil infused with a synthetic product that simulates one of the numerous aromas found in truffles. These products are not highly recommended.

If available, use only naturally flavored black or white truffle oil to enhance the flavor of fresh truffle-based foods, or to dribble over simple dishes such as scrambled eggs, beef carpaccio, or smashed boiled potatoes. Never heat or cook with truffle oil or the flavor and aroma will dissipate.

When purchasing truffle oil, read the label carefully. It should contain real truffles and nothing else. For example: *Olio extravirgine di olive, infusione di tartufo* (extra-virgin olive oil, infusion of truffle). You may also see small bits of truffle sediment on the bottom of the bottle. When opened, real truffle oil will have an almost overpowering perfume. If searching online, check the advertising carefully for how the oil is presented and look for words such as "natural."

/ TRUFFLES

Truffles are an underground variety of mushroom that form a symbiotic relationship with the roots of certain trees. Although there are hundreds of different kinds of truffles, only a few are considered delicacies. These emit a particular aroma similar to a male pig sex hormone, and are usually hunted with the help of female pigs or trained dogs. They are difficult to find and vary in price depending on the variety.

The Italian white truffle, *tartuffo bianco*, considered the most valuable on the market, is native to the foothills and mountains of northern and central Italy. It is the most flavorful and delicate of all truffle varieties and is never cooked, but usually shaved raw over simple cold or warm dishes that enhance its flavor. Harvested from September to December, the white truffle can be purchased fresh or preserved or infused in olive oil.

Umbria is the biggest producer of the Italian black truffle, *tartufo nero*. It is less aromatic and less expensive than the white truffle, and has a very earthy flavor that can withstand cooking, which makes it popular for use in sauces or spreads for bruschette. The main harvesting season is from November to March, although black truffles and various black truffle products can also be purchased preserved in jars at other times of the year. Check your local Italian market, or mail order from Amazon. Urbani is one of the largest producers in Umbria and is readily available.

OTHER INGREDIENTS

The following ingredients, commonly found in Italy, are used in some of the gnocchi recipes. They will also make a welcome addition to your pantry when cooking other signature Italian dishes.

/ BOTTARGA

Bottarga is preserved fish eggs made from either tuna or mullet. Most popular in Sicily and Sardinia, it comes as a dry, hard slab that is grated or shaved to garnish a dish. It's good over eggs, pasta dishes, risotto, and salads, and has a distinct, very delicate salty flavor — similar to, but milder than, caviar. It's available in some Italian markets or by mail order. Any extra will keep for weeks refrigerated or months frozen, sealed in plastic. Avoid powdered bottarga available in bottles as the pre-grating significantly reduces its flavor.

/ FAVA BEANS

Fava beans have a very long history in the Mediterranean. Also known as horse, field, pigeon, and/or broad beans, they've been a major food source in the Middle East and Europe for thousands of years. Although available year round in dried form, they're best eaten fresh.

When very young, fava bean pods are split open and the beans are eaten raw with a chunk of pecorino cheese and maybe some olive oil. Italian farmers have been known to carry this with them for a snack while working the fields. As the beans mature, they become meatier and develop a tough outer skin that needs to be removed by blanching, then popping the inner bean from the loosened skin. One kilo, or 2.2 pounds of favas in the shell, usually produce about 2 cups skinned beans, ready to use as desired.

Fava beans are one of the first crops to ripen in late spring in Italy. I look forward to fava season every year and spend a couple of evenings preparing kilos of them for soup, salads, and sauces as well as for longer storage in the freezer.

If you can't find fresh fava beans in your local markets, canned ones will make an OK substitute. Dried ones will not.

/ FENNEL POLLEN

Collected from wild fennel, the pollen is sweeter and more intense than fennel seed. Just a pinch will add an extraordinary flavor to any dish including vegetables, roasted meats, sauces, and even baked goods. Ground fennel seed can be substituted if absolutely necessary, but you will need to use more of it and the taste will not be the same.

It's worth purchasing some fennel pollen for your pantry to keep on hand for a variety of dishes. It's available from a number of California mail-order sources.

/ MIRTILLI ROSSI (RED BERRIES)

These small tart berries, common in the mountains of northern Italy, are close cousins to our cranberry. They are commonly used to make a sweet-tart *marmalata*, or jam, used in desserts, on toast, and in crepes.

I've successfully used cranberries in the U.S. to make my own version of marmalata to sauce or garnish various dessert gnocchi. Look for a simple cranberry jam recipe that calls for just berries, water, pectin and sugar, and you'll have the closest alternative to *mirtilli rossi* you can get without making a trip to the Dolomites.

TOOLS

There are very few tools required to make gnocchi — and you probably already have most everything you need in your kitchen. I've listed the most important tools below; if you can't find them in your local kitchen store, check the internet for mail-order sources.

/ CHEESE GRATER

This is the cheese grater I always use when making gnocchi. It has small holes, is hand-held, and easy to use.

Specially-designed Parmigiano cheese graters and commercially grated Parmigiano-Reggiano produce cheese that is too fine to use in the recipes in this book — and many of the new standard microplane graters produce a cheese that is too fluffy and difficult to measure. A standard medium-to-large-holed grater produces cheese that is too coarse to blend well into the dough. Always grate cheese as you need it from a solid chunk.

/ FLEXIBLE CURVED PLASTIC BOWL SCRAPER

This is the perfect tool for getting every last bit of gnocchi dough out of your bowl. You'll find lots of other uses for this handy scraper as well.

/ GNOCCHI PADDLE

I prefer using a wooden paddle instead of the back of a fork when forming dimples in gnocchi. It has some "tooth" to it and the dough doesn't slip the way it does on a fork's metal surface. But it's not necessary to use either one. Many of my Italian friends have never used anything to shape their gnocchi; instead, they shape their gnocchi by flipping them over on a lightly floured surface with the flick of their finger. Formed this way, the gnocchi won't have ridges, but the sauce-retaining dimple is there.

/ DOUGH SCOOPS

I keep a variety of sizes of these scoops on hand for quick and easy measuring. Scoop and drop! They're much easier than using a tablespoon. Be sure to buy the design with the squeeze handle that releases the dough.

/ LARGE, LIGHTWEIGHT 6-QUART
  STOCKPOT WITH LID

A lightweight, deep stockpot that helps the water return to a boil as quickly as possible — and one large enough to give the gnocchi room to "swim" — is the most important tool for cooking good gnocchi and/or pasta. More often than not, non-Italians make the mistake of not using enough water. The water temperature drastically falls, and when the gnocchi are added, the pot becomes crowded and the gnocchi stick together before they have a chance to cook.

/ LARGE, ROUND METAL SPOON WITH HOLES

It's so easy to lift out an entire serving of gnocchi or small pasta from cooking water with one of these large, flat spoons. They come in a variety of designs and are sold by most kitchen stores.

/ METAL BENCH SCRAPER

This is undoubtedly one of the more important tools I have in the kitchen. It's indispensable for handling dough, cleaning work surfaces, transporting large amounts of chopped vegetables or other ingredients to a cooking pot, and more. Every kitchen should have one.

/ FOOD MILL OR POTATO RICER

Either one of these tools will rice potatoes and other vegetables perfectly for gnocchi-making. The food mill is more versatile, so you may also wish to consider the other kinds of cooking you do and expand your possibilities with the food mill. If you like smooth tomato sauce, for instance, the food mill is your choice for separating out the skins and making a smooth paste.

SERVING GNOCCHI

The suggested serving quantities for the gnocchi and sauce recipes in this book are loosely based on how Italians serve and enjoy gnocchi: Italians eat gnocchi with sauce; Americans eat sauce with gnocchi.

As a general guideline, I suggest 10 to 12 gnocchi or 6 small canederli as one first-course serving, and 15 to 20 gnocchi or 10 small canederli as a main course serving.

Another way to look at servings: Recipes calling for two pounds of potatoes will generally yield six generous main-course servings.

There are too many sauce variables — such as differences in personal taste regarding the quantity of sauce, which sauce is used on which gnocchi, and whether it is served as a first or second course — to recommend a definite amount per serving. Pestos, for example, are used in small amounts, just enough to barely coat the gnocchi. Browned butter is to taste, and basic tomato sauces are more often ladled on generously.

You could start with two tablespoons pesto for a first course serving of 10 to 12 gnocchi. Increase the volume to a half-cup for other sauces dressing the same serving size. Most sauce recipes can be refrigerated or frozen or added to a soup or stew, so I suggest you follow the given recipes and save any leftovers for another use.

Serve gnocchi in shallow, preheated soup bowls if possible. Pass extra freshly grated cheese at the table if desired.

In Italy, bread is not served with a first course of pasta, risotto, or gnocchi. It's eaten, instead, with the second course, usually as a way to sop up any juices on the plate. When serving gnocchi as a main course, which is becoming more popular as people choose to eat more lightly, I usually add a salad and a crusty, rustic bread to the meal.

Leftover gnocchi can be added to a simple, broth-based soup or used to top a salad.

FREEZER NOTES

Making gnocchi takes some time and planning, and the convenience of being able to freeze it is a definite plus. Many varieties of gnocchi and sauce can be frozen in individual servings, which means dinner can be on the table in less than an hour. It also means you can prep gnocchi in advance for a dinner party. All you need are some sheet pans and plastic freezer-weight bags.

To freeze, form the gnocchi and place it, uncooked, on a sheet pan layered with parchment or wax paper and a dusting of flour. Make sure the gnocchi don't touch each other. When the pan is full, place it in the freezer for a couple of hours or overnight, until the gnocchi are completely frozen. Then put the gnocchi in a bag, remove as much air as possible, label with the date, and return to the freezer. It's that simple.

Remember to use the gnocchi within two weeks for best results. Freezer burn and texture deterioration could set in after that.

That said, I've not always had the best of luck freezing potato-based gnocchi. Other chefs may contradict this, but I've had frozen potato gnocchi disintegrate in the water because, I've discovered, the dough was not initially compact enough. Gnocchi made with russet potatoes have a greater tendency to deteriorate in the freezer, as well as those made without egg, but you can expect the unexpected to happen at any time. Testing gnocchi before it's frozen doesn't guarantee success either. Therefore I highly recommend that you test-cook all frozen gnocchi (especially potato-based) well in advance of the time you plan to serve it — particularly if you've planned a dinner party.

If the gnocchi have the slightest tendency to disintegrate when dropped into the boiling water, do the following: Remove all the gnocchi from the freezer, let it thaw and reform the dough into a ball, lightly kneading it with a sprinkling of four, until it holds together. Reform the gnocchi and retest a few until you're convinced that they will hold together. I've done this a number of times and it works with practically no loss of quality.

The sauces and gnocchi varieties most suitable for freezing are noted at the end of each recipe. Polenta, some canederli, and alla Romano-style gnocchi do not freeze well. Freezing also negatively affects coarse flour-based gnocchi and bread-based canederli. Gluten-free recipes in this book are also not good candidates for freezing due to the lack of gluten that binds the dough. These are the general guidelines I've discovered after years of making all kinds of gnocchi. Sometimes, though, they still will freeze better than other times. You may want to experiment on your own.

HOW RESTAURANTS PREPARE GNOCCHI IN ADVANCE

I often think of a small restaurant my husband and I stopped at for lunch in the Veneto region of the Dolomites years ago. It was in the middle of a beautifully maintained forest — the same forest that supplied the trees that built Venice. While hiking in this beautiful place, we stumbled upon a restaurant praised locally for its potato gnocchi that was only accessible by foot trail or a small back road. The gnocchi were superb! And because so many different kinds were on the menu, I asked the chef before leaving if he would answer some questions about his recipes. He quickly answered that all was secret! When I suggested that all I wanted to know was how he stored so many kinds in advance for later cooking, he freely answered that he froze them at exactly 0 degrees centigrade. Perfect! For a restaurant anyway …

If making potato gnocchi in advance for use within a day or two, Italian restaurants often make it, cook it, coat it well with extra-virgin olive oil, and refrigerate it on a tray in a single layer. The gnocchi can then be reheated in simmering water with no ill effects, ready to serve when they bob to the surface.

WEIGHTS AND MEASURES

Most of the ingredients in the recipes in this book are measured by volume rather than by weight. One may argue that weights are more accurate, and that most of the world prefers to use a kitchen scale instead of cups and measuring spoons. I did learn to make gnocchi in Italy using a scale — but I teach Americans to use measures because it's a more familiar technique.

There are a number of easy-to-use kitchen conversion charts available on the internet, such as convert-me.com, and startcooking.com, if you prefer to use weights.

An important note: When using a cup to measure flour, it's important to spoon the flour into the cup and level it off with the back of a knife or spatula. All the recipes are written with this method in mind.

I've never found one system to produce a better gnocchi than the other. That's because no matter how one measures or weighs, there are too many variables that can have an effect on the final product. Eggs of the same size will differ; flour will vary in humidity; potatoes have a range of skin thicknesses; some potato is always left in the ricer; some ingredients will absorb more flour than others;

vegetables have different water-to-fiber ratios — even the temperature of your kitchen will affect the recipe.

Therefore I suggest you consistently use the measuring method that is most comfortable for you, pay attention to your habits, and note differences each time you make a recipe. After a few trials, you will gain a feeling for how the dough should feel and react and can make adjustments accordingly. It takes experience and practice. Read the tips at the front of this book and trust your instincts.

And test each and every batch of gnocchi before you cook it, no matter how many times you may have made the same variation in the past. Even after making many thousands of gnocchi, my experienced Italian friends and I always test before finishing a batch.

ACKNOWLEDGEMENTS

I'd like to thank the following people for the role they've played in bringing *Gnocchi Solo Gnocchi* to life:

Anna Maria Rodrigeuz d'Amato for opening the doors to my gnocchi-making over 25 years ago.

David Tanis for being my most influential mentor at the crucial point when I was searching for ways to make my love of cooking into a profession.

John Vollertson, alias Johnny V, the director of Las Cosas Cooking School in Santa Fe, for his years of support with cooking classes — and for the final push over the summit of procrastination that moved me to complete *Gnocchi, Solo Gnocchi*.

Mike & Karen Walker, owners of Las Cosas Kitchen Shoppe, for over 16 years of support for my cooking class teaching career and for lending us some of their beautiful dinnerware for the photo shoots.

The masterfully talented photo crew of Lois Ellen Frank, Daphne Hougard, and Walter Whitewater, with whom I spent over a week capturing plate after plate of "all those balls."

Carole Gardner for her ability to represent many of the tools used in gnocchi-making in a simple sketch.

Lisa Lavagetto, cooking class instructor at Ramekins Culinary School in Sonoma, California, for her enthusiasm and delicious recipe contributions.

Jennifer Hayes, former event manager at Ramekins, for her ongoing support with cooking classes in California.

Anne Ritchings for her never-ending dedication to recipe testing and contribution of recipes to the book. The first class she took with me was gnocchi-making 10 years ago, and she volunteered then as a tester. "Remember, when you need a tester, I'm here," she said, and she was — through all of it. I think she's eaten almost as much gnocchi as I have.

Others who helped with recipes testing: Jessica Cassirer, Jan Huizenga, Pat Greathouse, and students too numerous to mention who, over the years, were helping me test recipes — whether they knew it or not.

Pat West-Barker for her countless hours of superb editing and her ability to capture my voice. She has been a constant supporter of my idea and a good friend over the years.

David Chickey and Montana Currie of Radius Books for their talented design, which has made *Gnocchi Solo Gnocchi* as beautiful as I had always hoped it would be.

My husband Mark, for sharing my love of Italy and for encouraging me to follow my dreams. For the more than 25 years between the concept of this book and its birth, he never lost faith in my goal — or that I would accomplish it.

My Italian friends Lorenza Santo and Cinzia Ubaldi for their help in understanding the subtleties of Italian cuisine and for donating some of their personal recipes.

Chef Claudio Brugalossi for sharing his knowledge of what gnocchi mean to the Italians.

And finally, to all the Italians I've met, lived with, and worked with over the years: Thanks for being who you are and for creating one of the most delicious cuisines imaginable.

INDEX

Page numbers in bold indicate main recipe. Serving suggestions can be found under the individual main headings for each type of gnocchi and sauce.

ENDORSEMENTS

"Christine Hickman has spent much of her life cooking in Italy and in this book she explores one of her favorite subjects: gnocchi! A collection of recipes from all over Italy that is a delicious resource."

— ELIZABETH MINCHILLI

blogger, food tour guide, and author of Eat Italy apps

"A very personal love letter to the extended gnocchi family with a bit of history, a good bit of kitchen sense, and the promise of some excellent meals."

— MAUREEN B. FANT

principle, Elifant Archaeo-Culinary Tours, and author of *Pasta the Italian Way: Sauces & Shapes*, winner of the IACP award for best international cookbook

"Christine Hickman has been amazing in her research and discovery of the gnocchi recipes of Italy. This book is a tribute to Italy and to its wonderful people. It truly has come from Christine's heart. Mangia bene!"

— LISA LAVAGETTO

chef and educator, Ramekins Culinary School, Sonoma, CA; private chef, Guy's Grocery Games contestant

ISBN: 978-0-692-11092-8

Christine Hickman
sonomarcella.com
christine@sonomarcella.com

Library of Congress Cataloging-in-Publication Data
available from the publisher upon request.

Design: David Chickey & Montana Currie
Editor: Patricia West Barker
Color Proofing: Dexter Pre-media Ltd
Cover Image: Kyra Kennedy

Printed by Editoriale Bortolazzi-Stei, Verona, Italy